O9-BSA-066

9

No Longer the Property of
Hayner Public Library District

REFERENCE

The Roaring Twenties

Almanac and
Primary Sources

The Roaring Twenties
Almanac and
Primary Sources

Kelly King Howes
Julie L. Carnagie

U·X·L
An imprint of Thomson Gale,
a part of The Thomson Corporation

THOMSON
™
GALE

Detroit • New York • San Francisco • San Diego • New Haven, Conn. • Waterville, Maine • London • Munich

HAYNER PUBLIC LIBRARY DISTRICT
ALTON, ILLINOIS

The Roaring Twenties: Almanac and Primary Sources

Kelly King Howes

Project Editor
Julie L. Carnagie

Rights Acquisitions and Management
Kim Smilay; Margaret Abendroth

Imaging and Multimedia
Robyn Young, Lezlie Light, Dan Newell

Product Design
Jennifer Wahi

Composition and Electronic Prepress
Evi Seoud

Manufacturing
Rita Wimberley

©2006 Thomson Gale, a part of the Thomson Corporation.

Thomson and Star Logo are trademarks and Gale is a registered trademark used herein under license.

For more information, contact:
Thomson Gale
27500 Drake Rd.
Farmington Hills, MI 48331-3535
Or you can visit our Internet site at
http://www.gale.com

ALL RIGHTS RESERVED
No part of this work covered by the copyright hereon may be reproduced or used in any form or by any means—graphic, electronic, or mechanical, including photocopying, recording, taping, Web distribution, or information storage retrieval systems—without the written permission of the publisher.

For permission to use material from this product, submit your request via Web at http://www.gale-edit.com/permissions, or you may download our Permissions Request form and submit your request by fax or mail to:

Rights Acquisition and Management Department
Thomson Gale
27500 Drake Rd.
Farmington Hills, MI 48331-3535
Permissions Hotline:
248-699-8006 or 800-877-4253, ext. 8006
Fax: 248-699-8074 or 800-762-4058

Cover photographs reproduced by permission of AP/Wide World Photos (Model T) and ©Bettmann/Corbis (flappers dancing the Charleston, radio receiver, and "Variety" newspaper).

While every effort has been made to ensure the reliability of the information presented in this publication, Thomson Gale does not guarantee the accuracy of the data contained herein. Thomson Gale accepts no payment for listing; and inclusion in the publication of any organization, agency, institution, publication, service, or individual does not imply endorsement by the editors or publisher. Errors brought to the attention of the publisher and verified to the satisfaction of the publisher will be corrected in future editions.

LIBRARY OF CONGRESS CATALOGING-IN-PUBLICATION DATA

Howes, Kelly King. The roaring twenties almanac and primary sources / Kelly King Howes ; Julie L. Carnagie, project editor.
p. cm. – (The roaring twenties reference library)
Includes bibliographical references and index.
ISBN 1-4144-0212-0 (hardcover : alk. paper)
1. United States–History–1919-1933–Juvenile literature.
2. United States–History–1919-1933–Sources–Juvenile literature.
3. Almanacs, American–Juvenile literature.
I. Carnagie, Julie. II. Title.
E784.H69 2005
973.91′5–dc22
2005007800

This title is also available as an e-book.
ISBN 1-4144-0609-6
Contact your Gale sales representative for ordering information.

Printed in the United States of America
10 9 8 7 6 5 4 3 2 1

R
973.915
HOW

b17186122

Contents

Primary Sources

Reader's Guide

The Roaring Twenties is one of the most colorful eras in U.S. history. Bordered on one side by the end of World War I (1914–18) and on the other side by the Great Depression (the severe economic downturn that began in 1929 and lasted until the early 1940s), this short period would later be remembered by historians largely as a time of excitement and fun. It was the decade, after all, when daring young women called flappers danced the Charleston, and Charles "Lucky Lindy" Lindbergh crossed the Atlantic Ocean in a small airplane. It was a time when the economy was strong, and many had extra money in their pockets. Yet this was also a period of changes. Some of these changes, such as advances in technology and medical care and new freedoms for women, were welcomed by many people. There were others, however, who found some of the changes— such as the new reliance on science over religion, or the large number of immigrants living in the nation's cities, or the fact that not everyone shared in the economic prosperity of the Twenties—more troubling.

The Roaring Twenties: Almanac and Primary Sources presents a comprehensive overview of events and everyday life that occurred within the United States during the 1920s. The volume is divided into two sections: the Almanac section, containing nine chapters, and the Primary Sources section, containing eleven chapters.

The Almanac section begins with some background to the Roaring Twenties, followed by coverage of the political, economic, technological, and social events and changes that occurred during the decade. Some of the darker aspects of life in this period are explored, such as the rise of organized crime and the effects of nativism (favoring established inhabitants over new immigrants), then the focus shifts to developments in arts and entertainment and finally to the 1929 stock market crash, which launched the United States into the Great Depression, and its aftermath. The Primary Sources section tells the story of the 1920s in the words of the people who lived and shaped the decade. Excerpted and full-text documents provide a wide range of perspectives on this period of history. Included are excerpts from political speeches; influential books of the era; and reflections by individuals who lived through the decade.

Features

The Roaring Twenties: Almanac and Primary Sources contains sidebar boxes that highlight people and events of special interest, and each chapter offers a list of additional sources students can go to for more information. More than fifty-five black-and-white photographs help illustrate the text. The volume begins with a timeline of important events in the history of the 1920s; a "Words to Know" section that introduces students to difficult or unfamiliar terms; and a "Research and Activity Ideas" section. The volume concludes with a general bibliography and a subject index so students can easily find the people, places, and events discussed throughout *The Roaring Twenties: Almanac and Primary Sources*.

Format of Primary Sources section

The Primary Sources chapters in *The Roaring Twenties: Almanac and Primary Sources* are formatted uniformly for ease of use. Every chapter opens with a historical overview, followed by the reprinted document.

Each excerpt includes the following additional features:

- **Introductory material** places the document and its author in a historical context.

- **Things to remember while reading** offers important background information about the featured text.

- **Excerpt** presents the document in its original spelling and format.

- **What happened next**... discusses the impact of the document and/or relevant historical events following the date of the document.

- **Did you know**... provides interesting facts about the document and its author.

- **Consider the following**... poses questions about the material for the reader to consider.

- **For More Information** offers resources for further study of the document and its author as well as sources used by the authors in writing the material.

The Roaring Twenties Reference Library

The Roaring Twenties: Almanac and Primary Sources is only one component of the two-part U•X•L The Roaring Twenties Reference Library. The other title in the set is:

- *The Roaring Twenties: Biographies* (one volume) presents the life stories of twenty-five notable personalities of the 1920s drawn from the worlds of politics and government, literature, music, sports, aviation, religion, art, anthropology, and crime. Included are baseball great Babe Ruth, anthropologist Margaret Mead, comedy king Charlie Chaplin, artist Georgia O'Keeffe, author Zora Neale Hurston, composer George Gershwin, and gangster Al Capone. Profiles are also provided for lesser-known though no less interesting figures, including evangelist Aimee Semple McPherson, writer H.L. Mencken, and boxer Jack Dempsey.

Comments and Suggestions

We welcome your comments on *The Roaring Twenties: Almanac and Primary Sources* and suggestions for other topics to consider. Please write: Editors, *The Roaring Twenties: Almanac and Primary Sources*, U•X•L, 27500 Drake Rd. Farmington Hills, Michigan 48331-3535; call toll free: 1-800-877-4253; fax to (248) 699-8097; or send e-mail via http://www.gale.com.

Timeline of Events

1859   British naturalist Charles Darwin publishes his influential work, *On the Origin of the Species,* in which he attempts to show that different animals could have descended from common ancestors and describes changes in species over millions of years as a process called "natural selection" (also known as survival of the fittest).

1859   African American leader W.E.B. Du Bois illuminates black history, dreams, and concerns in *The Souls of Black Folk.*

1907   Auto manufacturer Henry Ford releases the Model T, fondly known as the Tin Lizzie, which will be much loved by the public for its reliability and low price tag.

1914   World War I begins in Europe. The results will be devastating, for an estimated ten million soldiers will be killed and twenty million wounded, while millions of civilians will also die from hunger and rapidly spreading diseases like influenza.

May 1915 The German navy sinks the British passenger ship *Lusitania,* killing more than one thousand passengers, including more than one hundred U.S. citizens. President Woodrow Wilson issues a warning to Germany.

April 1917 The United States enters World War I.

November 11, 1918 World War I ends.

1919 An epidemic of influenza spreads across the globe. About four hundred thousand U.S. citizens die of the disease.

January 1919 Congress passes the Eighteenth Amendment, which makes the manufacture and sale of alcoholic beverages illegal.

June 28, 1919 The Treaty of Versailles, the peace agreement that officially ends World War I, is signed. Its terms demand that Germany pay heavy reparations (compensation) for its role in starting the conflict.

July 4, 1919 Boxer Jack Dempsey, known as the "Manassa Mauler," wins the heavyweight title from Jess Willard.

October 28, 1919 Congress passes the Volstead Act, which spells out the terms of the Eighteenth Amendment. Defined as "intoxicating" beverages are those containing as little as 0.5 percent of alcohol, including not just distilled liquor but beer and wine.

1920 W.E.B. Du Bois becomes director of publications and research at the newly formed National Association for the Advancement of Colored People (NAACP), and soon founds the influential journal *Crisis*.

1920 Sinclair Lewis's best-selling novel *Main Street* is published.

1920 For the first time, airplanes are used to deliver mail from New York to California.

January 1920 The Red Scare begins as Attorney General A. Mitchell Palmer orders raids on several thousand individuals thought to hold radical political views.

January 3, 1920 Baseball great George Herman "Babe" Ruth signs with the New York Yankees. He hits fifty-four home runs his first season; in 1927, he hits a career high of sixty-two home runs and leads the Yankees to victory in the World Series.

January 16, 1920 The Eighteenth Amendment goes into effect.

March 1920 F. Scott Fitzgerald begins his ascent to fame with the publication of his novel *This Side of Paradise.*

May 1920 The Negro National League is formed, allowing African American baseball players and fans more structured opportunities to play and enjoy the sport.

May 5, 1920 Italian immigrants and labor activists Nicola Sacco and Bartolomeo Vanzetti are arrested for the murder of two employees of a shoe factory in Massachusetts. On what many consider flimsy evidence, they are convicted and sentenced to death.

August 18, 1920 Congress passes the Nineteenth Amendment, giving women the right to vote.

September 28, 1920 Eight players on the Chicago White Sox baseball team are charged with intentionally losing a game in exchange for money. As a result they are banned from the sport for life.

November 2, 1920 Having campaigned on the promise of a "return to normalcy," Republican candidate Warren G. Harding is elected president by a wide margin. For the first time, the election results are broadcast over the new technology of radio.

1921 Margaret Sanger founds the American Birth Control League (later named the Planned Parenthood Federation of America). Two years later, she opens the first physician-run birth control clinic in the United States.

September 8, 1921 The first Miss America pageant is held in Atlantic City, New Jersey.

1922 Marcus Garvey, charismatic leader of the United Negro Improvement Association (UNIA), is convicted of defrauding investors in his shipping company. He spends several years in prison.

1922 Sinclair Lewis's novel about a middle-class businessman, *Babbitt,* is published, and its title soon becomes a general term for a complacent conformist.

1922 T.S. Eliot's complex, book-length poem *The Waste Land,* is published.

1922 Irish writer James Joyce's influential modernist novel *Ulysses* is published.

1922 A period of economic prosperity begins; it lasts until the U.S. stock market crash in 1929.

April 1922 Secretary of the Interior Albert Fall leases government-held oil reserves in the West (including one near Teapot Dome, Wyoming) to private oil companies. Fall is later convicted and imprisoned for bribery.

October 4, 1922 For the first time, play-by-play coverage of baseball's World Series is heard over the radio. The New York Giants beat the New York Yankees.

October 28, 1922 Benito Mussolini leads a fascist (an extremely right wing, authoritarian form of government) march on Rome and takes control of Italy.

November 26, 1922 The tomb of King Tutankhamen is discovered in Egypt by British archaeologist Howard Carter.

1923 The Frigidaire Company introduces the first electric refrigerator. The electric shaver is also patented.

1923 Poet Edna St. Vincent Millay wins the Pulitzer Prize for Literature.

1923 The New York Yankees open their new stadium, which is known as "The House That Ruth Built" because it is financed by tickets sales boosted by the stellar performance of Babe Ruth.

1923 The great blues singer Bessie Smith makes her first recording.

1923 Sales of automobiles are booming. One of every two cars sold in the United States is a Ford.

1923 "The Weary Blues," written by poet Langston Hughes, is published.

January 3, 1923 The first issue of *Time* magazine appears on newsstands.

August 2, 1923 President Harding dies unexpectedly in San Francisco, California. Vice President Calvin Coolidge is sworn in as president the next day.

1924 Congress passes the National Origins Act, which sets new limits on the number of immigrants allowed into the United States (especially those from southern and eastern Europe and Asia).

1924 Following the death of Russian ruler Vladimir Lenin, Josef Stalin takes power. He will serve as Russia's dictator until 1953.

1924 The Florida land boom is underway. Many investors will lose large amounts of money on get-rich-quick land-buying schemes.

February 12, 1924 George Gershwin's jazz symphony *Rhapsody in Blue* premieres at a concert led by bandleader Paul Whiteman at New York's Aeolian Hall.

May 1924 Teenagers Nathan Leopold and Richard Loeb are convicted of murdering a fourteen-year-old Bobby Franks. Defense attorney Clarence Darrow argues successfully that they be spared the death penalty and sentenced to life in prison.

November 1924 President Calvin Coolidge is reelected.

1925 *The New Negro* anthology, edited by Howard University professor and Harlem Renaissance mentor Alain Locke, showcases the work of African American writers and artists.

1925 *The New Yorker* magazine begins publication.

1925 Charlie Chaplin delights moviegoers with his performance as the Little Tramp in the classic comedy film *The Gold Rush*.

1925 In a speech to newspaper editors, President Coolidge declares that "the business of America is business."

1925 F. Scott Fitzgerald's novel *The Great Gatsby*, a classic portrait of the Roaring Twenties, is published.

July 1925 In Dayton, Tennessee, high school teacher John Scopes is tried for violating the Butler Act, which prohibits the teaching of the scientific theory of evolution in public schools. William Jennings Bryan leads the prosecution team, while the defense is headed by Clarence Darrow.

October 8, 1925 A Ku Klux Klan parade in Washington, D.C., draws approximately forty thousand participants.

1926 Humorist Will Rogers begins writing a weekly, syndicated newspaper column for *The New York Times* that is enjoyed by an estimated twenty million readers.

1926 Ernest Hemingway's novel about U.S. and British expatriates in Europe, *The Sun Also Rises,* is published.

May 1926 Aimee Semple McPherson disappears while swimming in the Pacific Ocean and is presumed drowned. She reappears six weeks later, claiming to have been kidnapped and taken to Mexico.

July 19, 1926 A devastating hurricane ends the Florida land boom.

August 26, 1926 Swimmer Gertrude Ederle crosses the English Channel, beating the previous record by two hours.

1927 *The Jazz Singer,* the first motion picture to incorporate sound, stars Broadway performer Al Jolson.

1927 Babe Ruth hits sixty home runs (a record that will stand for the next thirty-four years), and this season's New York Yankees are called the greatest baseball team ever.

1927 The Duke Ellington Orchestra begins a thirty-eight-month engagement at Harlem's premier night spot, the legendary Cotton Club.

1927 At the peak of its popularity, the *American Mercury* magazine, founded by writer H. L. Mencken, has a circulation of seventy-seven thousand readers.

April 4, 1927 The first scheduled passenger flight travels from Boston, Massachusetts, to New York City.

May 16, 1927 The first Academy Awards ceremony is held.

May 20, 1927 Flying in an airplane called *The Spirit of St. Louis,* Charles Lindbergh takes off from Long Island, New York. Thirty-three and a half hours later, he becomes the first pilot to make a solo, nonstop flight across the Atlantic Ocean when he lands in Paris, France.

August 23, 1927 Despite protests and demonstrations on their behalf, Sacco and Vanzetti are executed.

October 1927 Dorothy Parker begins writing a weekly book review column, which she signs "Constant Reader," for the *New Yorker* magazine.

December 2, 1927 Henry Ford introduces the eagerly awaited Model A. Spectators by the thousands line up at dealerships to catch a glimpse of the new automobile.

1928 The influential book *Coming of Age in Samoa,* the result of anthropologist Margaret Mead's field work among a group of adolescent girls in the Pacific Island nation of Samoa, is published.

1928 Alexander Fleming discovers penicillin.

August 27, 1928 Fifteen nations sign the Kellogg-Briand Pact, agreeing to use peaceful means to resolve conflicts and to resort to war only as a last measure. Eventually more than sixty other countries sign the agreement.

November 6, 1928 Republican candidate Herbert Hoover is elected president of the United States.

1929 Artist Georgia O'Keeffe begins spending each summer in New Mexico, creating paintings of that environment, such as *Cow's Skull: Red, White and Blue* (1931), for which she becomes well known.

1929 Louis Armstrong appears on Broadway in the hit show *Hot Chocolates,* singing his famous song "Ain't Misbehavin'."

1929 William Faulkner's complex novel *The Sound and the Fury* is published.

1929 Robert and Helen Lynd's *Middletown,* a sociological study of an Indiana town, is published.

1929 Ernest Hemingway's *A Farewell to Arms,* a novel about World War I, is published.

February 14, 1929 In what comes to be known as the St. Valentine's Day Massacre, men from Al Capone's gang enter a Chicago warehouse and kill seven members of the rival gang of George "Bugs" Moran.

March 1929 In his inaugural speech, President Hoover describes the future of the United States as "bright with hope."

September 3, 1929 Prices on the stock exchange reach record highs.

October 1929 Charged with creating a task force to fight organized crime, Prohibition Bureau agent Eliot Ness hires the nine men who will become known as the Untouchables, due to their honesty and integrity.

October 24, 1929 On a day known as Black Thursday, a huge and alarming sell-off of stocks occurs.

October 29, 1929 The stock market crashes on Black Tuesday, heralding the beginning of the severe economic downturn known as the Great Depression.

1930 More than one thousand banks close, and many customers lose their life savings.

1930 One in five U.S. citizens owns an automobile.

1930 Sinclair Lewis becomes the first U.S. citizen to win the Nobel Prize for Literature.

1931 More than eight hundred banks close.

1931 Al Capone, leader of a hugely profitable organized crime empire in Chicago, Illinois, is convicted of tax evasion and sent to federal prison for eleven years.

1932 At the peak of the Depression, 56 percent of black workers and 40 percent of white workers (a total of thirteen million) are unemployed, and wages are 60 percent less than what they were in 1929.

March 1932 The twenty-month-old son of aviator hero Charles Lindbergh is kidnapped and ransomed for fifty thousand dollars. The child is found dead seventy-two days later, and German immigrant Bruno Hauptmann is later convicted of the murder and executed.

May 20, 1932 Amelia Earhart flies solo across the Atlantic Ocean.

November 1932 Democrat Franklin Delano Roosevelt is elected president, ending more than a decade of Republican dominance and promising a "New Deal" to ease the nation's suffering.

1933 President Roosevelt launches his New Deal, including jobs created through new federal programs and changes to the monetary system.

1933 Nazi leader Adolf Hitler takes power in Germany.

1933 Dust storms devastate farms in the midwestern United States, causing a migration of impoverished families westward toward California.

1933 Playing for the Negro League's Pittsburgh Crawfords, pitcher Satchel Paige wins an astounding thirty-one out of forty-two games, including a run of twenty-one consecutive wins.

December 5, 1933 Prohibition ends as the Eighteenth Amendment is repealed.

November 1936 Roosevelt is reelected to a second term as U.S. president.

1937 Zora Neale Hurston's most acclaimed work, *Their Eyes Were Watching God,* is published.

July 3, 1937 In the middle of an around-the-world flight, Amelia Earhart's airplane mysteriously vanishes. No trace of her is ever found.

1938 Germany takes control of Austria.

1939 Germany invades Poland. France and Great Britain declare war on Germany, beginning World War II.

1940 Under the leadership of dictator Benito Mussolini, Italy joins forces with Germany.

1940 The U.S. unemployment rate falls as orders for war materials and supplies flow in from Europe.

November 1940 Roosevelt is reelected to a third term as U.S. president.

December 1941 The Japanese attack U.S. naval forces at Pearl Harbor, Hawaii. The United States declares war on Japan and its allies, Germany and Italy.

Summer 1943 Race riots ravage the cities of Los Angeles, California, and Detroit, Michigan, and the African American community of Harlem in New York City.

June 6, 1944 Allied forces invade the Normandy region of France (D Day).

November 1944 Roosevelt is reelected to a fourth term as U.S. president.

April 12, 1945 Roosevelt dies and Vice President Harry S Truman takes office.

May 8, 1945 The war in Europe ends (VE Day).

August 6, 1945 The Allies drop an atomic bomb on Hiroshima, Japan, killing eighty thousand people. Forty thousand more die the next day, when a bomb falls on Nagasaki.

August 15, 1945 The war in the Pacific ends (VJ Day).

Words to Know

A

assembly line: A factory innovation consisting of a waist-high, belt, along which parts move while workers (each performing one task over and over) gradually assemble the product.

B

Barnstormers: Pilots from the early days of aviation, who performed daring feats (such as rolling their airplanes, flying upside down, and even walking on the wings) at county fairs and other exhibitions.

birth control: The use of contraceptives, which are devices or methods to prevent pregnancy. During the Roaring Twenties, it was illegal in many states to disseminate birth control or even information about it, yet growing numbers of women were beginning to use it.

Black Thursday: October 24, 1929, when orders to sell stocks rose at an alarming rate while prices fell, leading to hysteria and panic on the streets of New York City's financial district and elsewhere.

Black Tuesday: October 29, 1929, when the stock market crashed. Banks that were suddenly forced to pay back loans ran out of cash and closed their doors. Many people lost their life savings, and the severe economic downturn known as the Great Depression began.

Bolshevik Revolution: The 1917 takeover of the Russian government by communists, which, in the United States, led to fear and distrust toward foreigners and those believed to hold radical political views.

bootlegging: The sale and distribution of alcoholic beverages made illegal by Prohibition.

C

capitalism: A political and economic system in which a country's trade and industry are controlled by private interests, for profit.

communism: A political and economic system in which all property is owned by the community and each person contributes and receives according to his or her ability and needs.

consumerism: The preoccupation with acquiring goods, which began to dominate U.S. society in the 1920s and which many feel has continued into the twenty-first century.

Coolidge Prosperity: A popular term for the revival of the U.S. economy that occurred in the 1920s, during the administration of President Calvin Coolidge.

creationists: Those who believe in the Biblical version of human creation, in which God created Earth and all its plants and animals in a week, and all people are descended from Adam and Eve, the first humans. In the 1920s, creationists were opposed to the teaching of the scientific theory of evolution in the public schools.

E

Eighteenth Amendment: Popularly known as Prohibition, this amendment to the U.S. Constitution made the manufacture, transportation, and sale of alcoholic beverages illegal.

Eugenics: A pseudo-science that not only claimed to prove the inferiority of anyone who was not of northern-European heritage but warned of the dangers of so-called "mongrelization" (the mixing of superior white blood with that of the inferior immigrants).

evangelists: Those who seek to convert others to their religious faith.

evolution theory: The idea originated in the middle of the nineteenth century by British naturalist Charles Darwin, who proposed that different animals could have descended from common ancestors; it describes changes in species over millions of years as a process called "natural selection" (also known as survival of the fittest).

F

Federal Highway Act: The 1921 legislation that provided for federal funds to states for the creation and maintenance of interstate highways.

Federal Radio Commission: The federal government agency set up in the 1920s to regulate the new technology of radio broadcasting.

flappers: Young women whose bold, carefree manner of dress and behavior signified a change in attitudes toward women's roles, and who came to symbolize for many years to come the free-wheeling spirit of the Roaring Twenties.

Florida land boom: The craze in the 1920s for buying land in Florida, with purchases often made on credit and without the buyer ever seeing or visiting the property. Many investors lost large amounts of money on these get-rich-quick land-buying schemes. The boom ended in 1926, when a hurricane devastated Miami.

Freudianism: The popular application of theories proposed by Austrian psychiatrist Sigmund Freud (1856–1939). These include the influence of childhood experiences on adult behavior, the subconscious (the part of the mind of which one is unaware) as a source of neurotic (abnormally sensitive, anxious, or obsessive) behavior and psychological problems, and the use of psychoanalysis, or talk therapy, to reveal and treat deeply buried emotional damage.

Fundamentalism: A very conservative form of Christianity that includes a literal interpretation of the Bible; that is, the Bible is considered a true account of factual events, rather than a collection of literary, mythical stories told to illustrate moral lessons.

G

Great Depression: The period of severe economic downturn and hardship when millions lost their life savings, their jobs, and the sense of security they had once known. It lasted from the stock market crash of October 1929 until about 1941, when orders for war materials and supplies for World War II (1939–45) invigorated the U.S. economy.

H

Harlem Renaissance: The period of achievement in African American culture—including literature, drama, music, visual arts, and journalism—that took place during the Roaring Twenties. Sometimes referred to as the New Negro Movement, it was centered in Harlem, the African American community in New York City.

I

influenza epidemic: An outbreak of influenza that spread across the world from late 1918 to 1919. It broke out first near Boston, Massachusetts, in September 1918, and within nine months it had killed four hundred thousand U.S. citizens (including seven hundred in one day in Philadelphia, Pennsylvania) as well as scores of others (almost twenty-two million) around the globe.

isolationism: The belief in avoiding political and economic relationships with other countries, and not getting involved in other nations' problems; a policy that dominated the United States during the Roaring Twenties.

J

jazz: A new, distinctly American form of music developed from the combined influences of European and African elements.

Jazz is said to have originated in New Orleans, Louisiana, with musicians playing on instruments discarded by Civil War-era bands. Their style incorporated offbeat rhythms and improvised solos.

Jazz Age: A term for the Roaring Twenties that originated as the title of one of F. Scott Fitzgerald's short stories and that seemed to capture perfectly the spirit of this decade of exuberance, creativity, and sometimes troubling change.

K

Kellogg-Briand Pact: An agreement intended to outlaw war between the nations of the world, justifying armed conflict only as a last resort. It was signed by fifteen nations in August 1928 and eventually by a total of sixty-two countries. The pact proved ineffective in preventing war, as World War II (1939–45) began about a decade later.

Ku Klux Klan: A white supremacist group that had carried out a brutally successful campaign against blacks during the Reconstruction Era (the period stretching roughly from the end of the American Civil War to the end of the 1870s). During the Roaring Twenties, the Klan was revived and extended its campaign of violence and harassment to include not just African Americans but also Jews, Catholics, and immigrants.

L

laissez-faire: The belief that government should loosen its control of the economy and society in general, which characterized the Roaring Twenties.

M

McNary-Haugen Bill: One of few measures intended to help farmers, who were one of several groups left out of the general economic prosperity of the 1920s. President Calvin Coolidge vetoed the bill in both 1927 and 1928.

Model T: The automobile introduced by manufacturer Henry Ford (1863–1947), also known as the Tin Lizzie, which became the best-selling and most popular car in the United States for its simple design and low price tag.

Monkey Trial: The popular name for the July 1925 Scopes trial, referring to the misconception that Darwin's theory of evolution meant that human beings had descended directly from apes.

N

National Origins Act: The 1924 legislation meant to slow the flow of immigrants from southern and eastern Europe and from Asia. It capped immigration from each country at 150,000 and lowered earlier country quotas to 2 percent of foreign-born residents at the time of the 1890 U.S. census (when very few southern and eastern Europeans had been in the United States). Immigration from Asia was banned altogether.

nativism: The practice of favoring established inhabitants over new immigrants.

Nineteenth Amendment: The amendment to the U.S. Constitution that gave women the right to vote.

O

organized crime: Groups of criminals who worked together, especially in the illegal liquor trade, and often fought each other for control of particular areas or cities.

P

petting: Various forms of kissing and touching, but usually not sexual intercourse, that increasing numbers of young people were said to be engaging in during the Roaring Twenties.

Progressive Era: The period from about 1900 to about 1914, when a variety of reform groups sought to improve society through such measures as child labor laws, Prohibition, and women's right to vote.

Prohibition: The popular name for the Eighteenth Amendment to the U.S. Constitution, which banned the manufacture, transportation, and sale of alcoholic drinks.

R

Red Scare: A period when people thought to hold foreign or radical political ideas came under suspicion. In a January 1920 action known as the Palmer Raids, Attorney General A. Mitchell Palmer authorized federal agents in 33 cities to raid homes and businesses and arrest several thousand suspects. About 250 of them were eventually deported to the Soviet Union.

Roaring Twenties: The period of 1920 to 1929, when a number of factors—including a population shift from the country to the city, an influx of immigrants, advances in technology, economic prosperity, and changing attitudes and values—converged to create a decade both exciting and troubling.

S

Sacco and Vanzetti Trial: The May 1920 trial in which Italian immigrants and labor activists Nicola Sacco and Bartolomeo Vanzetti were tried, on what many considered a lack of evidence, for the robbery and murder of two employees of a shoe factory in Massachusetts. They were convicted and sentenced to death, but their execution was not carried out until 1927, due to worldwide protests.

St. Valentine's Day Massacre: A multiple murder that occurred in Chicago, Illinois, on February 14, 1929, when it was alleged that men from Al Capone's criminal organization entered a warehouse and killed seven members of the rival gang of George "Bugs" Moran. No one was ever charged for this crime.

scientific management theory: The system devised by industrial engineer Frederick Taylor for making production more efficient. It involved breaking particular tasks into separate steps and calculating the minimum amount of time needed for each step, then requiring workers to complete tasks in these scientifically determined time allotments. Managers were given increased control over workers, functions, and procedures.

Scopes Trial: A Dayton, Tennessee, court case that took place in July 1925, centering on a debate between Biblical beliefs and the scientific theory of evolution. High school teacher John Scopes was charged with violating the Butler Act, which banned the teaching of evolution. The prosecution and defense teams were led by two famous public figures: William Jennings Bryan for the prosecution and Clarence Darrow for the defense.

Sheppard-Towner Act: A 1921 law that guaranteed federal funding to states to set up and run prenatal and children's health centers.

socialism: A political and economic system in which the means of production, distribution, and exchange are owned by the community as a whole, rather than by individuals.

Spirit of St. Louis: The name of the airplane Charles Lindbergh flew in May 1927 when he became the first pilot to make a solo, nonstop flight across the Atlantic Ocean. To make room for the amount of gas needed to get Lindbergh to his destination, it carried no unnecessary gear, such as a radio or special instruments for night flying, gas gauge, or parachute.

stock market: The economic structure that allows investors to buy stocks or shares in companies with the promise of sharing in any profits the company earns. During the Roaring Twenties, more U.S. citizens were investing in the stock market than ever before, sometimes borrowing money to do so. The rapid drop in stock values contributed to the October 29 stock market crash, heralding the beginning of the Great Depression.

T

talkie: A motion picture incorporating both images and sound (initially just music, and eventually both music and voices).

Teapot Dome: The scandal that unfolded during the administration of President Warren G. Harding, in which Secretary of the Interior Albert Fall leased government oil reserves to some private oil companies in exchange for money. He was eventually convicted of bribery and sent to prison, becoming the first Cabinet member in U.S. history to serve time in jail.

trickle-down theory: The economic strategy that involves reducing taxes in order to give ordinary consumers more money to spend while also allowing the wealthy to make more investments. The benefits are expected to eventually spread down through all levels of society. This theory, popular in the Roaring Twenties, would be revived in the 1980s under President Ronald Reagan.

U

Untouchables: The nickname for the squad of special agents headed by Eliot Ness of the Justice Department's Prohibition Bureau and charged with fighting organized crime. Ness and his nine men earned this nickname through their honesty and integrity.

V

Volstead Act: Legislation passed in October 1919 that spelled out the terms of the Eighteenth Amendment (Prohibition), defining as "intoxicating beverages" not only distilled liquor, like whiskey or gin, but fermented drinks, like beer and wine, which many had assumed would not be included in the ban.

W

World War I: The bloody conflict that took place in Europe from 1914 to 1918 in which Germany, having sought to expand its territory, was pitted against the Allies: France, Great Britain, and Italy. The United States entered the war on the side of the Allies in 1917.

Research and Activity Ideas

A World Suddenly Changed: World War I (1914–18) was such a bloody, devastating conflict that it changed many people's view of the world and profoundly affected the decade that followed. The terrorist attacks of September 11, 2001, might be said to have had a similar effect. Think about the similarities and differences between these two historical events, and investigate the consequences of each. Write a report or essay detailing your findings and conclusions.

Ford's Vision and Accomplishments: Pretend that you are an advertising copywriter working for the Ford Motor Company in the 1920s. Create a brochure to promote sales of Ford cars. Include a short biography of Henry Ford, along with information about the Model T and Model A. Use photos and drawings as well as text.

The Two Sides of Prohibition: With a group of students, stage a debate between the "Drys" (those who support the ban on alcoholic beverages) and the "Wets" (those who oppose it). If you want to include famous people in your debate, participants could impersonate politician William Jennings Bryan and evangelist Billy Sunday on the Dry side, and

New York governor Al Smith and gangster Al Capone on the Wet side.

Celebrities and Stars of the Roaring Twenties: Tape a radio broadcast made up of interviews with Roaring Twenties figures from the worlds of sports and entertainment. Talk to athletes such as Babe Ruth, Jack Dempsey, or Gertrude Ederle, as well as movie stars like Clara Bow and Douglas Fairbanks about their lives and careers. You might also interview some ordinary people to find out what they think about these celebrities.

Women's Changing Lives: During the Roaring Twenties, women's lives and roles were changing. Yet these changes were affecting different women in different ways. Find out what it would have been like to be a flapper, a farm wife, an African American domestic worker, and the middle-class white mother of a teenager during this decade. Write profiles of these four women.

Documenting the Harlem Renaissance: Create a magazine about the exciting developments and achievements centered in Harlem, New York City's African American community, during the Roaring Twenties. Include information about the writers, musicians, journalists, artists, and others who made up this exciting scene, as well as photos and art work that you find on the Internet.

Popular Music Reflects the Times: A number of memorable songs were written and enjoyed during the Roaring Twenties. In addition to being entertaining, these songs reflected the moods and events of this period. Analyze the lyrics of several and compare their content. You might consider using some from the beginning of the decade (such as "Ain't We Got Fun") and some from the end (such as "Brother, Can You Spare a Dime?").

Prelude to the 1920s

It is tempting to think of the 1920s as a distinct period bordered on one end by World War I (1914–18), the bloody conflict that was supposed to spread democracy across the globe, and on the other by the Great Depression (1929–41), the period of economic downturn and hardship when millions lost their life savings, their jobs, and the sense of security they had once known. Yet the events of the 1920s had their roots in the past, and their influence strayed into the future. The political isolationism (the belief in staying apart from international politics and economics) that dominated the United States in this period, for example, grew out of people's disillusionment with war and desire to keep out of other countries' troubles. On the other hand, the changing role of women that was set in motion during the 1920s would continue to evolve in coming years.

The period often called the Roaring Twenties or the Jazz Age is popularly remembered for the jazz and blues music and colorful characters it spawned—especially the young women called flappers, who dressed and behaved in a carefree, bold, modern way. The 1920s are famous for the speakeasies, where

Four men drinking illegal alcohol at a 1920s speakeasy. *(© Bettmann/Corbis. Reproduced by permission.)*

people drank liquor made illegal by Prohibition (the popular name for the Eighteenth Amendment to the U.S. Constitution, which banned the manufacture and sale of alcoholic drinks); for the gun-toting gangsters who shot it out on the streets of Chicago; and for the young people leaning exhausted on each other during dance marathons or sitting on top of flagpoles for hours and hours. Although photographs, written records, and the memories of people still alive show that all of these things really did happen, not everybody took part in all of them.

For example, if you were a wealthy young white woman living in a large city, you might indeed have been a flapper. But if you were an Italian-born factory worker in the same large city, or a black sharecropper in the South, or a middle-aged homemaker in a small western town, or a midwestern farmer, your experiences during the 1920s would have been very different. Although it is generally true that the economy was booming during this period, not everybody—especially farmers, African Americans, and recent immigrants—shared in the prosperity. And not everybody embraced the cultural changes that were taking place.

Changes are both exciting and frightening

The 1920s were in many ways an outrageous time. Changes were happening fast and old ways of doing, being, and thinking were questioned. New ways are exciting, but they are also frightening, so it is not surprising that some people welcomed the changes that came during this decade, while others resisted them. These changes, however, could not be slowed down or stopped. They would shape modern life for many years to come.

Unsettling things like suspicion, inequality, and machine gun-toting gangsters gave the 1920s a dark side. Among the most troubling of these darker trends was the hostility toward immigrants from places like southern Europe (e.g., Italy), eastern Europe (e.g., Poland), Asia, and Mexico, who brought traditions different from those of the white Protestant majority of U.S. citizens. The nation's long-standing and complex conflicts over race relations also increased during this period. There were renewed attacks on African Americans, whose differences from the white mainstream were more familiar than those of the new immigrants but just as unwelcomed.

Women cast their vote for president for the first time in November 1920. This was one of the changes taking place in the United States during the 1920s. *(© Bettmann/Corbis. Reproduced by permission.)*

Still, more neutral or even positive changes were also taking place. Women could now vote, and they also had somewhat easier access to education, employment, and birth control. The family was taking on a warmer, more nurturing role, and young people found themselves more respected. Important discoveries and inventions made people healthier and safer and brought unheard-of conveniences to daily life. Many people could afford automobiles and telephones, and almost everybody had a radio. In new magazines like *Time* and *Reader's Digest,* people were dazzled by advertisements for products and appliances that promised to improve their lives, and that they could buy on credit.

A lively new culture

The 1920s saw the birth of a lively mass culture: people from very different places and backgrounds could watch the same movies (now enhanced by sound), laugh at the same radio comedy shows, and worship the same sports heroes. Before the decade was over, advances in transportation made it possible to travel by road or air from one far-off region to another. While these kinds of developments gave many people confidence in the future, others worried that traditional values—especially the individualism that U.S. citizens had always treasured—would be lost. Events like the Scopes Monkey Trial (1925), which centered on a debate between biblical beliefs and the scientific theory of evolution, highlighted the doubt and insecurity that many ordinary people felt.

Meanwhile, the writers of the 1920s were busy producing original literature and commenting on the society around them. Some of the best-known works featured the social criticism of novelist Sinclair Lewis (1885–1951); the biting satire of reporter H.L. Mencken (1880–1956); the powerful dramas of playwright Eugene O'Neill (1888–1953); and the racially charged poems, fiction, and essays of the African Americans who made up the Harlem Renaissance (the period of achievement in African American culture that took place during the 1920s). Musicians were creating the new forms of jazz and blues that would astound the world, and dance both modern (like that performed by Martha Graham [1893–1991]) and popular (like the Charleston and the Black Bottom) was thrilling audiences. Painters, sculptors, architects, and clothing designers were all finding new ways to express themselves.

There is no doubt that the decade of the 1920s was exciting enough to justify the adjective "Roaring" that is often attached to it. But it was also a time of confusion and conflict, as new and old ideas, beliefs, and practices collided with each other. As previously mentioned, the roots of the changes that caused so much excitement and so much struggle may be found in the years leading up to the 1920s.

Industry and immigrants

For more than a century after the colonization and founding of the United States in 1776, the nation's people were occupied with expanding across and settling the immense land they inhabited. The vast majority of them were farmers. But as the twentieth century approached, parts of the country, especially the cities in its eastern half, became more and more industrialized as discoveries and developments made it easier, faster, and cheaper to produce things and to get places. At the same time immigrants from other nations, some pulled by the promise of a better life and some pushed by hardships and mistreatment in their own societies, streamed into the United States.

The nation was changing. The cities were growing larger and more crowded, with vast numbers of mostly poor people crammed together. Corruption was also on the rise, as political "machines" (organizations with seemingly unlimited power and influence) came to control city and state governments. Society itself was changing, too, as people from a wider variety of ethnic and religious backgrounds came together in a new mixture that was not always well blended.

For the first two centuries of its existence, the United States had been dominated by the worldview of people whose ancestors came from such northern European countries as England and the Netherlands. They were white and mostly Protestant, and their values were shaped by the Victorian Age (defined by the years 1837 to 1901, the reign of England's Queen Victoria), which emphasized hard work and a strict moral code based on sobriety, restraint, and traditional Christianity. With the dawn of the twentieth century, though, these values were challenged as a new kind of culture took shape. The new society would introduce different views of women and the family and different approaches to both work and leisure.

The Progressive Era

Meanwhile, in the years that fell between the end of the old and the beginning of the new, came a period called the Progressive Era. It lasted from about 1900 to about 1914 and was led by a loose group of leaders from business, agriculture, and labor as well as radical thinkers like Socialists (who believe in shared or government ownership of the means of production and distribution of goods), anarchists (who believe that no form of government is desirable), and feminists (who support equal rights for women). Although each of these groups had its own ideas and aims, all were reformers; that is, they believed that society needed improvement.

Many reform-minded people were worried that the large corporations that had formed near the end of the nineteenth century had too much power. Thus they sought to give government more ability to protect the rights of individuals, especially workers and consumers. This kind of "activist" government, they hoped, could counterbalance the loss of individuality brought about through modern inventions like the assembly line (which made for much faster production but also boredom, by requiring each worker to perform one task over and over) and the scientific management theory (based on more rigidly structured companies).

Some of the reforms introduced during the Progressive Era included public health measures, workmen's compensation, and laws to restrict child labor and the formation of monopolies (companies with exclusive control of one product or industry). This period had strong threads of morality and nativism (favoring native inhabitants over immigrants) running through it, especially in regard to women's right to vote and the temperance movement (which tried to persuade people to stop drinking alcohol). The suffrage movement had been fighting to win the vote for women since the middle of the nineteenth century, but it was not until 1920, with the passage of the Nineteenth Amendment, that women finally earned this right. Supporters had worked hard to convince the public that, because women were thought to be naturally more pure, more virtuous, and more morally upright than men, they should be allowed to vote so that they could have a good influence on society.

Similarly, many people considered drinking a sinful practice that led to poverty and violence. Groups like the Anti-Saloon League (founded in 1893) argued for a ban on alcohol not only because it would, they believed, improve the lives and productivity of U.S. citizens but also because it would force the new wave of immigrants to behave more like the well-established majority. Whereas the white Protestants of the United States tended to disapprove of alcoholic beverages, these beverages formed an important part of many newcomers' cultures. Thus these immigrants were among those disappointed when the temperance movement managed to push

Amending the Constitution

The Roaring Twenties was a time of major social change and conflict as the values of the earlier centuries were altered or replaced by modern ones. The document at the heart of the U.S. political system, the Constitution, reflected these changes. Two amendments added at the beginning of the decade were both the product of many years of work by reform groups. They sought to improve U.S. society by banning one practice and allowing another.

Nearly a century of efforts by the temperance movement resulted in what was called the "Noble Experiment" of Prohibition. In early 1919 Congress passed the Eighteenth Amendment to the U.S. Constitution, which made it illegal to manufacture, transport, or sell alcoholic beverages. The amendment was meant to put an end to what reformers felt were the negative consequences of drinking, such as decreased worker productivity and family violence.

Prohibition remained a controversial and divisive issue throughout the 1920s. Society was divided into the "Wets," who thought that people should be free to drink alcohol if they chose, and the "Drys," who believed that Prohibition was necessary. Those who suffered most from the ban were the urban poor. Many were immigrants who came from cultures in which alcoholic beverages were accepted and valued.

As the decade wore on, though, it was the increase in crime that captured the attention of most U.S. citizens. Despite Prohibition, many people still wanted to drink, and bootlegging

was hugely profitable. Organized crime was making millions, and law enforcement agencies seemed unwilling or unable to do much about it. The mounting violence and lawlessness shocked ordinary people and made it easier for the Wets to campaign for the repeal, or overturning, of Prohibition.

Led by New York governor and Democratic presidential candidate Alfred E. Smith, the repeal effort resulted in the February 1933 passage of the Twenty-First Amendment, which overturned the Eighteenth Amendment. Prohibition was now seen as a relic of an earlier, more simple time, and something that no longer suited the modern, more sophisticated U.S. society.

Also reflective of social change was the Nineteenth Amendment, which gave women the right to vote and signaled the beginning of a major shift in women's roles. Led by feminist Elizabeth Cady Stanton, the suffrage movement had begun in 1848 at a meeting called the Seneca Falls Convention. Just as Prohibition was intended as a positive social force, supporters of suffrage held that women could exert more of a moral influence on society if they were allowed to vote.

On August 26, 1920, the Nineteenth Amendment was signed into law. Its positive effects were not as immediately obvious as its supporters had expected, though, for the enthusiasm and activism of the Progressive Era receded during the 1920s, and many women chose not to exercise their new right. Nevertheless, winning access to the ballot box was an important step in the evolution of women's rights that took place throughout the course of the twentieth century.

through the Eighteenth Amendment in 1919, which made it illegal to make or sell most alcoholic drinks. Prohibition would play an important role in the mood and practices of the 1920s, but it would eventually prove unenforceable.

African Americans migrate to the North

Another important trend in the years leading up to the 1920s was that of African American migration from the southern states to the northern cities. Beginning in the seventeenth century, black people who had been captured in Africa and transported across the ocean had been forced to work as slaves on the farms and plantations of the South. By the time of the American Civil War (1861–65), there were about four million slaves in the United States.

Although the Civil War had made all African Americans free, they still faced many hardships and injustices. Poor economic conditions, the Jim Crow laws that made discrimination legal, and violent attacks by hostile whites all provided reasons for blacks to leave the South. During the first quarter of the twentieth century, they traveled north in great numbers, hoping to create better lives.

Between 1916 and 1918, for example, five hundred thousand blacks had moved to such large northern cities as Chicago, Illinois; New York City; and Pittsburgh, Pennsylvania. By the end of the 1920s this number doubled. Crowded into poor and racially separated neighborhoods and still limited to the lowest-paying jobs, African Americans found that many of their dreams were still out of reach. Yet the 1920s would also be a time of racial pride and achievement. The writers, musicians, artists, and thinkers of the Harlem Renaissance, for example, would demonstrate the range and depth of black talent.

Meanwhile, though, racial violence was all too common. In 1917 forty blacks were killed in a racially sparked riot in East St. Louis, Missouri. Race riots also erupted two years later in Chicago, Illinois; Knoxville, Tennessee; and Longview, Texas. Even more troubling was the re-emergence in 1915 of the Ku Klux Klan, the white terrorist group that had carried out a brutally successful campaign against blacks during the Reconstruction Era (the period stretching roughly from the

Civil War to the end of the 1870s, when the political and social structure of the defeated South was reorganized). This time the Klan would extend its hatred beyond African Americans to include Jews, Catholics, and immigrants. Playing on the fears and suspicions that many whites felt toward those they perceived as different from themselves, Klan members would claim to be the defenders of tradition and morality.

World War I

While the citizens of the United States struggled with change and division, a conflict between nations was brewing overseas. Beginning in 1914, World War I pitted the Allies—France, Great Britain, and Italy—against Germany, which was seeking to expand its territory. At first the United States seemed determined to stay clear of the conflict. The nation's leader at this time was President Woodrow Wilson (1856–1924; served 1913–21), a Democrat elected in 1912. The son of a Presbyterian minister and the former president of Princeton University, Wilson was an idealistic, reform-minded man. During his first term he presided over several Progressive Era crusades. Through a program he called the New Freedom, he sought to curb the power of business interests by expanding government's influence.

Wilson at first vowed to keep the United States out of the European conflict; in fact, he won re-election in 1916 on the strength of the slogan "He Kept Us Out of War." But then German submarines began attacking merchant ships in the Atlantic Ocean, resulting in the deaths of several U.S. citizens. Finally, in April 1917, the United States declared war on Germany.

The earlier reluctance of U.S. citizens to join the fight now turned to enthusiasm since this effort was intended, as was commonly said, to "make the world safe for democracy." The economy boomed as orders came in from overseas for war materials, equipment, and food. The addition of U.S. troops helped the Allies win the war, but the conflict—waged with new, more effective weapons, airplanes, and trench warfare—was incredibly bloody. More than 15 million people died. The United States, however, suffered a comparatively low 320,000 casualties, including 130,000 killed.

Many people around the world were both horrified by the high cost of war and disillusioned with its results. According to historian Nathan Miller in his book *New World Coming: The 1920s and the Making of Modern America,* "The universal presumptions of the Victorian Age—progress, order, and culture— were blown to bits. For those who had endured the savagery of the fighting and those who lost husbands, fathers, brothers, lovers, and friends, life would never be the same again."

Within the United States, the war had led to even more suspicion of foreigners, radicals, and even just people who disagreed with the government. Several acts were passed to prevent people from expressing their opinions in public, including the Espionage Act of 1917 and the Sedition Act of 1918. During the war Wilson had also taken steps to put the government in charge of functions previously performed by private businesses and industries (such as the railroads).

Wilson's plan for peace

World War I ended in November 1918 when Germany agreed to an armistice, or peace agreement. Armed with a plan for peace he called the Fourteen Points, Wilson traveled to Europe to negotiate a treaty with the leaders of the other nations involved in the war. Meeting with Wilson in Versailles, France, were French premier Georges Clemenceau (1841–1929), British prime minister David Lloyd George (1863–1945), and Italian premier Vittorio Emanuele Orlando (1860–1952). Greeted as a hero by European crowds, Wilson nevertheless faced a difficult struggle in pushing through his ideas for what he called "peace without victory."

An important part of Wilson's plan involved the establishment of the League of Nations, an organization of countries that would agree to work together to resolve conflicts before declaring war. Although the Treaty of Versailles did finally include the League of Nations, many of Wilson's other ideas were ignored. The treaty laid down very harsh terms for Germany (for example, it had to pay the outrageous sum of $33 billion for losses suffered by the Allies during the war), which many correctly predicted would one day lead to another war.

Back in the United States, Wilson faced opposition to the League of Nations. Some members of Congress wanted to

President Woodrow Wilson faced opposition to his plan for the League of Nations back in the United States.

(AP/Wide World Photos. Reproduced by permission.)

change it in various ways, but Wilson refused to compromise. Although the United States eventually signed a document that officially ended the war, the nation never did join the League of Nations (which would later provide a model for the United Nations, formed in 1945). Bitterly disappointed, Wilson waited out the rest of his term, and in March 1921 he left office. The new president was Warren G. Harding (1865–1923; served 1921–23), who would preside over the first part of a decade marked by optimism and prosperity as well as conflict and doubt.

The war's aftermath

For U.S. citizens, the immediate aftermath of World War I was marked by both a sense of relief and new problems. The end of the war spelled the end of European orders for U.S. products and food, resulting in drastic cuts in production and worker layoffs. This meant that many of those who had been hired to work in factories and other businesses during the war, especially African Americans and women, became unemployed as returning soldiers entered the work force again. Stock market prices fell, and farming entered a depression that would last through the 1920s.

These economic troubles led to major labor unrest in 1919, when more than four million workers (or 22 percent of the work force) went on strike to demand better wages and working hours. They also wanted employers to accept and work with unions (organizations of workers formed to protect their interests), as they had during the war. Major strikes occurred across the country, from Seattle to Pittsburgh to Boston. The strikes generally failed, however, as profits continued to fall, wages were cut, and layoffs continued. The economy would soon improve, but the labor movement would not grow strong again until the 1930s.

The Red Scare

At the beginning of the 1920s, the suspicion of foreigners and foreign ideas had been growing along with the increase in immigration to the United States. This had been deepened by the onset of World War I and resulted in a series of events called the Red Scare. The color red was often associated with Communism, the belief that all property should be distributed between all citizens equally. Communism was one of the ideas that many people in the United States believed was being introduced into their country from the outside. Fear that Communists might take over the nation and destroy its democratic system was inflamed by the Bolshevik Revolution (1917) in Russia, in which Communists overthrew the czar (the traditional ruler of Russia) and established a Communist state called the Soviet Union.

The Communist Party did exist in the United States, and even though it did not have very many members, some U.S. citizens blamed such problems as unemployment, strikes, and even the influenza epidemic on Communists. In early 1919 several well-known public figures, including Supreme Court Justice Oliver Wendell Holmes (1841–1935), were the victims or attempted victims of bomb attacks, some involving bombs sent through the mail. Found near the attack sites were printed materials calling for a worker revolution. One of the victims was Attorney General A. Mitchell Palmer (1872–1936), whose home was bombed. Previously, Palmer had been a strong defender of individual rights, but now his views had changed. He became one of the leaders of a movement aimed at promoting what its members called "100 percent Americanism."

Palmer used his power to organize a campaign against Communists and others with radical ideas. The targets of the campaign, however, would include many people who were just suspected of belonging to the wrong group or having the wrong ideas. On January 2, 1920, federal agents in thirty-three cities raided homes and businesses—such as pool halls, restaurants, and community centers—and arrested more than 4,000 suspects. In many cases, the agents did not have the proper warrants needed to make these arrests legal. Among the people rounded up, those who did not have citizenship papers were held for deportation hearings (legal proceedings to determine if they could be forced to leave the country), and 249 of them were eventually sent back to the Soviet Union.

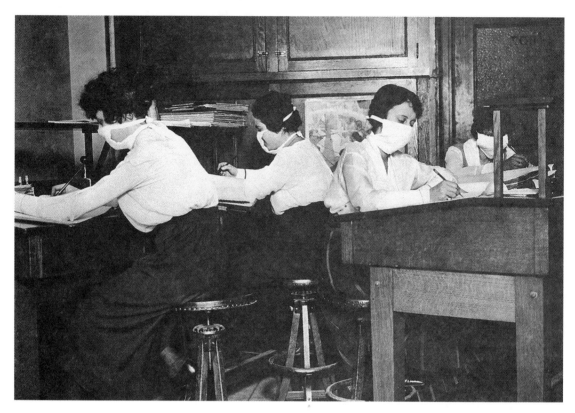

Female office workers wear surgical masks to protect themselves against influenza during the worldwide epidemic. *(© Bettmann/Corbis. Reproduced by permission.)*

Despite the drastic measures taken during this period, the Red Scare did not last long. By the end of 1920 it was over, as most U.S. citizens realized that the threat posed by Communists and other radicals had been greatly exaggerated. Looking back on what happened during this period, it seems strange that the cherished values of freedom of speech and freedom of the press, which are guaranteed to all citizens of the United States by its Constitution, were actually more threatened by the federal government than by any outside forces.

The influenza epidemic

Also adding to the rather grim tone of the period between the end of World War I and the beginning of the 1920s was a worldwide epidemic of influenza. Overall, this quickly spreading illness killed more people than had died in the war. Influenza broke out first near Boston, Massachusetts, in September 1918, and within nine months it had killed five hundred thousand U.S. citizens (including seven hundred in one day in Philadelphia, Pennsylvania) as well as almost twenty-two million people around the globe. Schools were closed and public gatherings were banned. In some places, spitting or coughing in the streets was even forbidden. People walked around wearing gauze masks over their mouths, and coffin makers worked overtime.

Strangely, though, the influenza epidemic did not get much media coverage, as newspapers were filled with news of the war and armistice. After about a year, the disease died out as quickly and as mysteriously as it had appeared. Some have said, however, that the horrible costs of both war and disease contributed to the escapist mood that would characterize the 1920s.

For More Information

Books

Allen, Frederick Lewis. *Only Yesterday: An Informal History of the 1920s.* New York: Perennial, 1964.

Boer, Lawrence, and John D. Walther, eds. *Dancing Fools and Weary Blues: The Great Escape of the Twenties.* Bowling Green, OH: Bowling Green University Press, 1990.

Heckscher, August. *Woodrow Wilson: A Biography.* New York: Scribner, 1991.

Higham, John. *Strangers in the Land: Patterns of American Nativism.* New York: Atheneum, 1965.

Katz, William Loren. *The New Freedom to the New Deal 1913–1939.* Austin, TX: Raintree Steck-Vaughn, 1993.

Leavell, J. Perry, Jr. *Woodrow Wilson.* New Haven, CT: Chelsea House, 1987.

Levin, Phyllis Lee. *Edith and Woodrow: The Wilson White House.* New York: Scribner, 2001.

Miller, Nathan. *New World Coming: The 1920s and the Making of Modern America.* New York: Scribner, 2003.

Noggle, Burl. *Into the Twenties: The United States from Armistice to Normalcy.* Urbana: University of Illinois, 1974.

Perret, Geoffrey. *America in the Twenties.* New York: Touchstone, 1982.

Trani, Eugene P., and David L. Wilson. *The Presidency of Warren G. Harding.* Lawrence: Regents Press of Kansas, 1977.

Web Sites

"American Cultural History, Decade 1920–1929." *Kingwood College Library.* Available online at http://kclibrary.nhmccd.edu/decade20.html. Accessed on June 17, 2005.

Best of History Websites. Available online at http://www.besthistorysites. net/USHistory_Roaring20s.shtml. Accessed on June 17, 2005.

Clash of Cultures in the 1910s and 1920s. Available online at http://history. osu.edu/Projects/Clash/default.htm. Accessed on June 17, 2005.

Interpreting Primary Sources. Digital History. Available online at http:// www.digitalhistory.uh.edu/historyonline/us16.cfm. Accessed on June 17, 2005.

"Woodrow Wilson." *The White House.* Available online at http://www. whitehouse.gov/history/presidents/ww28.html. Accessed on June 17, 2005.

2

Politics in the 1920s

During the Progressive Era (roughly 1900–14), many U.S. leaders and citizens believed that the government should take an active role in protecting individuals, especially children, workers, and consumers. They wanted the government to be free to make laws that would, for example, limit the size of companies so that smaller businesses could compete or stop employers from hiring children to work in their factories. In fact, U.S. involvement in World War I (1914–18; the United States entered the war in 1917) could be seen as a large-scale application of this belief, because it was supposed to make the whole world "safe for democracy" (a common saying of the period).

But that extremely bloody, destructive war took a terrible toll on humanity. When it was over, many people in the United States began to call for an isolationist stance, meaning that the nation should stay out of other countries' affairs and look after its own concerns. At the same time, they adopted a different outlook on the role that government should play in day-to-day life.

The leader of the United States during the war and for much of the Progressive Era that preceded it had been the

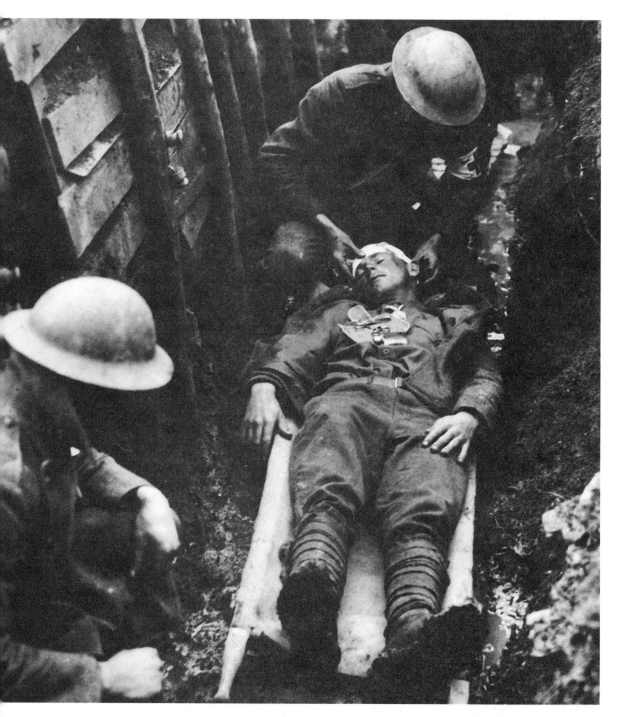

A wounded soldier is placed on a stretcher during World War I. (© Hulton-
Deutsch Collection/Corbis. Reproduced by permission.)

reform-minded, idealistic Woodrow Wilson (1856–1924; served 1913–21). He had been the candidate of the Democratic Party, whose members tended to believe that government should take an active role in improving people's lives. But after the war, and for the entire decade of the 1920s, the men chosen to lead the nation would come from the Republican Party. Members of this political organization were generally more business-oriented. They felt that those active in successful businesses were best suited to direct national affairs. They wanted government to act as a supportive partner to businesses but not try to limit or control them.

The economic growth and prosperity that occurred in the United States during the 1920s (following a short period of economic recession in the first years of the decade) convinced most people that the Republicans were right. Thus the story of politics and government during this period involves an unusually strong partnership between politicians and business. Although there were still voices calling for the government to take a stronger role in reform and people who worried about the poor and the oppressed, the laissez-faire philosophy (the belief that government should loosen its control of the economy and society in general) prevailed. The majority of U.S. citizens seemed to agree with this point of view. Only the crisis of the Great Depression, the period of economic downturn and hardship that began at the end of the 1920s and lasted until the early 1940s, would finally change their minds.

The 1920 election
After World War I ended in 1918, President Wilson had traveled to Europe to take part in peace talks with the heads of the countries—Great Britain, France, and Italy—known as the Allies. Held in Versailles, France, these discussions were to decide on the terms of the Treaty of Versailles, the document that would officially end the war, including the price that Germany would have to pay for starting the war. Wilson brought with him his own plan for the shape that peace should take, which he called the Fourteen Points. The most important of these points involved the establishment of a League of Nations, an organization that would help the countries of the world avoid another terrible war.

Norman Thomas Crusades for Liberal Causes

In a decade dominated by the Republican Party, Norman Thomas was something of a political maverick, or an independent-minded person. As leader of the Socialist movement in the United States, he represented liberal views that were out of the mainstream in a period in which most citizens were conservatives. Yet in his six bids for the presidency, Thomas attracted considerable support.

Born on November 20, 1884, in Marion, Ohio, Thomas was the son of a Presbyterian minister. He studied first at Princeton University in New Jersey, then at a theological seminary. He was ordained a minister in 1911 and assigned to the East Harlem Presbyterian Church in New York City, working among the urban poor.

Thomas was opposed to World War I and joined a pacifist organization called the Fellowship of Reconciliation. He later became one of the founders of the American Civil Liberties Union (ACLU), which provided support for conscientious objectors, who refused to serve in the military because they believed that armed conflict was wrong.

In 1918 Thomas resigned his ministerial position and became an activist for the Socialist Party, succeeding labor leader Eugene V. Debs as the organization's director after Debs's death. In this role, Thomas spoke out in favor of public ownership of industry, natural resources, and transportation. He also pushed for labor reforms like the five-day workweek and the minimum wage. Thomas ran as the Socialist Party's presidential candidates in six elections between 1928 and 1948, earning an impressive number of votes for a third-party candidate (especially in 1932, when 884,781 voters cast ballots for him).

Thomas's relative success suggested that not all U.S. citizens were happy with the laissez-faire government, which featured loosened control of the economy and society in general, the Republicans had put in place. Nor were these people benefiting equally from the general economic prosperity of the Roaring Twenties. The Socialist Party gradually lost supporters, however, when the New Deal program introduced by President Franklin D. Roosevelt incorporated many of its ideas. The party also grew increasingly divided over U.S. foreign policy.

Although Thomas retired from politics in 1948, he continued to actively promote such causes as global peace, nuclear disarmament, and antipoverty measures. He died on December 19, 1968.

Wilson's dream of international cooperation would not be realized, however. Although some of his Fourteen Points, including the League of Nations, were accepted by the Allies, others were not, and Wilson was disappointed by their determination (which he saw as greed) to get as much money as possible from the defeated Germany. As it turned out, predictions that this would create great bitterness among Germans and lead to another war were correct. Meanwhile, Wilson faced opposition at home to the League of Nations. Wilson saw his proposal fail because he was unwilling to compromise on some requested changes to the League. Although the United States eventually signed a document officially ending the war, the nation never did sign the Treaty of Versailles.

Two political conventions

Exhausted and discouraged, Wilson suffered a stroke and lay gravely ill for many months. As the summer convention to choose a Democratic candidate for the 1920 election approached, he had mostly recovered. Democrats wondered if he would pursue a third term as president. Wilson's delay in facing the question meant that his party was not quite prepared when, in the end, he decided not to run. They were divided on several important issues, including whether Prohibition (the ban on the sale or manufacture of alcoholic beverages that had been written into the U.S. Constitution with the Eighteenth Amendment) was a good idea, and what should be done to help struggling farmers.

In the early twentieth century political conventions were unlike those of the twenty-first century. When the convention began, the delegates really had no idea who their candidate would be, and it often took many ballots or votes for them to choose one. This was certainly the case in 1920, when the Democrats went through forty-four vote counts before deciding on Ohio governor James M. Cox (1870–1957) as their rather lackluster, middle-of-the-road candidate. Assistant Secretary of the Navy and future president Franklin D. Roosevelt (1882–1945) was chosen as Cox's vice presidential running mate. The Democratic platform (a set of official positions on various issues) included support for the League of Nations, the Nineteenth Amendment (which would give women the right to vote), and agricultural and labor reform measures. It also supported free speech and freedom of the press and opposed lavish campaign spending.

At their own 1920 convention, the Republicans had less trouble coming up with a candidate to challenge Cox. On the tenth ballot, they chose another Ohioan, a former newspaper publisher and current senator named Warren Gamaliel Harding (1865–1923; served 1921–23) who was known for his moderate views and for his strong party loyalty. The vice presidential candidate was Massachusetts governor Calvin Coolidge (1872–1933; served 1923–29), who had impressed his fellow Republicans with his firm handling of a police strike in Boston. The Republican platform supported cuts in government spending and taxes and more anti-immigration legislation.

A landslide victory

Harding took a relaxed approach to campaigning. He went back to his hometown of Marion, Ohio, and let it be known that he would share his views with anyone who cared to visit him there. A steady stream of people did indeed gather in front of Harding's front porch, where he stood doing what he called "bloviating" (making speeches that were peppered with grandiose phrases and patriotic cliches). Harding was friendly and personable, and he actually enjoyed meeting and chatting with people; he also got along well with the press, partly due to his position as a former newspaper publisher. The vice presidential candidate, whose personality was in many ways the opposite of Harding's, did not campaign very aggressively either, making only one eight-day tour through the southern states (which were traditionally Democratic strongholds).

The Democrats, on the other hand, put a lot of effort into campaigning. Roosevelt was especially energetic, averaging ten speeches a day during the campaign season. His hard work did not pay off, though. The Democrats faced some major obstacles, including their association with the unpopular Woodrow Wilson. Ordinary U.S. citizens approved of the Republican program of lower taxes and less government interference, and Harding's promise of a "return to normalcy" appealed to their postwar need for peace and quiet. (See Warren G. Harding's "Return to Normalcy" primary source entry.) Harding won by a landslide, gaining 404 electoral votes to Cox's 127, as well as 60 percent of the popular vote to Cox's 37 percent. This was the widest margin by which any U.S. president had ever been elected.

A partnership between business and government

Thus began a decade of Republican dominance of the U.S. government. As Harding took office in the early spring of 1921, the economy was in something of a downturn caused by the dips in manufacturing and employment that had followed the end of the war. The reason for this downturn was that foreign orders for war materials and other goods dried up and returning soldiers flooded the job market. Convinced that the economy would improve and prosper if the federal government would give it space to do so, Harding went about putting into place his program of cooperation between government and business.

Harding chose some well-qualified men to head up this program, including Secretary of Commerce Herbert Hoover (1874–1964), who would himself be president by the end of the decade. Hoover called for more efficiency and for a system he called "cooperative capitalism" (in a capitalist system, a country's industry and trade are controlled by private owners for profit), which involved loosening many regulations while leaving some in place.

Warren G. Harding's landslide victory over James M. Cox was the widest margin by which any U.S. president had ever been elected. *(AP/Wide World Photos. Reproduced by permission.)*

Another important figure in Harding's administration was Andrew Mellon (1855–1937), who would serve as Secretary of the Treasury under all three Republican presidents of the 1920s. Mellon was a strong champion of tax reform. He believed it was essential to reduce government spending while also lowering taxes, so that wealthy people could make more investments. According to what has become known as the "trickle-down" theory of economics, the result would be more jobs and benefits for everybody. This philosophy would become popular again in the 1980s under President Ronald Reagan (1911–2004; served 1981–89).

Harding's two years in office were characterized by this partnership between business and government and by the general promotion of expansion in industry and business. Between 1922 and 1927, the economy would grow at an impressive rate of 7 percent per year. The nation would become steadily more prosperous throughout the decade, with a corresponding rise in consumerism.

Farmers are in trouble

The picture was not so bright in the agricultural sector, however. Even though the 1920 census (a population count taken every ten years) had shown that more U.S. citizens now lived in urban than rural areas, much of the nation was still dominated by agriculture. The United States had 400 million acres of farmland, on which lived and worked about one-third of the country's population. As the 1920s began record amounts of crops were being grown, yet farmers were in trouble. The problem was that farmers were producing many more crops than were needed while also paying high prices for the materials and equipment they used to operate their farms. This meant that they earned very low profits and incurred large debts.

Even the formation of a farm bloc (a group of legislators or others who band together to lobby in favor of a special interest) that called for more generous credit for farmers, higher tariffs (taxes) on exports, and cooperative marketing proved ineffective. The core problems, especially those of production surpluses and the gap between low prices for crops and high operating costs, remained unresolved. By the time the Great Depression arrived in 1929, farmers had already endured a decade of hardship.

Restricting immigration

Another important aspect of Harding's administration was its support for new restrictions on immigration. During the 1920s the traditional image of the United States as a welcoming refuge for those seeking better lives shifted dramatically. Once foreigners had been encouraged to move to the United States, because their willingness to take low-paying jobs made them attractive as employees. Early waves of immigrants had been

Even though the Roaring Twenties were prosperous for most Americans, this was not the case for farmers who suffered greatly during the decade.

(Courtesy of The Library of Congress.)

dominated by people from northern European countries like England and the Netherlands, whose values and habits were similar to those of most native-born U.S. residents. But the early years of the nineteenth century had seen a big increase in immigrants from southern Europe, especially Italy, and eastern Europe, such as Poland and Yugoslavia. Whereas the United States had historically been dominated by Protestants—such as Baptists, Methodists, and Presbyterians—many of the newcomers were Catholic or Jewish. They came from unfamiliar cultures. Importantly, many of these immigrants did not share mainstream citizens' disapproval of liquor.

The fear and distrust that many U.S. residents felt for foreigners was increased by World War I and by the Communist takeover that resulted from Russia's Bolshevik Revolution in 1917.

(Communism is a system where all property is jointly owned by the whole community.) Native-born people worried that their beloved U.S. culture was under attack by outsiders with unsavory habits and radical political views. The result was a movement toward "nativism" (favoring native-born citizens over immigrants) and toward new laws to curb the influx of immigrants from places seen as undesirable. In 1921 Congress passed an emergency law that limited immigration to 355,000 immigrants per year (those from Asia had already been severely restricted). Each nation would be allowed a quota (fixed number) of 3 percent of whatever number of residents from that country had been in the United States at the time of the 1910 census.

Despite some resistance from business leaders, who hated to lose so much cheap labor, this trend continued. It was helped by the popularity of eugenics, a pseudoscience that not only claimed to prove the inferiority of anyone who was not of northern European heritage but also warned that U.S. society would be doomed if its white citizens mixed with people who were biologically inferior. In 1924 Congress passed the National Origins Act, which capped immigration at 150,000 and lowered the earlier country quotas to 2 percent of foreign-born residents at the time of the 1890 census when very few southern and eastern Europeans had been in the United States. Immigration from Asian countries was banned altogether.

An unexpected loss

Even though Harding had made some wise choices in staffing his administration—including Hoover, Mellon, and Secretary of State Charles Evans Hughes (1862–1948)—he had also made some poor ones. Harding was not just a loyal Republican, he was a loyal friend, but some of his friends proved unworthy of his faithfulness. In the middle of 1923 rumors began circulating that Harding's administration was riddled with corruption. Key figures in the scandals would include not only attorney general Harry M. Daugherty but also Interior Secretary Albert B. Fall and Charles Forbes, who was the head of the Veteran's Bureau.

It is thought that by the summer of 1923, when Harding embarked on a speaking tour to the West, he probably already knew something about the scandals that were soon to break wide open. In any case, Harding would not be around when the truth was revealed. On August 23, he died suddenly in a hotel in San Francisco, California, of an unidentified ailment that was probably related to heart disease.

When word of the president's death reached Vice President Calvin Coolidge, he was vacationing at his family home in Plymouth Notch, Vermont. Coolidge's father woke him up with the news at 2:30 A.M. The elder Coolidge was a notary public, and as such, was authorized to deliver the oath of office to his son. Upon returning to Washington, D.C., Coolidge took the oath of office again.

As vice president, Coolidge had been an especially quiet, unassuming presence in the Harding administration, and became know as "Silent Cal" due to his unwillingness to engage in small talk. When he took over as president, he vowed to continue with the policies that Harding had established. Coolidge's calm, low-key manner and his reputation for honesty and integrity did much to reassure the U.S. people after the unexpected loss of their elected president. Just as Coolidge took office, the scandals that had swirled beneath the surface of Harding's presidency broke through. Coolidge quickly took steps to see that the wrongdoers were investigated and prosecuted, which also helped to distance him from the corruption that had been exposed.

The Teapot Dome scandal

All of the scandals involved public officials who had taken advantage of their positions to gain something for themselves at public expense. Some commentators have suggested that the close links forged between business and government during the 1920s created an atmosphere in which corruption could, and did, thrive. In any case, some of the perpetrators were among those closest to Harding, including his old friend Harry Daugherty, who was accused of taking bribes from former clients in exchange for political favors, and Charles Forbes of the Veteran's Bureau, who was convicted of cheating his agency out of thousands of dollars that went into his own bank account. Of all the political misdeeds that occurred during the 1920s, however, the Teapot Dome scandal is perhaps the best known.

Teapot Dome involved some rights to oil reserves in the western United States. During the Progressive Era, conservationists (people who believe in protecting or restoring the natural environment) had sought to preserve these areas by making them federal property. Thus these areas were off limits to private oil companies that would have liked to lease these lands so that they could drill for and sell the oil located there. Because the oil was eventually to be used to fuel warships, the reserves were under the control of the Department of the Navy.

When Harding took office, he appointed a staunch anti-conservationist, New Mexico senator Albert B. Fall, as secretary of the interior (the federal department responsible for looking after government-owned land). Fall persuaded Secretary of the Navy Edwin Denby to transfer the rights to the western oil reserves to the Interior Department. Then he started granting oil drilling rights to several of his friends in the oil industry. Edward L. Doheny of Pan-American Petroleum and Transport Company got the rights to reserves in California, while Harry Sinclair of Mammoth Oil Company got those at Teapot Dome, Wyoming.

Conservationists who were concerned about these developments, along with some members of Congress, started an investigation that led to public hearings that began on October 23, 1923. The case began to get a lot of attention after it was learned that Fall had, as he put it, "borrowed" about $100,000 from Doheny. The hearings, which lasted through the spring of 1924, resulted in Fall's conviction on bribery charges. Fall became the first member of a president's cabinet to go to prison, while Daugherty and Denby were both forced to resign; two other men who were probably involved in the scandal committed suicide. Coolidge, meanwhile, emerged untouched by the taint of corruption.

Coolidge wins reelection

Coolidge was true to his word, continuing with the same conservative, pro-business policies, as well as many of the same administration officials, that Harding had promoted. As 1924 unfolded, Coolidge decided to run for reelection, hoping to win the presidency on his own merits rather than by chance.

Albert B. Fall (left), U.S. secretary of the interior, and Harry F. Sinclair, president of the Mammoth Oil Company, two of the participants in the Teapot Dome Scandal. *(© Bettmann/Corbis. Reproduced by permission.)*

Once again the Democrats found it difficult to choose a candidate. For a while the favorite was the widely respected William McAdoo (1863–1941), who had been both Wilson's treasury secretary and his son-in-law. But McAdoo's reputation had been scarred, even though he was a Democrat, because he had served as a legal adviser to one of the men involved in the Teapot Dome scandal, and because he had accepted support from the Ku Klux Klan. (The Ku Klux Klan is a white terrorist group first formed in the South just after the American Civil War, which once again emerged in the early 1920s.)

Eventually the Democrats selected John W. Davis (1873–1955), a lawyer and diplomat with a conservative, pro-business approach not very different from that of Coolidge. This election also featured the participation of a third-party candidate,

Senator Robert LaFollette (1855–1925) of Wisconsin, who ran on the Progressive Party ticket. LaFollette's platform included support for a tax increase for wealthy citizens, an end to child labor, encouraging urban and rural workers to unite, and condemning the Ku Klux Klan.

Coolidge's approach to campaigning was in keeping with his nickname: he was almost completely silent on the issues. Instead he allowed his vice presidential running mate, Charles G. Dawes (1865–1951) to take on the burden of active campaigning. (Part of the reason may have been that Coolidge's son Calvin Jr. had died of blood poisoning that summer after getting a blister on his toe while playing tennis on the White House grounds.) In the end Coolidge's low-key approach—his slogan was "Keep Cool with Coolidge"—to the election mattered not at all, because he won decisively. He earned an impressive 54 percent of the popular vote to Davis's 29 percent; LaFollette won a surprisingly large 17 percent.

Coolidge continues laissez-faire policies

Coolidge's victory had shown that the laissez-faire approach to government he favored was strongly supported by the majority of U.S. citizens. The second (and first full) term of his presidency was marked by his belief that private enterprise was the backbone of U.S. society and that the main purpose of government was to assist business in every way possible. His most famous line was that "the chief business of America is business," uttered in a speech he made a few months after his inauguration. He pushed for high tariffs, low taxes, and prompt payment of the loans the United States had made to the Allies during World War I. He and Treasury Secretary Mellon sought to cut government expenses dramatically while also loosening the government's grip on many industries. For example, budget cuts meant that there were fewer inspectors to keep track of the quality of the food and drugs that U.S. citizens consumed.

Despite his general popularity, Coolidge was disliked by farmers because he did not support efforts to provide government assistance to the agricultural sector. In both 1927 and 1928 Coolidge vetoed the McNary-Haugen Bill, which called for price supports for agricultural products (in other words, farmers would charge higher prices for their crops than the market demanded to help close the gap between their profits and expenses). Although the bill was flawed, it did call attention to the problem of surpluses and to the idea of paying farmers to reduce the number of acres they cultivated. This reform strategy would be used later, after the Great Depression made the farmers' problems inescapable.

The revival of the U.S. economy that occurred during the 1920s was so closely associated with the man who was president during much of the decade that it was often referred to as Coolidge Prosperity. The country was producing more goods and wages were rising, allowing many people to buy things like cars and appliances. The unemployment rate fell from 11.7 percent to 5 percent. At the same time, though, the country was dominated by a get-rich-quick mood that led to widespread speculation on the stock market, with investors buying stocks on credit in the hope of making huge profits with which to pay back their debts. This and other indicators were already warning some more cautious observers that trouble was on the way.

Foreign affairs

On the international front, Coolidge's approach to foreign affairs was not really as isolationist as it may seem. For one thing, U.S. businesses were still interested in selling their products to foreign markets. For another, the United States was intervening in several troubled countries in the Caribbean and Central America, including Haiti, Honduras, and the Dominican Republic. In Nicaragua, concerned about the region's stability and about preventing the spread of radical political ideas, the United States lent support to a conservative government, despite protests that it should stay out of other nations' affairs.

Another notable political event of Coolidge's presidency was the signing of the Kellogg-Briand Pact, an agreement intended to outlaw war between the nations of the world, justifying armed conflict only as a last resort. (See the Kellogg-Briand Pact Primary Source entry.) The idea of taking such a step had been discussed among peace activists since the end of World War I, when many began to fear that Germany's harsh treatment under the Versailles Treaty would lead that country to start another war. One of these activists was a

Columbia University professor named James T. Shotwell, who proposed a peace agreement to French foreign minister Aristide Briand (1862–1932).

Briand subsequently announced that France would be willing to sign such an agreement with the United States. Secretary of State Frank B. Kellogg (1856–1937) was initially cool to the idea, but pressure exerted by members of Congress, peace activists, and the press finally changed his position. The Kellogg-Briand Pact was signed by fifteen nations in August 1928 (eventually a total of sixty-two countries signed the agreement) and approved by the U.S. Senate by a vote of eighty-five to one. Although the pact is now seen as having been totally ineffective (another world war broke out in the late 1930s), it did represent some willingness on the part of the United States to cooperate with other nations.

The 1928 election

As the 1928 election approached Coolidge's admirers assumed that he would run for president again. He seemed to be at the height of his career and enjoyed widespread support. Coolidge surprised everyone when he announced that he would instead return to a quiet life in Vermont. Some historians have suggested that Coolidge had read the warning signs and, knowing what was coming—that is, the Great Depression—wanted to put himself as far away from the trouble as possible. Others argue that he was simply tired of being president and that all the joy had gone out of the job after the death of his beloved son. In any case, the Republicans were left with the task of choosing someone else as their candidate.

The man they chose was already fairly familiar to U.S. citizens and admired by many. Herbert Hoover was a self-made man: born in California and orphaned at ten, he had graduated from Stanford University, worked as a mining engineer, and become a millionaire before he was forty. He had also built a stellar career in public service.

During World War I, Hoover had done an outstanding job in the role of administrator of food distribution in Europe. As commerce secretary under Coolidge, he had promoted efficiency and self-regulation in government, with such success that people began to use the word "Hooverize" to stand for economizing and saving. Hoover managed to combine the typically Republican, laissez-faire approach to government with his own concern for minorities, women, and children, even earning the nickname "The Great Humanitarian." In fact, during the terrible flood that occurred in Mississippi in 1927, Hoover personally took charge of the relief effort, overseeing the set-up of tent cities to house the more than a million people who were left homeless and the building of a thousand wooden boats that were used in rescue and evacuation efforts. Another of Hoover's accomplishments as commerce secretary is still a major U.S. landmark: he encouraged several western states to cooperate in the building of the large and much-needed dam that bears his name on the Colorado River.

At the Republican convention in the summer of 1928, Hoover was nominated on the first ballot. His running mate was Charles Curtis (1860–1936) of Kansas, who was chosen mainly for his appeal to midwestern farmers. The party's platform endorsed the main positions of the Coolidge administration, especially lowering taxes, reducing the federal debt, and maintaining an isolationist stance in foreign affairs.

Once again, the Democrats were suffering from deep divisions. Theirs was a party that tended to appeal to people from a wide variety of backgrounds, with members from both rural and urban, native-born and immigrant, Catholic and Protestant backgrounds. They disagreed on the issue of Prohibition, with some supporting the ban on alcohol and some opposing it. The deciding factor in choosing a candidate for this election was that the Democrats needed to win New York, with its high electoral vote count. Thus they chose the governor of that state, Alfred E. Smith (1873–1944), as their candidate.

Smith was a controversial figure because of his Irish-Catholic background (there had never been a Catholic president, and in fact would not be until the 1960s, when John F. Kennedy was elected) and his anti-Prohibition stance. He also favored again opening up immigration. But the Democrats hoped that adding vice presidential nominee Joseph T. Robinson (1872–1937), a senator from Arkansas, would increase their ticket's appeal in the South.

They hoped in vain, however. In fact, Hoover won many more votes across the South than Smith, in spite of that region's usual tendency to vote for Democrats. Smith won only eight states, gaining a relatively impressive 41 percent of the popular vote. At his inauguration Hoover expressed the same confidence and optimism that had characterized the national mood for most of the decade. As quoted in Erica Hanson's *The 1920s,* Hoover said, "I have no fears for our country. It is bright with hope."

Signs of trouble to come

Hoover would have only eight months in office that could be called bright or hopeful. During those eight months he proved himself an able and even progressive leader, taking positive steps toward improving child welfare, prison reform, conservation, and better treatment of African Americans. Yet it is not these accomplishments for which Hoover is remembered. Because of the events that took place before the end of his first year in office, his name would always be linked to the Great Depression.

When Hoover's presidency began, things really did seem positive. The country had enjoyed nearly a decade of rising prosperity, and it seemed that things would continue along this same path. Yet there were warning signs that the economy was not as strong as most people assumed. For one thing, construction was declining, which can be seen as a negative economic indicator. For another, more goods (such as cars) were being produced than people were buying; in addition, poor economies overseas were affecting U.S. investors. Banks were lending money at high interest rates (the cost borrowers pay for the money they receive) to people who were using it to invest in the stock market.

When a person buys stock in a company, he is giving that company some money to help it operate, with the promise of a share in the profits later, when the company performs well. When a stock price goes up, it means that more people want to buy that stock, so it is more valuable. When the price goes down, it means that the stock has lost value, and an investor may lose money. During the 1920s many more U.S. citizens, especially ordinary people who were not wealthy, were investing in the stock market than had ever before. Sometimes they used their own savings, and sometimes they borrowed money or bought stocks on credit with the hope of making huge profits and paying back their debts.

By 1928 the New York Stock Exchange was trading six to seven million shares (or stocks) per day, compared to a more normal rate of three to four million. The prices of stocks had risen higher and higher, but these prices did not reflect the stocks' real value or the real earning capacity of companies. All across the country people were frantically playing the stock market, hoping to get rich fast. Some thought this could go on forever, but it could not. In the fall of 1929, the stock market started taking big dips downward.

Investors began to worry, and even to panic, which meant that many were selling off all of their stocks. Then came Black Thursday. On Thursday, October 24, orders to sell stocks rose at an alarming rate, while prices fell and fell. On the streets of New York City's financial district, crowds gathered and panic and hysteria mounted. This led to even more selling that took place across the nation. Five days later, on what is known as Black Tuesday, the devastation was complete, as banks with no cash in their safes began to close their doors. Many people had lost their life savings, with no chance of getting them back again.

Hoover's efforts to restore people's confidence in the U.S. economy failed as things grew worse and worse. Scores of businesses closed, and unemployment rose from 700,000 to 3 million. Suddenly the country was deep in the worst depression in its history. The nation's mood shifted from the joyous confidence of the 1920s to doubt and fear of what the future would bring. Unable to find a way to mend things, Hoover was voted out of office in the next election. In 1932, a dynamic Democrat named Franklin D. Roosevelt would convince the U.S. people that his New Deal program of government and economic reform would light the way out of the Great Depression.

Warning signs from overseas

While many U.S. citizens of the 1920s were overlooking the warning signs at home, fateful things were occurring in Europe that would soon impact the entire world. World War I had ended with Germany's surrender, and many of its citizens

Investors rush to withdraw their savings from a bank before it is wiped out during the 1929 stock market crash.
(Hulton Archive/Getty Images. Reproduced by permission.)

were enraged by the harsh terms of the Treaty of Versailles. One of these was a war veteran named Adolf Hitler (1889–1945), who blamed his nation's Jewish population for many of its problems, including the economic depression under which Germany (like other European countries) was suffering.

In the early 1920s Hitler became the head of the National Socialist German Workers Party, also known as the Nazis. In November 1923 he was involved in a failed attempt to take over the government. Jailed for nine months, he wrote *Mein Kampf,* a book that expressed his theory of Aryans (white people) as the Master Race and Jews in particular as undesirable aliens. He spent the rest of the decade rebuilding the Nazi Party and gathering more and more supporters. In 1934 he would become head of state and begin a campaign of aggression and terror (including the murder of six million Jews and a million others) that would lead to the outbreak of World War II (1939–45). In that conflict, Germany would be allied with Italy, under the control of dictator Benito Mussolini (1883–1945). Also joining what would come to be known as the Axis countries would be Japan, whose military strength and desire to expand its empire were growing during the 1920s.

For More Information

Books

Abels, Jules. *In the Time of Silent Cal.* New York: Putnam, 1989.

Burner, David. *Herbert Hoover: A Public Life.* New York: Knopf, 1978.

Downes, Randolph C. *The Rise of Warren Gamaliel Harding: 1865–1920.* Columbus: Ohio State University Press, 1970.

Fausold, Martin. *The Presidency of Herbert C. Hoover.* Lawrence: University Press of Kansas, 1985.

Ferrell, Robert H. *The Presidency of Calvin Coolidge*. Lawrence: University Press of Kansas, 1998.

Hanson, Erica. *The 1920s*. San Diego, CA: Lucent Books, 1999.

Haynes, John Earl. *Calvin Coolidge and the Coolidge Era: Essays on the History of the 1920s*. Washington, DC: Library of Congress, 1998.

Heckscher, August. *Woodrow Wilson: A Biography*. New York: Scribner, 1991.

Higham, John. *Strangers in the Land: Patterns of American Nativism*. New York: Atheneum, 1965.

Katz, William Loren. *The New Freedom to the New Deal 1913–1939*. Austin, TX: Raintree Steck-Vaughn, 1993.

Leavell, J. Perry, Jr. *Woodrow Wilson*. New Haven, CT: Chelsea House, 1987.

Levin, Phyllis Lee. *Edith and Woodrow: The Wilson White House*. New York: Scribner, 2001.

McCoy, Donald R. *Calvin Coolidge: The Quiet President*. Lawrence: University Press of Kansas, 1988.

Miller, Nathan. *New World Coming: The 1920s and the Making of Modern America*. New York: Scribner, 2003.

Moore, Edward A. *A Catholic Runs for President: The Campaign of 1928*. New York: Ronald Press, 1956.

Nash, George H. *The Life of Herbert Hoover, Vol. I*. New York: Norton, 1983.

Nash, George H. *Teapot Dome: Oil and Politics in the 1920s*. Westport, CT: Greenwood Publishing Group, 1980.

Slayton, Robert A. *Empire Statesman: The Rise and Redemption of Al Smith*. New York: Free Press, 2001.

Sobel, Robert. *Coolidge: An American Enigma*. Washington, DC: Regnery, 1998.

Weiner, M.R., and John Starr. *Teapot Dome*. New York: Norton, 1965.

Web Sites

"American Cultural History, Decade 1920–1929." *Kingwood College Library* http://kclibrary.nhmccd.edu/decade20.html. Accessed on June 17, 2005.

Best of History Websites. http://www.besthistorysites.net/USHistory_Roaring 20s.shtml. Accessed on June 17, 2005.

"Calvin Coolidge: 30th President of the United States." *The Calvin Coolidge Memorial Foundation*. Available online at http://www.calvin-coolidge.org/ index.html. Accessed on June 17, 2005.

Clash of Cultures in the 1910s and 1920s. http://history.osu.edu/Projects/ Clash/default.htm. Accessed on June 17, 2005.

"Coolidge and Foreign Affairs: Kellogg Briand Pact, August 27, 1928." *U-S-History.com.* Available online at http://www.u-s-history.com/pages/h1485.html. Accessed on June 17, 2005.

"Herbert Clark Hoover (1929–1933)." *American President.* Available online at http://www.americanpresident.org/history/herberthoover/. Accessed on June 17, 2005.

Interpreting Primary Sources. Digital History. http://www.digitalhistory.uh.edu/historyonline/us16.cfm. Accessed on June 17, 2005.

Warren G. Harding. Available online at http://www.whitehouse.gov/history/presidents/wh29.html. Accessed on June 17, 2005.

3

The Business of America: The Economy in the 1920s

T he story of the 1920s is in large part a story about money. After a few slow years at the start of the decade, money began to flow through many, though not all, people's hands. The flow continued right up until those fateful few days near the end of 1929, when it suddenly stopped. After the seemingly endless prosperity of the previous years, the stock market crash and the onset of the Great Depression (the period of economic downturn and hardship that would last until the beginning of World War II; 1939–45) came as a great surprise to almost everybody. A few sharp observers had predicted that the good times of the Roaring Twenties were too good to last, that certain practices and attitudes popular during the decade could lead to disaster. But while the money flowed, few paid attention to the warning signs.

Ordinary people were only following the lead, after all, of the nation's most powerful figures. The federal government was now dominated by men who considered business the lifeblood of the United States. One of the most famous remarks of the 1920s was made by President Calvin Coolidge (1872–1933; served 1923–29), who declared in a

A man selling his car after losing everything in the stock market crash.

(© Bettmann/Corbis. Reproduced by permission.)

1927 speech delivered to newspaper editors that "the business of America is business." The administrations of all three presidents who served during the 1920s—Warren G. Harding (1865–1923; served 1921–23), Coolidge, and Herbert Hoover (1874–1964; served 1929–33)—followed the same laissez-faire approach. That is, they believed that if government would just stay out of business affairs, for example, by lowering taxes and loosening regulations, the economy would thrive and everyone would benefit. Up until the close of the decade, most U.S. citizens agreed.

A different United States

The first two decades of the twentieth century were dominated by a major shift not only in the work done by most people in the United States but in the very makeup of those people as well. Previously, a majority had worked either on farms or as skilled craftsmen. They toiled in small, relatively quiet settings where the emphasis was on doing a job well, not on getting it done quickly. But at the dawn of the twentieth century, more people moved out of rural areas and into cities. Factories began springing up everywhere. They were big, noisy places in which it was important to work fast. The concerns and accomplishments of individual workers took a backseat to increasing production numbers. A large number of laborers, including young children, were working long hours for low wages, often under harsh conditions. To protect themselves, workers began forming labor unions and taking part in strikes, many of which had violent outcomes.

At the same time, the population of the United States was changing. The early years of the century saw a huge surge of immigrants, many from the countries of southern and eastern Europe (such as Italy, Greece, and Poland). Grateful for the fresh start and future prosperity that the United States promised, these people were willing to work for little money. African Americans from the rural South were also migrating north in search of better jobs and an escape from prejudice, discrimination, and white terrorist groups like the Ku Klux Klan. Increasing numbers of women were also entering the workforce, though, like immigrants and blacks, most of them were working as unskilled laborers. The cities were growing and expanding past their earlier boundaries, and this growth, combined with the new mix of people, brought social, economic, and political tensions. During the Progressive Era (which lasted roughly from 1900 to 1914), reformers would try to ease some of these tensions.

Rise of big business sparks reform efforts

During the 1800s the United States became an increasingly industrialized country. As the century progressed, major advances in technology brought machines that increased productivity. At the same time, new ideas about the efficient management of that production became popular.

The railroad industry was one of the most important industries of the nineteenth century. By 1900, there were 200,000 miles of track crisscrossing the United States, compared with the 65,000 miles that had existed at the end of the American Civil War (1861–65). Not only could goods now be easily transferred from one far-flung place to another, but people could also communicate with residents of regions that had previously been far out of reach. In one way, that made the country seem smaller, but in another, it led to a new and important concern. The rapid growth of the railroad system and the great wealth and power it brought to those who controlled it, who sometimes took actions to protect their interests, like price-fixing, that did not benefit the people who used the trains, led to questions about government regulation. Many believed that only government rules would keep the big railroad companies in line.

Other kinds of companies were also forming and expanding during this period, such as those producing steel and oil and those processing and packing meat. It took a lot of money and people to run these large corporations, and proper management became a key issue. The men who sat at the top of these new corporate structures, well-known examples include J.P. Morgan (1867–1943) at U.S. Steel and John D. Rockefeller (1839–1937) at Standard Oil, inspired awe and fear for their almost unimaginable wealth and power. Working under them were networks of lesser managers, who followed the principle that productivity, efficiency, and profits were more valuable than anything else, including the rights or concerns of individual workers.

Reform-minded leaders and activists feared that the new corporations had become too big and powerful and that workers were in danger of being crushed by the companies that depended on their labor. These reformers, who became known as Progressives because of their belief in positive change, pushed for protections for factory workers and consumers. They considered women and children especially vulnerable and worked with particular passion on protecting these groups.

World War I brings a shift in attitude

Among the new laws enacted during the Progressive Era were public health measures, workmen's compensation, and restrictions on child labor. Through such legislation as the

Sherman Antitrust Act of 1890, the Clayton Antitrust Act of 1914, and the founding of the Federal Trade Commission in 1914, reformers tried to prevent the formation of monopolies (companies with exclusive control of one product or industry). They believed that such corporations not only threatened society's weakest members but also unfairly limited competition by pushing smaller companies out of business. The pro-business atmosphere of the 1920s would, however, drain these measures of power.

It might be said that the sentiments of the Progressive Era, the idea of helping the weak and taking an active approach to improving society, led to the entry of the United States into World War I (1914–18) in 1917. This global conflict was popularly called a war to "make the world safe for democracy." Yet when the war, with its huge toll of death and destruction, was over, the mood of the vast majority of U.S. citizens had

In the early 1900s, men such as John D. Rockefeller inspired awe and fear due to their almost unimaginable wealth and power. *(© Bettmann/Corbis. Reproduced by permission.)*

changed. The activist government of the Progressive Era gave way to the laissez-faire approach that would dominate the 1920s. Instead of being feared for his power, the businessman would now be embraced and respected by both government leaders and ordinary people for his management skills, his wisdom, and most of all his ability to make astounding quantities of money.

During World War I the federal government had tightened its control on several industries, especially the railroads, that were crucial to the production and transportation of materials and equipment needed for the war effort. When the war was over, however, government leaders favored the loosening of these controls. In the twenty-first century U.S. citizens take the safeguards guaranteed by the Environmental Protection

Agency, consumer protection laws, and Social Security for granted. In the 1920s none of these existed. Instead businesses were left to their own devices, with the blessing of the federal government. Under Treasury Secretary Andrew Mellon (1855–1937), who served under all three presidents of the decade, taxes were also lowered. Mellon's idea, which has since come to be known as the "trickle-down" theory of economics, was that if wealthy companies and individuals had money to invest, the overall economy would improve, benefiting even the poorest members of society.

The economy starts to prosper

In the years immediately following the end of the war, the nation experienced something of an economic recession, or temporary decline. This occurred because the orders for materials, weapons, and equipment that had kept U.S. industry humming during the conflict were no longer being received. Similarly, U.S. farmers who had struggled to keep up with the demand for food to feed armies and ordinary people in war-torn Europe now found themselves with too few customers. In fact, the farming sector entered a slump that would continue through the 1920s. The rest of the economy, however, would soon begin to flourish. A major factor in the economic prosperity of the 1920s would be the development and popularity of new technologies used both by industry and by consumers, especially automobiles, airplanes, radios, and appliances like washing machines and vacuum cleaners.

Between 1922, when the recession ended, and 1927, the U.S. economy grew by 7 percent, which is the largest increase it has ever achieved in such a short period. Throughout the 1920s, each year saw a rise in every leading economic indicator (signs that the economy is thriving). Income levels rose (workers, for example, made 26 percent more in 1929 than they had in 1919), as did business growth, new construction, and stock market trading. Production rose by 64 percent between 1920 and 1930, while only 2 percent of workers were unemployed. Not everybody was rich, but many more people than before had more money to spend. Significantly, the old ideas about saving were no longer so popular, and people wanted to spend their money.

Frederick Taylor: A New Kind of Management

The expansion of business and industry that occurred during the Roaring Twenties had its roots in earlier decades of the late nineteenth and early twentieth centuries. A case in point is the theory of scientific management, which developed prior to 1920 but influenced many of the decade's leading business and industry leaders. The inventor of scientific management was Frederick Taylor, an industrial expert who devised more efficient and productive ways to manage workers.

Born in 1856, Frederick Taylor worked as a machinist and then as a foreman in machine shops. His work convinced him that productivity was not as high as it could be, and he spent the 1880s and 1890s publishing papers describing how industry should be run. In 1901 he left his job at Bethlehem Steel after the company's directors rejected his productivity ideas. Taylor became a management consultant and in June 1903, after a presentation made to industrial engineers, his work began to achieve recognition. He was elected president of the American Society of Mechanical Engineers in 1906.

In 1911 Taylor's book *Principles of Scientific Management* was published. It detailed Taylor's vision for making workers more efficient: study a particular task in detail, breaking it down into separate steps; calculate the minimum amount of time needed for each step in order to determine the most time-efficient means to perform it; if a worker could not complete the task within this time, he would be fired.

Previously, their special knowledge had given skilled workers a certain amount of power. Under Taylor's revolutionary system, managers had more knowledge of tasks and thus more control over them. Because certain tasks were assigned to individual workers, it also isolated them from one another and made them more dependent on managers. If workers recognized that their interests were closely linked to those of their managers, Taylor theorized, they would want to work more efficiently.

Industry and business leaders such as automobile manufacturer Henry Ford were not the only ones to adopt Taylor's ideas. They were also applied in areas of education, medicine, and the military. By the time of Taylor's death in 1915 scientific management was the dominant trend and it would remain so throughout much of the twentieth century.

Consumer demand spurs new approach

Consumer demand for various products led to great leaps for industry. Early in the century, an industrial engineer named Frederick Taylor (1856–1915) had created a theory called scientific management that promised to make corporations more efficient and thus allow for maximum mass production. Taylor performed studies to determine how to get men and machines to work together smoothly and quickly.

His theory emphasized the importance of managers to lead the functions of sales, budgeting, research, financing new ventures and getting rid of old ones, and hiring and firing employees.

As a result of widespread public faith in these kinds of practices, business schools such as the Harvard Graduate School of Business (founded in 1924) sprang up as the study of business gained legitimacy. Business was now considered a profession, and the businessman was viewed as a well-qualified leader of society.

This attitude is reflected in one of the most popular literary works of the decade, Sinclair Lewis's 1924 novel *Babbitt*. Despite some self-doubts that were probably felt by few actual businessmen of the period, George Babbitt is considered the model businessman and upstanding small-town citizen of the 1920s. Even though Lewis (1885–1951) had intended the novel as a criticism of U.S. society, its widespread popularity suggests that many readers of the 1920s found something they liked in George Babbitt. Nevertheless, the character's name has since become a synonym for spiritual emptiness and complacency (being uncritically satisfied with oneself or one's society).

Henry Ford's innovations

One of the first industry leaders to employ the ideas of scientific management was Henry Ford (1863–1947), founder of the Ford Motor Company. Although he is often thought of as the inventor of the automobile, he was not. His actual achievement was to take an invention that others were already making and figure out how to produce it in large numbers, so that it could be offered at a low cost to the consumer. He did so by pioneering the use of the assembly line, which involved dividing the work of producing a car among many laborers, each of who performs one specific task repeatedly. A constantly moving belt transports the parts along until the vehicle is assembled. A passage quoted in Lynn Dumenil's *Modern Temper: American Culture and Society in the 1920s* from an account by Hugh Grant, an Australian who came to the United States to observe production methods, illustrates what this kind of work was like for the average laborer:

> At 8 A.M., the worker takes his place at the side of a narrow platform down the centre of which runs a great chain moving at the rate of a foot a minute. His tool is an electrically-driven riveter. As he stands, riveter

poised, the half-built framework of the car passes slowly in front of him. . . . Once, twice, . . . once, twice . . . and so on for six, eight, or ten hours, whatever the rule of the factory may be, day after day, year after year. . . . There is not a job on the mass-production chain more complicated technically than that. The chain never stops. The pace never varies. The man is part of the chain, the feeder and the slave of it.

Determined to produce a small, cheap car that would be available to as many consumers as possible, Ford watched his workers carefully to constantly improve and simplify production methods. He sought to cut time and waste of both materials and human motions. His efforts paid off spectacularly, as Ford produced more than 60 percent of the cars sold during the 1920s. The Model T, which Ford had introduced in 1908, took twelve hours to make in 1912. Three years later Model Ts were being turned out at the rate of one every ninety minutes. Just as predicted, the cost of a Model T fell accordingly, from $850 in 1910 to as low as $260 by the end of the decade.

At the beginning of the 1920s, a number of automobile companies had competed for customers' business. By the end of the decade, however, many of these smaller operations had been pushed out of the market by the success of Ford, the Chrysler Corporation (headed by Walter P. Chrysler; 1875–1940), and General Motors (headed first by William C. Durant and then by the more modern-thinking Alfred P. Sloan [1875–1966]). These companies, which came to be known as the "Big Three," would dominate the automobile industry for the remainder of the century.

A new approach to spending

Automobile ownership was now within the reach of many ordinary U.S. people, and they embraced it with gratitude and joy. A car gave a person or family the freedom not only to travel between work and home but from region to region as well. Cars provided more opportunities to pursue leisure activities, even if that just meant a drive in the countryside. For young people, cars were a way to escape from parents' watchful eyes.

Owning a car was now practically a necessity, but not everybody had the ready cash to buy one. As previously

Workers producing Ford Model T automobiles on an assembly line. Henry Ford pioneered the use of the assembly line to make automobiles. *(AP/Wide World Photos. Reproduced by permission.)*

mentioned, the majority of U.S. residents had traditionally saved their money, buying only what they really needed. If they did not have the cash for something, they did not buy it. With the 1920s, though, came another major societal shift: people started purchasing things on credit. Their eagerness to own radios, electrical appliances, and especially automobiles (60 percent of which were bought on credit during the 1920s) led them to sign up on installment plans, by which consumers made regular payments, including interest, until they had purchased the item. This was commonly known as the "buy now, pay later" mentality, part of the general consumerism (the preoccupation with acquiring goods) that many people feel has continued to dominate U.S. society.

A passion for the stock market

The newfound comfort that the average U.S. resident displayed toward buying on credit also extended to the stock market. A stock represents a share in a company. When a person buys stock in a company, he or she offers it money with which to operate. In exchange the buyer receives a share in any profits the company makes. A rise in the price of a stock means that more people want to buy it, often because the company has gained a reputation as a successful moneymaking operation, which makes it more valuable. If the price goes down, the stock has lost value, and investors may lose money if they choose to sell the stock. Instead they may decide to hold on to it in the hope that the value will rise again.

Before the 1920s, most ordinary people had been unfamiliar with the buying and selling of stocks, but now a wide variety of individuals invested with enthusiasm. Some used their own savings, while others borrowed the money to buy stocks. Still others purchased stocks "on the margin," which meant that they paid a small amount of the price of the stock while the stockbroker (an individual authorized to conduct stock sales) paid the rest. If prices rose, they could pay back their debt while also making a profit. The problem with this method was that if prices fell, investors would have to pay the full amount back to the stockbroker right away.

Across the nation, people believed in the prospect of instant wealth. By the late 1920s the New York Stock Exchange was trading six to seven million shares, or stocks, per day, compared to a more normal rate of three to four million. The prices of stocks had risen so high that they often far surpassed the stocks' real value or the amount of profit the companies could possibly earn. Yet people kept up their frantic pace of investment, convinced that this boom could go on forever.

It could not, however, and in the fall of 1929 came a rude awakening. The stock market started taking big dips downward until, on two fateful October days known as Black Thursday and Black Tuesday, it crashed. The result was devastating financial losses that left individuals penniless, caused banks to fail, and forced companies to close their doors. The long period of hardship and suffering known as the Great Depression had begun (see Chapter 9 for more details).

The new art of advertising

Also closely linked to the advent of consumerism and credit buying was the rising importance of advertising. With so many people eager to spend their money, companies were in hot competition with one another. Advertising had existed in earlier days, but its main purpose had been to deliver the straight facts about products to consumers. In the 1920s the focus of advertising shifted. Advertisements became a kind of art form, with the purpose of persuading people to buy things. This was done by convincing them that these things were necessary through appeals to people's emotions, personal goals, or dreams.

Today's consumers are accustomed to slick, often entertaining ads on television or in print, but it was in the 1920s that this kind of approach was first practiced. Advertisers tried to show how much better people's lives could be if they owned certain products. A homemaker's burden, for example, would be lightened if she could use a Hoover electrically powered vacuum cleaner instead of using a broom to beat the dust out of her carpets. A young man who owned a Playboy car from the Jordan Motor Car company would enjoy the freedom of the open road as well as, the ads implied, the admiration and company of equally adventurous young women.

Already existing advertising agencies expanded and new ones sprang up, all of them making healthy profits from the public's new interest in sales, marketing, and public relations. One such company was the J. Walter Thompson agency, which saw profits rise from $10.7 million in 1922 to $37.5 million in 1929. Selling ad space in print publications also became increasingly profitable, which spurred the growth of mass circulation magazines (such as *Time* and *Life*) that were printed on the kind of slick paper that showed off advertisements to best advantage.

The Florida land boom

One of the most notable uses of advertising to appeal to people's dreams, and to cash in on their new willingness to buy on credit, led to a phenomenon known as the Florida land boom. Before the 1920s Florida was sparsely populated and mostly undeveloped, with few industries and a weak economy. Suddenly the state's image changed as advertisers hired by real estate agents and developers began to lure consumers with images of Florida's sunshine, palm trees, and fragrant, colorful flowers. Entranced by the promise of a warm climate and inviting beaches, thousands of residents of colder, drearier parts of the United States, especially the Northeast, rushed to buy land in Florida.

Often these purchases were made on the installment plan without the buyer ever seeing the property. Many bought with the intention of immediately selling the land and gaining the kind of instant wealth that seemed, during the 1920s, to be within everybody's reach. Prices for plots of land in Florida rose dramatically as people caught what Gertrude Matthews Shelby, in an article in *Harper's Monthly Magazine,* called "the smell of money in Florida."

Success stories abounded, right up until November 1926. That is when a devastating hurricane hit Miami, Florida's largest city. The storm left 100 people dead and 40,000 homeless, and it alerted many new property owners to the reality of the sunny realm they had imagined. A considerable number of buyers now found that the land they owned was worthless, much of it located in swampy areas or far inland, away from Florida's fabled beaches and palm trees. Houses said to have been built had never existed, and promised golf courses and harbors were never constructed. The Florida land boom was over.

The 1920s saw an increase in advertising like the advertisement pictured here for an electric washing machine. *(The Advertising Archive Ltd. Reproduced by permission.)*

Labor unions struggle

Although most working people in the United States— especially those in the skilled trades, such as printers, carpenters, and shoemakers—shared in the general prosperity of the 1920s, the labor unions did not. These organizations had been formed during the last quarter of the nineteenth century and first years of the twentieth century, with the goal of protecting workers from the dangers of big business. Many of them had focused on organizing skilled craftsmen or railroad employees. But U.S. industry had changed, with mass production dominated by unskilled workers, many of them immigrants or migrants from the rural South, who were not familiar with the benefits of union membership.

Labor unions needed to adjust to a new kind of workforce. Before, the majority of young people usually chose either to work on family farms or to learn skilled trades. But now they could work in factories where they made relatively high pay (Henry Ford caused a sensation by offering workers the incredible wage of five dollars a day) despite little education or training. Of course, factory work was boring and sometimes unpleasant, and there were frequent layoffs and few chances for advancement.

For African Americans, many of whom had migrated to the northern cities during World War I, when there was a labor shortage, racial discrimination was still a fact of life, even in the North. Women's opportunities were also limited. For the most part they were kept out of the professions, such as doctors and lawyers, and higher-level jobs, and hardly anybody considered it unfair if they received less pay for the same work performed by men. Women did, however, find factory work as well as jobs as office workers, teachers, nurses, social workers, and telephone operators.

Following a brief period of labor unrest and strikes resulting from the unemployment that followed World War I, public attitudes toward labor unions changed. During the 1920s union leaders were no longer viewed as heroic protectors of people's rights. They were seen as holding radical political views and anti-American ideas that they had imported from overseas. The suspicion and distrust that many U.S. citizens felt for labor unions was highlighted during the famous trial of Nicola Sacco and Bartolomeo Vanzetti, Italian immigrants and union organizers who were found guilty of robbery and murder (see Chapter 6). Despite a lack of evidence and the undeniable influence of prejudice on the court proceedings, the two men were executed for the crime in 1927.

The scientific management technique called for good relations between employers and workers, but this cooperation did not extend to labor unions. Instead, some large corporations, such as General Electric and Bethlehem Steel, began to employ a system called welfare capitalism. This meant that the company itself was supposed to take a protective role in workers' lives, thus eliminating the need for labor unions. They were to provide benefits like dental and health care and life insurance while ensuring better wages and working conditions. In the end, though, this system involved only about 5 percent of U.S. workers. The rest would have to wait until the 1930s, when the harsher circumstances of the Great Depression brought about another shift, for the newly strengthened labor unions to come to their aid.

Farmers suffer through the 1920s

Farmers were another group that did not share in the general economic prosperity of the 1920s. In fact, they experienced hard times throughout the entire decade. During World War I, U.S. farmers had risen to the great demand to supply food for the Allied troops as well as hungry Europeans. They had increased their production by 15 percent or more, purchasing tractors and other equipment and cultivating 35 million more acres than before. But the new machinery meant that fewer people were needed to work the farms, and all the extra purchases either ate into farmers' profits or put them in debt.

When the war ended these problems got even worse. With the European demand gone, there was an oversupply of food in the United States, and prices dropped dramatically. For example, a bushel of wheat that had cost $2.57 in 1920 cost only $1.00 a year later. By the middle of the decade the average farmer was making only about a thousand dollars a year, compared with the three thousand dollars per year that was considered a middle-class income. As a result, many people began to move off the farms and into the urban centers, especially the northern cities, in search of better opportunities. Yet some of the northern industries were also struggling; cotton manufacturers, for example, were affected by the development of man-made fabrics like rayon.

Meanwhile, the federal government showed little interest in what was happening in the farming sector. Both Harding and Coolidge seemed much more concerned about business. In fact, Coolidge twice vetoed the McNary-Haugen Bill, which farming advocates had pushed as a way to provide government aid to farmers.

Ignoring the warning signs

Despite the continuing problems experienced by some parts of society—especially labor unions, African Americans, and farmers—the United States was generally dominated by a mood of optimism and prosperity as the end of the decade approached. Some observers, however, were concerned about the tremendous rise in stock prices, which they considered dangerous. Construction starts were also beginning to decline, as was consumer demand for some products, such as automobiles, while people maintained their carefree approach to buying on credit. These warning signs were either unnoticed or ignored by most.

Thus when President Herbert Hoover, who had served as Secretary of Commerce under both Harding and Coolidge and might be considered an economic expert, took office in 1929, he predicted a prosperous future. In his inaugural address, he declared that he had "no fears for the future of our country. It is bright with hope." Chapter 8 describes the events that proved Hoover's optimism misguided.

For More Information

Books

Allen, Frederick Lewis. *Only Yesterday: An Informal History of the 1920s*. New York: Perennial, 1964.

Burlingame, Roger. *Henry Ford: A Great Life in Brief*. New York: Knopf, 1969.

Dumenil, Lynn. *The Modern Temper: American Culture and Society in the 1920s*. New York: Hill and Wang, 1995.

Hanson, Erica. *The 1920s*. San Diego, CA: Lucent Books, 1999.

Lears, Jackson. *Fables of Abundance: A Cultural History of Advertising in America.* New York: HarperCollins, 1994.

Marchand, Roland. *Advertising the American Dream: Making the Way for Modernity, 1920–1940.* Berkeley: University of California Press, 1985.

Miller, Nathan. *New World Coming: The 1920s and the Making of Modern America.* New York: Scribner, 2003.

Parrish, Michael E. *Anxious Decades: America in Prosperity and Depression.* New York: Norton, 1992.

Perret, Geoffrey. *America in the Twenties.* New York: Touchstone, 1982.

Stevenson, Elizabeth. *Babbitts and Bohemians: The American 1920s.* New York: Macmillan, 1967.

Wilson, Joan Hoff. *American Business and Foreign Policy, 1920–1933.* Boston: Beacon, 1973.

Web Sites

"American Cultural History, Decade 1920–1929." *Kingwood College Library.* Available online at http://kclibrary.nhmccd.edu/decade20.html. Accessed on June 17, 2005.

Best of History Websites. Available online at http://www.besthistorysites. net/USHistory_Roaring20s.shtml. Accessed on June 17, 2005.

Clash of Cultures in the 1910s and 1920s. Available online at http:// history.osu.edu/Projects/Clash/default.htm. Accessed on June 17, 2005.

Interpreting Primary Sources. Digital History. Available online at http:// www.digitalhistory.uh.edu/historyonline/us16.cfm. Accessed on June 17, 2005.

"Prosperity and Thrift: The Coolidge Era and the Consumer Economy." *Library of Congress.* Available online at http://lcweb2.loc.gov/ ammem/coolhtml/coolhome.html. Accessed on June 17, 2005.

4

Technology Changes Daily Life

A wide range of exciting discoveries, developments, and advancements whose seeds had been planted in earlier years blossomed during the 1920s. What had once been the dreams and visions of farsighted scientists, researchers, and inventors became, to varying degrees, normal parts of many people's daily lives.

Perhaps the leading example is the automobile. This vehicle was already in existence at the beginning of the twentieth century, but it was not a common sight on the roads of the nation until the 1920s, when car ownership rates skyrocketed. It was during this decade that Henry Ford (1863–1947) and other automobile manufacturers made cars that almost anybody could afford to buy. In 1919 there had been 6.9 million passenger cars in the United States, but by 1929 there were 23 million.

A similar story is told in the development of the airplane. The first manned flight had taken place in 1903, when an airplane designed by Orville (1871–1948) and Wilbur Wright (1867–1912) lifted off the sands of Kitty Hawk, North Carolina. Something of a gap in aviation progress then occurred,

Once thought to be a farsighted dream of inventors, the automobile became a common site during the 1920s. *(AP/Wide World Photos. Reproduced by permission.)*

followed by a period of renewed accomplishment when World War I (1914–18) began. Beginning in the early 1920s aviation ceased to be limited to the daring feats of barnstormers (pilots who performed stunts with their airplanes to entertain the public). By the end of the decade there were regularly scheduled flights linking U.S. cities, and one of the greatest U.S. heroes of twentieth-century, Charles Lindbergh (1902–1974), had made his famous flight across the Atlantic Ocean.

Scientists were also gaining fame in the realms of astronomy and medicine. Research done during the 1920s revealed the nature of the universe as well as more effective treatments for diabetes and other illnesses. A mold was discovered that would later be made available as penicillin, a drug that could kill the bacteria that caused many deadly diseases.

Technology also brought conveniences and safety into the home. By the end of the decade most people, especially those living in cities, enjoyed the benefits of electrical power and indoor plumbing, one of the most dramatic changes from life in previous centuries. Many homes had radios, which gave people instant access to news and information as well as entertainment. Labor-saving devices like washing machines and vacuum cleaners were much in demand, although still too expensive for most members of the working and lower classes. Generally, though, everyone benefited from the widespread expansion of electricity and water services and the improvements in hygiene and health care that occurred during the 1920s.

The craze for automobiles

Near the end of the nineteenth century, young Henry Ford left his family's farm in Dearborn, Michigan, determined to make something of himself. He became a mechanic and soon developed a passionate interest in the automobiles that were beginning to be seen, in very small numbers, on the roads of cities and towns around the nation. (For example, in 1895 only 4 automobiles were registered in the United States; by 1920 there were 8.5 million, and more than twice that number were registered in 1927.) After building himself a car, Ford decided to make this new technology his life's work. He founded the Ford Motor Company and began making automobiles in line with the expectations of the day: they were big and expensive. But Ford grew increasingly convinced that he could produce a smaller car that would be cheap enough (that is, costing less than $1,000) for almost anybody to buy. Other manufacturers laughed at Ford, but in 1908 he introduced his compact, inexpensive Model T, which quickly gained massive popularity with consumers.

Making a smaller, cheaper car

Ford could hardly keep up with the demand for the Model T. Looking for ways to increase production, he turned to the scientific management techniques then being proposed by industrial engineer Frederick Taylor (1856–1915). Taylor had conducted studies to determine the best ways to coordinate the motions of men with the industrial machines they used, and he suggested more efficient ways of managing businesses. In addition to these concepts, Ford employed a new method in his factories. He set up what would come to be called an assembly line, a moving belt along which the approximately five thousand parts that made up a car would be put together by workers performing single, specific tasks. The parts moved past the workers at waist height, and the workers were forbidden to sit, whistle, smoke, or even make small talk with each other as they worked.

By this method and by strict and careful overview of his workers and their surroundings, Ford soon reduced the time it took to make a Model T from one every twelve hours to one every ninety minutes. In order to cut down on worker turnover, that is the rate of workers starting and quitting jobs, Ford made an amazing offer: he would pay his workers five dollars a day, an incredibly high wage for factory work during this period. Despite the unpleasant aspects of working in a Ford plant, especially the boredom and the rigid rules, men lined up for jobs and kept them. As a result, Ford was able to speed up the line even more, and production rose to an incredible ten thousand cars per week.

Although other auto manufacturers laughed at him, Henry Ford knew he could build an automobile inexpensive enough for the common consumer to purchase.

The importance of cars in U.S. culture

U.S. consumers developed a strong fondness for the car that became known as the "Tin Lizzie." Despite its drawbacks—such as the fact that it was only available in black, included no fancy extras (not even a gas gauge), and tended to break down a lot—the Model T was simply designed and thus easy to fix. The best part, of course, was the car's price tag: at its cheapest, a Model T cost only $260, and a used Model T could be bought for as little as $50. Meanwhile, Henry Ford became not only extremely wealthy but also a folk hero to ordinary people, a self-educated man who had worked hard and lifted himself to great heights. Ford also gained the gratitude of the labor unions through his progressive policies, which included not only high wages but also a work week of only forty hours, rather than the usual forty-eight.

It was in the 1920s that automobiles took up their important role in U.S. culture. Called "the supreme machine of the 1920s" by historian Geoffrey Perret in his book *America in the Twenties,* the automobile provided jobs for five million people, who were involved not only in the assembly of cars but also in the manufacture of the raw materials used to make them, dealerships, the manufacture and sale of parts and supplies, the gasoline industry, and service stations. Car ownership allowed people to commute to work, thus leading to the expansion of the suburbs, as workers no longer needed to live close to their jobs, and to take family outings and vacations. Social life and dating were enhanced by the greater privacy that automobiles allowed. In *Middletown,* their study of the changes occurring in a small U.S. town during the 1920s, Robert and Helen Lynd reported that the automobile was now considered "an accepted essential of normal living."

The mass popularity of the automobile was highlighted by the public response when, in 1927, Ford introduced a new car, the Model A. People waited for its unveiling with eager anticipation and traded guesses on what it would look like and the features it would have. The day that the car was to be introduced, Ford ran full-page advertisements in newspapers across the country, and people flocked to the showrooms of Ford dealerships. In New York so many came to the city's largest dealership that the exhibition had to be moved to Madison Square Garden. Scores of people also gathered in smaller cities like Cleveland, Ohio, and Kansas City, Missouri. And they were not disappointed, for the Model A came with such exciting new features as a choice of colors (from Florentine Cream to Niagara Blue) and enough power to reach speeds as high as 70 miles per hour.

Alfred P. Sloan: Challenging Ford's Dominance

Alfred P. Sloan was an innovative business-man who, along with Henry Ford of the Ford Motor Company and Walter P. Chrysler of the Chrysler Corporation, helped to make automobile manufacturing a leading industry. Serving as chief executive officer, president, and chairman of the board, Sloan built General Motors (GM) into one of the most successful of all U.S. companies.

Born in 1875 in New Haven, Connecticut, Sloan grew up in New York City. He received a degree in engineering from the Massachusetts Institute of Technology (MIT) in 1895. His first job was at the Hyatt Rolling Bearing Company, a company whose chief product was billiard (pool) balls. By the time he was twenty-six, Sloan was the company's president. He revived the failing business by selling steel roller bearings, which were used to reduce friction in moving machine parts, to the growing automobile industry. When Sloan discovered that GM might begin manufacturing its own bearings, he made a deal with William C. Durant, who was then head of GM, to make Hyatt part of United Motors Corporation (a division of GM). By 1918 Sloan was a vice president at General Motors.

Two years later, the company's new director, Pierre Du Pont, put Sloan in charge of operations. Sloan became president in 1923, when Du Pont retired. Sloan would spend the next three decades introducing technological innovations, such as four-wheel drive, and a better way of running the company. He centralized the administrative functions of GM, especially its finances, and decentralized production. The company was divided into five divisions, each responsible for the production and marketing of a different line of cars. The lines were targeted to different markets, from the low-priced Chevrolets to the luxury Cadillacs.

During the 1920s GM doubled its pro-duction rate and increased sales dramati-cally, eventually passing industry leader Ford. Meanwhile, Sloan encouraged the man who had been in charge of GM's Buick division, Walter P. Chrysler, to strike out on his own. Before long Chrysler's com-pany would become the third largest auto-mobile manufacturer.

In 1937 Sloan became chair of GM's board of directors and the highest-paid executive in the United States. Like Henry Ford he resisted the efforts of the labor movement in the 1930s and 1940s to unionize GM workers. After the United Automobile Workers (UAW) staged a sit-down strike at GM's plants, Sloan was forced to recognize the union.

Sloan was well known for his generous contributions to charities. In the middle of the Great Depression he founded the Alfred P. Sloan Foundation, which would provide millions of dollars in grants for scientific and technological research. Sloan also funded the Sloan School of Management at MIT, and the Sloan-Kettering Institute for Cancer Research in New York City. Sloan died on February 17, 1966, in New York City.

Although he was probably the most successful in capturing the imagination of the U.S. public, Ford was not the only automobile manufacturer on the scene. Between 1900 and 1930 there were more than two thousand such companies in business in the United States. Some of the best-known smaller companies include Packard, Nash, and Pierce-Arrow, all of which focused on making expensive, very high-quality cars that only the wealthy could afford. These manufacturers were overshadowed by the Big Three: the Ford Motor Company, General Motors (GM), founded in 1908 by William C. Durant and later run by Alfred P. Sloan (1875–1966), who made GM a thoroughly modern and very successful corporation, and Chrysler Corporation (under Walter P. Chrysler; 1875–1940). These companies accounted for 75 percent of car sales. This industry, which produced 4.2 million cars in 1926, would remain the nation's largest industry through the twentieth century.

Road improvements made

The large and ever-increasing number of cars and trucks on the roads of the United States led to concerns about the condition of those roads. In 1920 there were about 3 million miles (4,827,000 kilometers) of road in the nation, but only about 36,000 of those miles (57,924 kilometers) were paved. Most of the country's highways and byways were made of hard-packed dirt, as they had originally been built for horses. They were subject to all kinds of damage and obstacles, and they were not well-maintained. Help arrived in the form of the Federal Highway Act in 1921, which offered federal funds to states for the creation and maintenance of interstate highways. It was agreed that those running east to west would be labeled with even numbers, and those running north to south would be given odd numbers.

By 1929 more than 10,000 miles (16,090 kilometers) of road were being paved annually. It was now much easier for people to travel, and travel they did. A big increase in the rate and mode of family vacations led to the establishment of so-called "car camps," which served as early motels by offering bathroom facilities and tents for the use of weary travelers. Other businesses sprang up along popular routes, including roadside diners and gas stations.

Aviation gets off the ground

In 1903, when the Wright brothers made their famous flight, the public imagination was dazzled by the idea of soaring above the earth in a flying machine. Nevertheless, the aviation industry took some time to get off the ground. The entry of the United States into World War I provided a needed spark, as the U.S. military began for the first time to use airplanes in combat. But for a short period after the war, the only planes in the air were flown by pilots called "barnstormers." In exhibitions that were commonly known as "flying circuses," which often took place at country fairs, these men performed such daring feats as rolling their airplanes, flying upside down, and even walking on the wings. Many were flying old aircraft that had formerly been used by the military and that underwent no inspections. Pilots were not formally trained, and there were no regulations governing flight.

Three pilots are congratulated following their first successful airmail trip between Boston and New York. Airmail helped to spur the development of the aviation industry during the 1920s. (© Bettmann/Corbis. Reproduced by permission.)

Airmail spurs development

A change came about with the introduction of airmail, a faster way to deliver mail than had ever been used before. The federal government began giving out airmail contracts to pilots, and in 1920 the U.S. Post Office established airmail service from New York to San Francisco, with stops at major cities along the way. By 1925 private airlines were being formed to carry both mail and passengers. Designers like Igor Sikorsky (1889–1972), who had immigrated to the United States from the Soviet Union in 1919, began turning out new and better aircraft.

Sikorsky developed a fourteen-passenger plane that was made of metal, not the usual wood, followed by his S37 and S38 models, the latter of which he sold to the new Pan Am airline. William Boeing (1881–1956) of Seattle, Washington, who had learned to fly in order to reach the more remote fishing spots of the Northwest, began producing the durable, effective 40A airplane in 1925. He went on to become the largest airplane manufacturer in the world, followed closely by Donald Douglas (1892–1981) and Anthony Fokker (1890–1939). By 1929, aviation had become a $200 million industry.

The first passenger flight took place on April 4, 1927, when Colonial Air Transport flew between Boston and New York. That same year, the first scheduled commercial flights began, and by 1929 airlines were offering cross-country passenger flights. Many aviation firsts and records were set during the 1920s. In 1925, for example, U.S. Army Air Corps pilot Lieutenant James Doolittle (1896–1993) flew 233 miles (375 kilometers) per hour in a Curtiss R3C-2 airplane, breaking the world speed record. Three years later Amelia Earhart (1898–1937) became the first woman to cross the Atlantic by air (as a passenger); the same year, Earhart made the first round-trip solo flight from New York to Los Angeles and back.

Lindbergh's daring feat

The most famous aviation feat of the 1920s, however, and the one that most thrilled and captivated people around the world, was without doubt the one achieved by a twenty-five-year-old pilot from Minnesota. In 1919 New York hotel owner Raymond Orteig had offered $25,000 to the first pilot who succeeded in flying nonstop from New York to Paris, a distance of 3,500 miles (5,632 kilometers). For eight years no one succeeded, though six aviators lost their lives attempting the feat. In 1927 a new contender emerged: former barnstormer and airmail pilot Charles Lindbergh (1902–1974) believed he could make it with a special one-engine plane with adequate fuel capacity, if he flew alone and with minimal equipment to make the craft as light as possible.

Using his own money as well as a contribution from a group of businessmen from St. Louis, Missouri, Lindbergh arranged for San Diego's Ryan Airlines to build the airplane. The *Spirit of St. Louis* (named in honor of Lindbergh's benefactors) carried no radio or special instruments for night flying, no gas tank gauge, and no parachute. It did carry enough gas to get Lindbergh to his destination. He left New York's Roosevelt Island on May 20 and flew northeast over Nova Scotia, then Newfoundland. Early the next morning Lindbergh spotted the rocky coast of Ireland. He flew south from there toward France, landing in Paris at 10:22 p.m. after a thirty-three-and-a-half-hour flight. He was met by a wildly enthusiastic French crowd and carried off the landing field.

When he returned to the United States, Lindbergh was treated to a reception even more enthusiastic than the one he had received in France. The shy, modest pilot was honored by a parade through the streets of New York City, looking down on what seemed to him, as quoted in Erica Hanson's *The 1920s,* "oceans of friendly upturned faces." Lindbergh's journey had been followed with intense interest by U.S. citizens, and their joy and pride in his success could hardly be contained.

The Guggenheim Fund aids Goddard

The further development of aviation was helped along by a wealthy mining executive named David Guggenheim, who established the Guggenheim Fund as a source of money for research and development. The fund offered grants to university researchers, sponsored contests, and gave financial support to those working to make flight safer; one project resulted in the practice of flying by instruments, rather than just by sight, which led to greater safety on night flights or in conditions of low visibility.

One of the beneficiaries of the Guggenheim Fund was Robert H. Goddard (1882–1945), a physicist at Clark University in Massachusetts who had been conducting experiments on high-altitude rockets. He had created devices that mixed liquid hydrogen and gas in metal cylinders, which at first tended to explode before takeoff. Scorned by some of his fellow scientists, Goddard attracted the attention of Lindbergh, who persuaded the Guggenheim Fund to finance his work. Goddard's achievements in rocket research and development would later serve as the basis for the technology that took human beings into space beginning in the 1960s.

Radios become commonplace

In 1899 Italian scientist Guglielmo Marconi (1874–1937) had invented a technology called wireless telegraphy, which sent signals through space using the same dot-dash code used in the telegraph (which had been invented by Samuel Morse in

Radios became an important part of people's lives during the 1920s.
(© Bettmann/Corbis. Reproduced by permission.)

the 1840s). Several years later, when it became possible to send voices by this method, it was called wireless telephony. The U.S. military began using this technology, changing its name to radiotelephony, which was shortened in common U.S. usage to radio. The British, however, continued to call it "wireless" for many years.

During World War I, radio signals began to be sent and received using vacuum tubes that gave the transmissions more power and precision. Similar to light bulbs, vacuum tubes were replaced by the transistors used in today's radios. Around the United States, amateurs interested in this technology began to tinker with it in their homes, and a few experimental radio stations were set up in New York, New Jersey, California, and Michigan. But it was not until 1920 that the first commercial radio station was established, in East Pittsburgh, Pennsylvania.

An engineer named Dr. Frank Conrad who worked for the Westinghouse company had been developing voice transmission equipment for use by the military. He became interested in ham, or home-based, radio and started communicating on his own with some like-minded friends. Conrad even played musical recordings over his radio, which attracted the attention of a local department store that began selling radios so that more people could hear Conrad's broadcasts. Sensing the marketing potential of radio, an executive at Westinghouse persuaded Conrad to set up a radio station in the company's plant. They applied to the federal government for something that did not yet exist, a broadcasting license, and were granted one by the Department of Commerce. The station was assigned the call sign KDKA, which was based on the system of call signs used for ships at sea.

Gradually more radio stations were established, so that by the end of 1922 more than five hundred were operating. This incredible growth led to the founding of a government agency, the Federal Radio Commission, to set up broadcasting rules and regulations. In 1922 about sixty thousand U.S. homes had radios. At the end of the decade, about twelve million families, or one-third of the total U.S. population, were reported to be listening to radios.

People were listening to news, live music, comedy shows, and programs that combined music, comedy, drama, and lectures. Sporting events such as boxing matches and baseball games were broadcast for the first time, creating instant and widespread fame for such figures as boxer Jack Dempsey (1895–1983) and baseball great Babe Ruth (1895–1948). Politicians, government officials—including President Calvin Coolidge (1872–1933; served 1923–29)—and religious leaders like Aimee Semple McPherson (1890–1944) were all using the airwaves to share their views with the public.

Motion pictures with sound and color

During the first two decades of the twentieth century, the U.S. public warmly embraced silent movies and the actors who appeared in them, even though they could not hear those actors' voices and had to rely on subtitles to know what they were saying. Ever since the invention of the motion picture, various inventors, including Thomas Edison (1847–1931), had tried unsuccessfully to develop a way to incorporate music and speech into movies. Finally, with the backing of the Warner Brothers movie studio, engineers at Western Electric came up with a system called Vitaphone.

Warner Brothers soon introduced the first movie with sound, *Don Juan* (1926); this was not, however, a full-length movie, and it featured only synchronized music and sound effects, not voices. The next year, Warner Brothers released the first full-length movie with synchronized dialog as well as music and singing. *The Jazz Singer,* starring well-known stage actor and singer Al Jolson (1886–1950), was hugely successful with the public and is still considered a milestone in motion picture technology. The only people made unhappy by the new technology were the silent screen actors whose voices or accents were considered unsuitable for what were called "the talkies."

The motion picture industry now began an ascent toward what is commonly referred to as the "golden age" of movies, the 1930s and 1940s. Walt Disney (1901–1966) made his first sound cartoon in 1928, the same year that Fox Studios released *In Old Arizona,* the first sound western. By the end of the decade, all the major studios, including Paramount, M-G-M, and Universal, had abandoned silent movies. The 1920s also saw the advent of color film in movies: the first full-length color movie, *The Toll of the Sea,* appeared in 1922; the second and third, *Wanderer of the Wasteland* and *The Black Pirate,* with screen idol Douglas Fairbanks (1883–1939), were released in 1924 and 1926. It would be about another ten years, though, before movies in color completely replaced black-and-white films.

During the 1920s researchers were also working on ways to transmit pictures through space; in other words, television was in its infancy. Efforts in the late 1920s by Bell Laboratories, General Electric, and NBC were interesting but not fully successful. In 1924, however, Russian immigrant Vladimir Zworykin (1889–1982) had patented a device called a kinescope, which used a glass tube to send a signal made up of black dots that formed a picture. This would form the basis of the technology that, several decades later, would evolve into television.

Scientific discoveries cause excitement and unease

Some of the uncertainty that many felt about the changes taking place during the 1920s might be linked to the groundbreaking discoveries that scientists were making during this period. One of the most unsettling had to do with the nature of the universe itself. In 1912 an astronomer named Vesto M. Slipher had been studying a nebula, then thought to consist of patches of gas that gave off light, at an Arizona observatory. He decided that nebulae were actually clusters of stars that made up complete galaxies, like the Milky Way of which Earth and its solar system are a part.

From Hubble to Mead: groundbreaking research

During the 1920s astrophysicist Edwin Hubble (1889–1953) was at the Mt. Wilson Observatory in Pasadena, California, studying the Andromeda nebula. Like Slipher, he believed that nebulae were collections of stars and possibly even entire galaxies. His calcu-

Astrophysicist Edwin Hubble, whose research provided the basis for the Big Bang theory proposed by French scientist Georges Lemaître. *(© Bettmann/Corbis. Reproduced by permission.)*

lations of Andromeda's great distance from Earth led him to the conclusion that this was, indeed, a separate galaxy. Further, he found that galaxies are constantly moving away from each other, which led him to conclude that the universe is expanding or even exploding. Hubble's research provided the basis for the later work of French scientist Georges Lemaître (1894–1966), who, in the late 1920s and early 1930s, would propose the Big Bang theory of the origin of the universe.

Some people were disturbed or unconvinced by the notion that the universe was expanding, especially those who relied more on religion than science to explain the world around them. Similar challenges to traditional beliefs came in a realm closer to Earth, through the work of anthropologist Margaret Mead (1901–1978). As a graduate student, Mead had studied with and been influenced by the renowned anthropologist Franz Boas (1858–1942). Boas sought to replace racist assumptions, such as the idea that some forms of humanity are genetically superior to others, with the concept that the environment in which people develop is much more important than the genes they inherit.

Mead conducted her own research in the Pacific Island nation of Samoa, where she observed and interviewed fifty adolescent females. She found that in contrast to U.S. culture, Samoans considered their teenaged years a calm, happy period, not one full of intense emotion and conflict. In *Coming of Age in Samoa* (1928), Mead concluded that the experience of adolescence was shaped by culture, not biology. Her book was considered an important and influential work for decades, though recent critics have questioned the validity of her conclusions.

Medical advances improve lives

Developments in the field of medicine that occurred or began in the 1920s would help to make life safer and more comfortable for the vast majority of people, especially in the generally prosperous United States. One change had to do with the role of the doctor, who had previously not been able to offer his patients much more than comfort and common-sense guidance. Advances in both science and education gave physicians more effectiveness and more status, as well as a less personal, more professional relationship with their patients.

Soon after the passage of the Nineteenth Amendment in 1920, which gave women the right to vote, reformers persuaded Congress to approve the Sheppard-Towner Act (1921). This law guaranteed federal funding to states to set up and run prenatal (before birth) and children's health centers. These centers would allow medical professionals to offer education and assistance designed to bring down high maternal and infant mortality rates (deaths of mothers and babies during or soon after birth). The Sheppard-Towner Act was opposed by some, especially the American Medical Association, an organization of doctors who feared competition from the free clinics, and the federal funds were withdrawn at the end of the decade.

Another important women's health issue was that of birth control. The use of contraceptives, and even the spreading of information about them, was illegal in some states and not much talked about anywhere in the United States. Determined to win for women the independence and freedom of choice afforded by the ability to avoid pregnancy, Margaret Sanger (1883–1966) and other reformers worked to overcome laws against the use and knowledge of contraceptives. In the course of her efforts, Sanger was jailed many times, but she persisted in promoting the use of birth control, especially among the working- and lower-class women she felt had the most to gain.

Great strides were also made during the 1920s in research on nutrition, as scientists discovered the existence of vitamins A, B, D, and E and laid the groundwork for the later discovery of vitamin C. They also made progress on cures, tests, or immunizations for pellagra (a disease caused by a lack of certain vitamins), pernicious anemia (caused by a shortage of red blood cells), and scarlet fever (a contagious disease that causes a red rash). The use of insulin to treat diabetes also dates to the 1920s. In 1928 British physician Alexander Fleming (1881–1955) discovered that mold called *penicillin notatum* had the ability to kill disease-causing bacteria. This discovery opened the way for the continuing research that would, during the 1940s, make penicillin available for general use as a drug.

Technology enters the home

Technological developments in the form of automobiles, airplanes, and medicine obviously affected the lives of many people, but what had an even more immediate effect were new devices meant to be used inside the home. Most basic, of course, were electricity and indoor plumbing, which brought light, warmth, better hygiene, and general comfort and convenience to more people in the 1920s than ever before. For example, only 34.7 percent of U.S. homes had electricity in 1920, but by 1930 the number had risen to 67.9 percent overall and to 84.8 percent of homes found in cities. Similarly, about 70 percent of homes had indoor plumbing by the end of the decade.

Middle-class families of the 1920s enjoyed an exciting new array of laborsaving devices, which helped them adapt

Several laborsaving devices, such as this Frigidaire refrigerator, were developed during the 1920s. *(© Bettmann/Corbis. Reproduced by permission.)*

to the shortage of people looking for work as domestic servants. (The shortage was due to better-paying jobs for unskilled workers in factories.) These devices included the vacuum cleaner, which eliminated the need to manually beat dust and dirt out of carpets and rugs, and washing machines, which made it easier to clean clothes, a process that had previously involved hauling water from wells and wringing out wet garments by hand. The electric iron was easier to use than the old, heavy iron that had to be heated in an oven, and it worked better. The electric refrigerator kept food fresh and cut down on the need for frequent shopping or store deliveries. Despite these conveniences, however, homemakers still put much time and effort into their domestic duties.

Telephones were already in use when the 1920s began, but the technology by which they worked improved during the decade. The 1920s saw the establishment of the first automated switching offices, which created the new occupation of telephone operator, a position available to the women who were now entering the workforce in greater numbers, and the first telephone cable to be placed on the ocean floor (between Key West, Florida, and Havana, Cuba). The first telephones had featured separate pieces holding the transmitter and the receiver, but in 1926 these were combined within the same handset.

For the most part, these new conveniences were available only to those who could afford them, which did not include most working- or lower-class families. For example, the price of a washing machine ranged between $60 and $200, while a typical factory worker might make only $100 a month. A wide range of people did benefit from the expanded availability of electricity, running water, and natural gas. In many rural homes, however, even these basic technologies were not available: by 1930, only 10 percent of farmhouses had electricity, and only 33 percent had indoor plumbing. Farm families would have to wait until the 1930s and 1940s for these services to arrive.

For More Information

Books

Allen, Frederick Lewis. *Only Yesterday: An Informal History of the 1920s.* New York: Perennial, 1964.

Berg, Scott. *Lindbergh.* New York: Putnam, 1998.

Burlingame, Roger. *Henry Ford: A Great Life in Brief.* New York: Knopf, 1969.

Chesler, Ellen. *Woman of Valor: Margaret Sanger and the Birth Control Movement.* New York: Simon & Schuster, 1992.

Douglas, Susan J. *Inventing American Broadcasting, 1899–1902.* Baltimore, MD: Johns Hopkins University Press, 1987.

Fisher, Jim. *The Lindbergh Case.* New Brunswick, NJ: Rutgers University Press, 1994.

Gwynn-Jones, Terry. *Farther and Faster: Aviation's Adventuring Years, 1909–1939.* Washington, DC: Smithsonian Institution Press, 1991.

Hanson, Erica. *The 1920s.* San Diego, CA: Lucent Books, 1999.

Howard, Jane. *Margaret Mead: A Life.* New York: Simon & Schuster, 1984.

Kennedy, David M. *Birth Control in America: The Career of Margaret Sanger.* New Haven, CT: Yale University Press, 1970.

Kent, Zachary. *Charles Lindbergh and the Spirit of St. Louis in American History.* Berkeley Heights, NJ: Enslow Publishers, Inc., 2001.

Lynd, Robert S., and Helen M. Lynd. *Middletown.* New York: Harcourt, Brace, 1929.

Miller, Nathan. *New World Coming: The 1920s and the Making of Modern America.* New York: Scribner, 2003.

Perret, Geoffrey. *America in the Twenties.* New York: Touchstone, 1982.

Walker, Alexander. *The Shattered Silents: How the Talkies Came to Stay.* London: Elm Tree Books, 1978.

Web Sites

"American Cultural History, Decade 1920–1929." *Kingwood College Library.* Available online at http://kclibrary.nhmccd.edu/decade20.html. Accessed on June 17, 2005.

Best of History Websites. Available online at http://www.besthistorysites. net/USHistory_Roaring20s.shtml. Accessed on June 17, 2005.

Clash of Cultures in the 1910s and 1920s. Available online at http://history. osu.edu/Projects/Clash/default.htm. Accessed on June 17, 2005.

Flaherty, Tarraugh. "Margaret Mead: 1901–1978." *Women's Intellectual Contributions to the Study of Mind and Society.* Available online at http://www.webster.edu/woolflm/margaretmead.html. Accessed on June 17, 2005.

"Henry Ford, 1863–1947." *A Science Odyssey: People and Discoveries.* Available online at http:www.pbs.org/wgbh/aso/databank/entries/ btford.html. Accessed on June 17, 2005.

Interpreting Primary Sources. Digital History. Available online at http:// www.digitalhistory.uh.edu/historyonline/us16.cfm. Accessed on June 17, 2005.

5

A Changing Society

In a book written just a few years after the end of the 1920s titled *Only Yesterday: An Informal History of the 1920s,* Frederick Lewis Allen noted that this decade had involved a "revolution in manners and morals." Indeed, many changes in ways of thinking and behaving, most of them actually rooted in the years leading up to the 1920s, were unleashed by this decade's special circumstances and atmosphere.

These changes were influenced by such factors as the impact of World War I (1914–18) and a falling birth rate, as well by the new work patterns, cultural diversity, and general prosperity that marked this period. They involved different roles for women, who entered the workforce and attended college in greater numbers, were more likely to use birth control, and interacted in society more freely. Families were smaller and were now more focused on emotional attachment and the nurturing of children. Young people were not as pressured to enter adulthood as they had been in previous years, and they spent more time in school. The 1920s saw the development of a distinct, lively youth culture and of a society that was much more youth-oriented than ever before.

During the 1920s, women entered the workforce in greater numbers.

(© Underwood & Underwood/Corbis. Reproduced by permission.)

Exciting and positive as these trends were for some, others found them alarming. The belief that the changes in society meant the downfall of traditional moral values led to an upsurge in religious fundamentalism. This kind of very conservative Christianity revolves around a literal interpretation of the Bible; that is, considering the Bible a true account of factual events, rather than a collection of poetic, mythical stories told to illustrate moral lessons. The success of evangelists (people who seek to convert others to their faith) like Aimee Semple McPherson (1890–1944) and the issues brought up in the Scopes Monkey Trial, which pitted fundamentalists against defenders of a teacher's right to teach the scientific theory of evolution (see William Jennings Bryan's undelivered closing statement from the Scopes Trial Primary Sources entry), demonstrate the resistance to the changes occurring during this period.

The roots of change

As the twentieth century began, a transition in U.S. society was already under way. The nation's population had shifted from one dominated by people of northern European ancestry (such as Great Britain, France, and Scandinavia) to a more diverse mix that included not only the African Americans and Native Americans who already lived in the country but also new immigrants from such places as Italy, Poland, and Mexico. For the first time, more U.S. citizens were living in cities than in rural areas, as the nation became increasingly industrialized. New technology and management methods that allowed for fast, efficient mass production changed work patterns, as fewer people became farmers and skilled craftsmen and more went to work in factories and offices. Technological improvements also increased communication between regions and broadened people's knowledge of the world around them. The expansion of print publications and radio broadcasting during the 1920s would help to blur the lines between people even more.

Then there was World War I, a global conflict so bloody and destructive that it seemed to shake the very foundations of society. Afterwards, many people, especially the young men who had fought in the war, were less innocent and more aware. Their perspective on life and on the world had changed, resulting in a new, inward focus and a willingness to embrace different ways of thinking and behaving.

New roles for women

One group with just such an altered perspective was women. During the war many of them had taken up a much more public role than in previous years, when they had been expected to remain behind the scenes, caring for homes and children and allowing men to take charge of society. Through involvement in volunteer work to support the war effort and by taking up jobs left by soldiers, women had enjoyed a degree of freedom that most had not experienced before.

Then came the passage of the Nineteenth Amendment, the result of decades of effort that had begun in 1848 at the Seneca Falls Woman's Rights Convention, where suffragists (those who worked to gain for women the right to vote) had first discussed how to achieve their goals. On August 18, 1920, twenty-six million U.S. women earned the right to vote. A number of them rejoiced, sure that women would now have the power to directly influence and change their society and to be a force for progress. As it turned out, though, the Nineteenth Amendment would not have as much political impact as the suffragists had hoped. Women had been united in the drive to gain the ballot box, but now they would be divided by differences of race, class, religion, and region. Different groups would express different ideas about needed reforms and how to achieve them.

Particularly divisive was the issue of the Equal Rights Amendment, which was supported by the most radical group of suffragists, the National Women's Party. They believed that equal rights could only be achieved through the passage of another constitutional amendment, this one making it illegal to discriminate against women in any way. Others, however, felt that such a broad amendment would sweep away laws meant to protect women. In addition, black women who had joined the struggle for suffrage now felt abandoned by women's organizations. They turned their energies toward the fight for racial justice, becoming especially active in the movement to end lynching (a brutal form of murder by hanging, often accompanied by torture, practiced by white terrorist groups against mostly African American victims).

A few women were elected to political office during the 1920s. Most prominent among them were Winnifred Mason Huck (1882–1936), who was elected to the House of Representatives in 1922, and Nellie Tayloe Ross (1876–1977), elected governor of Wyoming in 1925. By the end of the decade more than two hundred women were serving in state legislatures, compared with ten thousand men.

Women in the work force

Some accounts of the 1920s suggest that women achieved a very high level of equality during that decade, as if they suddenly became free to do and be exactly what they wished. The truth is more complicated. When the 1920s ended, opportunities for women were still very limited, and traditional views about their role in society and the family were still, for the most part, closely held. Still, some significant changes did occur. An important one was the entrance of more women into the workforce: their number rose from 8.3 million (23.6 percent) in 1920 to 11 million (27 percent) in 1930.

Winnifred Mason Huck was one of the first women to be elected to political office during the 1920s. (© *Corbis. Reproduced by permission.*)

The fact was, however, that most still worked in the lowest-paying jobs, either in factories or as clerical workers in offices. Significant numbers also worked as domestic servants or farmworkers, especially African American women who faced particularly harsh discrimination and unpleasant working conditions, and recent immigrants. Women did obtain professional jobs, but the vast majority were in traditional female fields such as nursing, teaching, and social work. It was still quite unusual for women to become lawyers or doctors, as obstacles were placed in their way before, during, and after they obtained the education they needed. And the practice of paying women less for the same work performed by men was still widely accepted by much of society. There were more married women in the workforce now, most by necessity, some by choice, but they faced not only disapproval from those who believed that wives and mothers should stay at home, but also the stress of balancing work with domestic duties.

Flappers symbolize the 1920s

A small group of women did manage to achieve a greater degree of freedom, at least on the surface, to have a lot of fun, and to make a lasting name for themselves. These women were called flappers, a term of British origin that referred to the unbuckled, floppy galoshes, or rain boots, worn by some of them. Though their number was small and their time in the spotlight short, flappers came to symbolize for many years to come the free-spirit of the 1920s.

The previous generation of women had worn high collars and ankle-length skirts, under which were layers of petticoats. Their long hair was coiled or piled on top of their heads. They wore uncomfortable corsets (stiff, laced undergarments meant to shape a woman's body in a certain way) in order to achieve the ideal "hourglass" figure: a small waist and wide hips. The women of the Victorian Age (roughly referring to the years 1837 to 1901, when Queen Victoria ruled England) were expected to be the guardians of morality and innocence; they were to obey their husbands, bear and raise children, and run their homes efficiently. Sex was a duty, the price they paid for the privilege of marriage and having babies, not something pleasurable. The flapper turned all of these expectations on their heads.

The flapper created a stir by her very appearance. Her hair was bobbed (cut short), her skirts short, her clothing simplified. She wore silk stockings, makeup—especially rouge for her cheeks, eyeliner to make her eyes look dramatic, and bold lipstick—long strings of beads, and close-to-the-head hats called cloches. The ideal flapper figure was thin and boyish, and in fact some women taped down their breasts to create that effect. In manner the flapper was independent, free-spirited, and fun-loving. She felt free to smoke and drink illegal liquor (both much-frowned-upon activities for women in the previous generation), to kiss her boyfriend in public, and to dance wildly to the daring new jazz music being played in the nightclubs of the nation's big cities. In general, the flapper thumbed her nose at tradition. Supposedly this extended to sexual freedom as well, but it is likely that few women were as sexually active as it seemed.

Here She Comes ... Miss America

In the Roaring Twenties, it was becoming clear that the notions about women's roles, appearance, and behavior that had prevailed during the Victorian Era were changing. In earlier decades, women had been expected to focus their energies on home and family, maintain a modest appearance, and behave in a quiet, polite, obedient manner. But by the 1920s, the bold young women called flappers were overturning these standards with their bobbed hair, short skirts, cigarette smoking, and modern attitudes about jobs, child-bearing, and sex.

Another sign of the times was a display of female beauty that had its start in 1921.

A group of Atlantic City, New Jersey, businessmen who were looking for a way to improve the tourism business after Labor Day came up with the idea of a beauty contest. On September 8, 1921, the first Miss America pageant took place, featuring eight young women dressed in daring, close-fitting, one-piece bathing suits. The winner was sixteen-year-old Margaret Gorman of Washington, D.C., who was said to resemble the famous movie star Mary Pickford.

Some people were shocked by this open display of flesh, which was extensively covered by the media. Nevertheless, the annual event grew increasingly popular, and by 1924 there were eighty-three contestants vying for the Miss America title.

The flapper's energy, independence, and provocative beauty were embodied on the motion picture screen by a number of movie stars, such as Louise Brooks (1906–1985) and Clara Bow (1905–1965). The latter, in fact, was nicknamed the "It Girl" because she seemed to possess a special quality, called "animal magnetism" by novelist Elinor Glyn as quoted in Nathan Miller's *New World Coming: The 1920s and the Making of Modern America*, that was popularly referred to as "It."

To many older or conservative people, the emergence of the flapper seemed proof that society was coming apart at the seams. Further, those who had fought for women's suffrage and who had hoped the younger generation would jump at the chance to become politically active were disappointed by the flappers' preference for fun and fashion over working to improve society. (This lack of interest in the wider world or in social reform seemed to apply, in fact, to most young people of the 1920s.) Nevertheless, modified versions of the fashions introduced by the flappers, if not some of their

Flappers symbolized the freedom that women seemed to achieve during the 1920s. *(© Hulton-Deutsch Collection/Corbis. Reproduced by permission.)*

wilder behaviors, caught on with a wide variety of women, who needed more comfortable clothing for their new, more active lifestyles.

The fight for birth control

One of the most important women's issues of the 1920s was that of birth control. For women, the ability to avoid pregnancy could have a significant impact on economic status, freedom of choice regarding family size and work, and health. Contraceptives were already in use by some women, but most of these were members of the upper classes. Working-class and poor women still had little access to or knowledge about birth control, and as many as fifty thousand U.S. women per year died from illegal abortions. In many places, it was against the law to use, make available, or even give out information about birth control. Contraceptives were considered immoral because they interfered with nature, and printed material about birth control was viewed as a form of pornography (material intended to stimulate sexual excitement).

Even before the 1920s, a reformer named Margaret Sanger (1883–1966) had begun an effort to change this situation. As a nurse working among underprivileged people, Sanger had seen for herself the sad results of unwanted pregnancies. She became determined to make information and advice about birth control available to as many women as possible, through public speaking and free birth control clinics that she hoped to establish around the country. "No woman can consider herself free," declared Sanger, as quoted in Miller's book, "until she can choose conscientiously whether she will or will not be a mother."

Arrested eight times for violating laws against birth control, Sanger fled to Europe in 1915. There she learned about a new, highly effective contraceptive device called the diaphragm, which she managed to smuggle back to the United States. Eventually Sanger felt she had to abandon some of the ties she had forged with more radical groups and activists in order to attract support from physicians and other, more conservative members of society. In 1921 she founded the American Birth Control League, which later became the Planned Parenthood Federation. By 1938 Sanger had opened more than three hundred clinics across the United States. Her efforts helped to bring about a shift in the way birth control was viewed, so that by the early twenty-first century most people considered it a legitimate medical service.

A new kind of family

During the eighteenth and nineteenth centuries, when the United States was being settled and developed and was primarily an agricultural nation, large families were common. More children meant more help with farmwork. As the country became more industrialized, though, children no longer represented an economic advantage. Most families of the 1920s were smaller, with two or three children being the norm. Both the lessened need for extra labor and new laws abolishing child labor meant that children stayed out of the workforce longer. At the same time, parents could focus more attention on their individual offspring, and childhood could be viewed as a sheltered, leisurely period of life.

In previous years family members had generally conformed to rigid roles: the father was the head of the family, in charge of laying down and enforcing the rules; the mother was obedient to the father and wholly devoted to her husband and children; and children were to obey their parents and to be "seen and not heard," as a popular expression said. Although these traditional values were deeply implanted and would take a long time to completely change, they did begin to shift somewhat during the 1920s.

This shift in ideas was partly due to a new interest in psychology and especially in the work of Sigmund Freud (1856–1939), who emphasized the importance of childhood trauma as a source of later mental imbalance. It now became accepted for family members to express their feelings openly, especially their affection for each other. In what became known as the "companionate" family, the parents were expected to be both friends and romantic partners, while parents and children were, in the slang of the day, "chums." This made for a somewhat more democratic family structure, even if basic roles remained the same.

With the increasing dominance of science as a source of knowledge and faith in the theories of those who claimed to be experts, parents also began to take a more scientific approach to child rearing. Whereas they had previously relied on instinct or their own parents' example, the adults of the 1920s read books, articles, and manuals to determine the best ways to handle such matters as feeding, toilet training, and discipline. One especially popular guide was child psychiatrist John B. Watson (1878–1959), who recommended a no-nonsense, strict approach to parenting. Contrary to the new tendency to show more affection for children, Watson recommended that parents control their emotions and enforce rigid rules and schedules to keep their offspring on the right track.

The younger generation

While parents of young children grappled with the correct ways to raise their children, parents of teenagers had different concerns. It was during the 1920s that, for the first time, a sharp division appeared between the older and younger generations. A lively youth culture emerged as young people created new ways to dress, amuse, and express themselves. One reason for this development was that teenagers and young adults were spending more time in school. During the 1920s, high school attendance doubled (between 1900 and 1930, it increased by 650 percent), going from 2.2 million to more than 5 million. During the first three decades of the twentieth century, college enrollments went up by 300 percent.

School now became more than just a place to acquire an education. It was a center of social interaction and recreation. Young people joined groups like the Young Men's Christian Association (YMCA), the Young Women's Christian Association (YWCA), the Boy Scouts, and the Girl Scouts and took part in other after-school and evening activities. They also took advantage of the new freedom provided by the family automobile to escape from watchful parental eyes and attend movies and dances with their friends. The increase in privacy resulted in the pairing-up of couples and the phenomenon of dating (previously, courtship had mostly consisted of boys and girls visiting each other in their homes, with parents present). The practice of petting, which involved various forms of kissing and touching, but not usually sexual intercourse, and petting parties also became popular, much to the dismay of the older generation.

During the 1920s, one in eight U.S. citizens between the ages of eighteen and twenty-two attended college, which was a much higher number than in any other developed nation in the world. College students of this period established many fads and trends that eventually influenced the rest of society. Young men and women, known respectively as "sheiks" and "shebas," were both satirized and glamorized in cartoons by artist John Held (1889–1958), whose work appeared in some of the decade's most popular magazines. Sheiks drove topless Model Ts (the inexpensive, very popular car produced by the Ford Motor Company; see Chapter 4), wore long coats made of raccoon pelts, and carried small containers full of illegal liquor and cigarettes in long, fancy holders. A sheba was either a full-fledged or modified flapper, dressed in a short skirt, adopting a breezy manner, and shocking her mother by failing to keep her knees together when she sat down. Both sheiks and shebas took great joy in dancing to jazz in a manner that looks tame to modern eyes but was quite outrageous at the time.

The sexual behavior of these young people was not as wild as it seemed. Despite all the talk about sexual freedom and the wider availability of birth control, most sex outside marriage generally seems to have taken place, if it took place at all, between very committed or engaged couples. Taboos against casual sex were still firmly in place. (The sex lives of married couples, however, did shift toward a new emphasis on romantic love and the pursuit of sexual pleasure for both partners.)

Fundamentalists react to change

Some members of U.S. society saw the changes in women's roles, in the family, and in young people, as well as the increasing mechanization of life in general, as

Vassar College holding commencement in 1929. During the 1920s more people attended college in the United States than any of the other developed countries. *(© Bettmann/Corbis. Reproduced by permission.)*

signs of moral collapse. An increasingly high divorce rate seemed to point to this conclusion; indeed, from 1914 to 1928, the number of marriages ending in divorce climbed from one in ten to one in six. The idea that traditional beliefs and values were apparently being replaced by faith in science and that society was becoming excessively secular (not bound by religious rules or standards) caused great alarm in some quarters.

The United States had traditionally been dominated by white Protestants (members of non-Catholic, Christian churches such as Baptists, Presbyterians, and Methodists). The influx of immigrants that took place in the late nineteenth and early twentieth centuries, however, had brought people of other religions, especially Catholics and Jews, into the mix. Worries about the radical ideas and negative influences these immigrants might introduce resulted in a number of efforts to curb them, such as the Red Scare of 1920 (see Chapter 1).

Many Protestants particularly disapproved of the role that alcoholic beverages played in the cultures of some immigrants. It was in large part the activism of traditional religious groups that had been responsible for bringing about Prohibition, the ban on the production and sale of liquor that was made law in 1919 in the Eighteenth Amendment to the U.S. Constitution. Supporters of Prohibition rejoiced in its passage, believing that now the whole U.S. population would again be held to the Protestant moral values established by those who had first founded and settled the United States. Prohibition would, however, prove to be a failure overall (see Chapter 6), and white Protestant dominance would be weakened during the 1920s.

Creationism versus evolution

One factor in this development was the splintering that occurred between Protestant groups on the basis of theology (religious beliefs and theory). On one side were those who felt that people of religious faith could and should adapt to the modern world, despite the sometimes unsettling changes it brought. On the other side were the fundamentalists, conservative Protestants who accepted the word of the Bible as literal truth. This conflict came to a head over the issue of evolution.

Since the nineteenth century, science had increasingly been replacing religion as a source of knowledge and guidance. The fundamentalists resisted this trend, and they focused their resistance particularly on the teaching of the scientific theory of evolution in public schools. During the previous century, the work of naturalist Charles Darwin (1809–1882) had provided an explanation for the origins of humanity by tracing the changes in human beings, animals, and plants over the millions of years of Earth's history. But this theory, known as evolution, contradicted the biblical story of the Creation, which traced the origin of humans back to Adam and Eve, the first man and woman.

People called "creationists" believed that the teaching of evolution would corrupt young people's minds, weaken their religious faith, and generally help to erode society's already endangered moral values. They misinterpreted Darwin's theory to mean that humans had descended directly from monkeys, and they concluded that hearing about this theory would lead children to behave like monkeys. Thus fundamentalist groups joined together to urge states to prevent teachers in public schools from educating their students about evolution.

The Scopes Monkey Trial

Their efforts reached a climax in Tennessee, which in January 1924 became the first state to pass such a law. A few months later the newly organized American Civil Liberties Union (ACLU) offered to defend any Tennessee teacher willing to test the law's constitutionality; that is, whether it violated the right to freedom of speech guaranteed by the U.S. Constitution, as the ACLU believed it did. Persuaded by a group of his fellow citizens in the small town of Dayton, high school biology teacher John Scopes agreed to get himself arrested by teaching a lesson on evolution. His subsequent trial for violating Tennessee's ban was a much-publicized, colorful affair and one of the most famous court cases in U.S. history.

William Jennings Bryan (1860–1925), a well-known public figure and former presidential candidate who was also active in the fundamentalist movement, signed on to help prosecute Scopes. Clarence Darrow (1857–1938), a Chicago attorney famous for his successful defenses of many underdog clients, led the defense team. Dayton filled up with journalists, street-corner preachers and evangelists, hot dog and soda vendors, and souvenir sellers hawking stuffed monkeys (the event was called the "Monkey Trial" in reference to the supposed connection between monkeys and humans). In a series of articles about the trial, *Baltimore Sun* reporter H.L. Mencken (1880–1956), nationally famous during the 1920s for his biting social criticism, called the scene, as quoted in *The Vintage Mencken,* "better than a circus."

The defense team was disappointed early in the trial by the judge's ruling that testimony on the scientific validity of the evolutionary theory could not be allowed because it did not involve the central question of whether Scopes had violated the law. Then Darrow made a bold move, calling Bryan to the witness stand as an expert on the Bible. Darrow spent an hour and a half mercilessly grilling Bryan on his religious beliefs, asking him whether he considered various Bible stories true in

Clarence Darrow (left) and William Jennings Bryan (right) fought on opposite sides of the Scopes Monkey Trial, one of the most famous trials of the 1920s. *(AP/Wide World Photos. Reproduced by permission.)*

the literal sense. To much of the U.S. public, Bryan seemed confused and foolish on the stand.

Even though Scopes was found guilty, and he was ordered to pay a $100 fine, it was generally believed that the fundamentalists had suffered a serious blow. In the wake of the trial, religious conservatives like Bryan, who died in his sleep only five days after the end of the trial, were increasingly seen as intolerant, backward remnants of a bygone era. The law was overturned a few years later, but the debate about creationism has continued into the twenty-first century.

A female evangelist gains followers

A significant number of people continued to cling to fundamentalist beliefs and practices, and many became followers of religious leaders calling them to turn away from the modern world and return to an older, stricter morality. Perhaps the most famous and effective of these leaders was Aimee Semple McPherson, whose flamboyant style would earn her a big enough following to allow her to establish her own church.

Born in Canada in 1890, McPherson converted at the age of seventeen to the Pentecostal Church, which emphasized such practices as speaking in tongues (when a participant in a worship service goes into a kind of trance and speaks in unidentified words, thought to be from a language of Biblical times), prophecy, and divine healing (in which God heals a person through a human being endowed with special ability). She married a preacher named Robert Semple and went on the road with him, appearing at revivals (large religious meetings, often held in the open air or under tents) and eventually starting to preach herself. She and Semple traveled to China to work as missionaries (people who attempt to convert the native residents of various places to their own Christian faith) in 1910. After the birth of a daughter and the death of her husband, McPherson returned to the United States.

She married again but eventually left her husband (who divorced her) and began to travel around the country, preaching to crowds of people wherever she could gather them. McPherson finally settled in Los Angeles, California, where she established the Full Square Gospel Church. Her ministry became so popular that she was able to build a new temple with space for three thousand worshipers. Converts were attracted not only by McPherson's impressive speaking skills but also by her magnetic personality, her great energy, and her physical appearance. Like other fundamentalists, McPherson preached salvation through an acceptance of Jesus Christ, a literal interpretation of the Bible, and a belief in the Second Coming of Christ. She prayed for the sick and was believed to have healed many. McPherson's many activities included opening the first full-time religious radio station in the United States.

Though beloved by her followers, McPherson was not immune from scandal. The most colorful one occurred in May 1926 when Aimee, as she was known by all, suddenly disappeared after going for a swim in the Pacific Ocean. For several weeks she was presumed dead. Then her mother received a ransom note demanding $500,000 for McPherson's safe return. A few days later, the missing evangelist called her mother from Arizona, reporting that she had been kidnapped, beaten, and taken to Mexico. She said that she had made a daring escape and walked for hours through the desert before being found.

Though joyfully welcomed home by her flock, McPherson was accused by the local authorities of having made up the whole story. For one thing, she had presented no evidence, including no physical injuries from her supposed ordeal, that it had actually happened. For another, several witnesses claimed to have seen her in the company of a male employee of her radio station, whose wife had recently accused him of having an affair with McPherson. Still, the case against McPherson came to nothing, and she returned to the revival trail, becoming even more famous due to the controversy. Her ministry continued successful, but McPherson herself was nagged by personal problems and lawsuits. She died of an overdose of sleeping pills at the age of fifty-four, but the church she established still exists.

In *Middletown* (1929), their detailed study comparing the beliefs and values of residents of a small Indiana town in 1920 with those of a previous generation, Robert and Helen Lynd reported that fewer people were attending church and that the values dominant in the nineteenth century seemed to be on the decline in the 1920s. Other commentators have since agreed. One of them, historian Geoffrey Perret writing in *America in the Twenties,* notes the "steady decline in the vitality of religious belief," asserting that fundamentalism was a "sad, distorted protest against the modern world, with its industrial disciplines, its lonely cities, and its economy of hard cash."

For More Information

Books

Allen, Frederick Lewis. *Only Yesterday: An Informal History of the 1920s.* New York: Perennial, 1964.

Chesler, Ellen. *Woman of Valor: Margaret Sanger and the Birth Control Movement.* New York: Simon & Schuster, 1992.

Cooke, Alistair. *The Vintage Mencken.* New York: Vintage Books, 1955.

De Camp, L. Sprague. *The Great Monkey Trial*. Garden City, NY: Doubleday, 1968.

Deutsch, Sarah Jane. *From Ballots to Breadlines: American Women 1920–1940*. Oxford: Oxford University Press, 1994.

Epstein, Daniel M. *Sister Aimee: The Life of Aimee Semple McPherson*. New York: Harcourt, 1993.

Glabb, Charles N., in John Braemen, Robert H. Bremner, and David Body, eds. *Change and Continuity in Twentieth Century America: The 1920s*. Columbus: Ohio University Press, 1968.

Hanson, Erica. *The 1920s*. San Diego, CA: Lucent Books, 1999.

Herald, Jacqueline. *Fashions of a Decade: 1920s*. New York: Facts on File, 1991.

Kennedy, David M. *Birth Control in America: The Career of Margaret Sanger*. New Haven, CT: Yale University Press, 1970.

Larson, Edward J. *Trial and Error: The American Controversy over Creation and Evolution*. New York: Oxford University Press, 1994.

Lynd, Robert S., and Helen M. Lynd. *Middletown*. New York: Harcourt, Brace, 1929.

Marsden, George. *Fundamentalism and American Culture: The Shaping of Twentieth Century Evangelism, 1870–1925*. New York: Oxford University, 1980.

Miller, Nathan. *New World Coming: The 1920s and the Making of Modern America*. New York: Scribner, 2003.

Mowry, George E., ed. *The Twenties: Fords, Flappers, and Fanatics*. Gloucester, MA: Peter Smith/Prentice Hall, 1963.

Perret, Geoffrey. *America in the Twenties*. New York: Touchstone, 1982.

Web Sites

Aimee Semple McPherson Resource Center. Available online at http://members.aol.com/xbcampbell/asm/indexasm.htm. Accessed on June 17, 2005.

"American Cultural History, Decade 1920–1929." *Kingwood College Library*. Available online at http://kclibrary.nhmccd.edu/decade20.html. Accessed on June 17, 2005.

Best of History Websites. Available online at http://www.besthistorysites.net/USHistory_Roaring20s.shtml. Accessed on June 17, 2005.

"Biographical Sketch." *The Margaret Sanger Papers Project*. Available online at http://www.nyu.edu/projects/sanger/msbio.htm. Accessed on June 17, 2005.

Clash of Cultures in the 1910s and 1920s. Available online at http://history.osu.edu/Projects/Clash/default.htm. Accessed on June 17, 2005.

Interpreting Primary Sources. Digital History. Available online at http://www.digitalhistory.uh.edu/historyonline/us16.cfm. Accessed on June 17, 2005.

Linder, Douglas. "Tennessee vs. John Scopes, The Monkey Trial, 1925." *Famous Trials in American History.* Available online at http://www.law.umkc.edu/faculty/projects/ftrials/scopes/scopes.htm. Accessed on June 17, 2005.

6

The Dark Side of the 1920s

The years between 1920 and 1929 are called the Roaring Twenties, a term that calls up images of happy people dancing the Charleston (a popular dance of the period), listening to jazz in Harlem nightclubs, or piling into Model Ts (an inexpensive car made by the Ford Motor Company) for rides through the city streets. In many ways this was a decade dominated by optimism, as people enjoyed the conveniences that technology brought into their lives, advances in medicine, and an economy that was generally prosperous. Yet the 1920s were also marked by some troubling trends and events, and not everybody enjoyed the era.

Prohibition, the popular name for the constitutional ban on alcoholic beverages that went into effect in early 1920, is often cited as a source of conflict in the United States. Designed by social reformers as a "noble experiment" that would bring more order and morality to society, Prohibition seemed to have the opposite effect. The heavy traffic in illegal liquor brought about an increase in criminal activity, with organized crime figures (groups of criminals who worked together and often fought each other for control of particular areas or cities)

A government official breaking open a barrel of illegal liquor during Prohibition. *(Courtesy of The Library of Congress.)*

raking in the money and stacking up the bodies. The public was shocked and frightened by the killings and lawlessness that seemed to result from Prohibition, which would be overturned at the beginning of the 1930s.

Another trend was the nativism (favoring inhabitants already living in the country over immigrants coming to the country) that flourished during the 1920s. Immigrants from southern and eastern Europe were widely viewed with suspicion and faced discrimination, both in the form of laws enacted against them and in legal efforts to harass and punish them. During the Red Scare of 1920, for example, hundreds of immigrants were rounded up and some were deported (forced to leave the country). The trial and execution of Nicola Sacco and Bartolomeo Vanzetti, Italian immigrants accused of murder, highlighted the prejudice against these newcomers. Other famous trials of the decade shed further light on the darker side of human nature, as well as the public's fascination with crime.

Also alarming was the revival of the Ku Klux Klan, a white terrorist group that had been active in the South during the Reconstruction Era (the period following the American Civil War; 1861–65). In its earlier days, the Klan had committed many violent acts against African Americans in order to prevent them from achieving political and social equality. In the 1920s it broadened its focus to include anyone perceived as different from the white Protestant majority, including immigrants, Catholics, and Jews.

Prohibition: noble or harmful?

It is ironic that a decade so often associated with carefree drinking is also one in which it was illegal to make or sell alcoholic beverages. On January 16, 1920, the Eighteenth Amendment went into effect. A ban on the manufacture and sale of liquor was now written into the U.S. Constitution. The evening before, many bars and saloons had held mock funeral services, with patrons throwing their glasses into wooden coffins and bands playing mournful music. Both private citizens and businesses had spent the previous weeks buying up bottles of liquor; for example, New York City's Yale Club had a supply that was supposed to last for fourteen years. Those who had worked hard to make the United States an alcohol-free society, however, rejoiced. As quoted in Nathan Miller's *New World Coming: The 1920s and the Making of Modern America*, the famous, conservative, and very pro-Prohibition politician William Jennings Bryan (1860–1925) declared that the "nation would be saloonless forever."

The temperance movement

Prohibition was the result of nearly a century of effort that began with the temperance movement of the early nineteenth century. It was made up of those who thought people should not drink alcoholic beverages. In the years following the American Revolution (1775–83), alcohol consumption in the United States had greatly increased. Saloons appeared in every city, town, and village as the hardworking men who were settling the western part of the country took refuge from their loneliness and exhaustion in drinking. In fact, the rate of alcohol consumption between 1800 and 1830 was three times the rate it was in the early twenty-first century. Saloons also provided a setting for such illegal activities as prostitution, which led to the spread of sexually transmitted diseases, and gambling.

Shocked by the real and imagined results of drinking's popularity, a number of reformers began efforts to curb it. At first they encouraged people just to cut down on the amount of alcohol they consumed, but eventually most began to call for total abstinence (drinking no alcohol at all). Drinking was described as a sinful activity that led to disease, crime, and damage to family relationships. Formed in 1836, the American Temperance Union urged abstinence from both distilled liquors, such as whiskey and rum, and fermented beverages, such as beer and wine. They asked people to sign a pledge and to write a "T" next to their name to stand for total abstinence; that is the origin of the popular term "teetotalers," still used to describe people who do not drink alcohol.

As time went on, the temperance groups turned increasingly to political action and government intervention. In 1851 the state of Maine banned the manufacture and sale of alcoholic drinks, and by 1855 twelve more states had done the same. These efforts resulted in a reduction in average consumption from 5 to 2 gallons (18.9 to 7.6 liters) to per year. Most of these laws were repealed soon after the end of the Civil War, but by the end of the nineteenth century, six states were still dry (meaning that alcohol was banned); hotels and bars, however, were allowed to sell liquor by the bottle.

The Prohibition movement gathers strength

In the early 1900s, there were still a large number of saloons in the United States, especially in the cities. At the same time, medical research was providing clear evidence of the toll alcohol took on people's health. There was also a concern about the power that the liquor interests, such as large beer breweries and distilling companies, many of which owned saloons, wielded as they pursued high profits. More groups now sprang into action, including the Methodist Church, the Women's Christian Temperance Union (1874), the Anti-Saloon League (1895), and the Prohibition Party (formed in 1872, this party sponsored anti-alcohol presidential candidates). Women played a particularly important role in this movement, both as leaders (because they were seen as the moral guardians of society) and as inspiration (because they were thought to suffer most from men's drinking habits).

Immigrants from countries in which alcoholic drinks had a cherished cultural role, such as Ireland and Germany, caused further concern and contributed to the nativism sentiments of the period. As the twentieth century dawned, industry was growing, with factories being built across the nation, but especially in the Northeast. Manufacturers needed a sober, reliable workforce to keep their factories going. Drinking became a leading issue of the Progressive Era (a period that lasted from about 1900 to 1914, during which reformers worked hard to improve society in a variety of ways), as Prohibition came to be seen as a way to help the poor and protect young people. During World War I (1914–18), Prohibition even became a patriotic issue: a number of the leading breweries were owned by people who had immigrated from Germany, the country against whom the United States and its allies fought.

All of these forces came together to propel the passage of the Eighteenth Amendment in 1919, followed closely by the Volstead Act, which laid out the terms of the new law. Many people were surprised to learn that the Volstead Act defined "intoxicating" beverages as containing as little as 0.5 percent alcohol, which meant that drinks like beer and wine were included. It is thought that the widespread public support for Prohibition before it took effect may have been based on a belief that it would ban only the so-called "hard" liquors, like whiskey. Over the next decade, the reforming mood that had dominated the Progressive Era would shift, and Prohibition would become increasingly unpopular.

Prohibition brings division

One argument against Prohibition was that it caused a deep division between the people of the United States, who identified themselves either as Wets (those who urged an end to Prohibition) or Drys (those who supported the law). Prohibition was particularly disliked in urban areas with large numbers of immigrants. They resented not only the ban on practices that were acceptable within their own cultures but also the loss of the saloons themselves. Saloons had previously served as neighborhood gathering places, where residents could go to find out about jobs, hold meetings, and even host dances and wedding receptions.

Meanwhile, despite the law, people continued to drink. Those with enough money could buy fairly high-quality liquor from sellers called bootleggers (the name refers to the practice of hiding liquor flasks inside boots). But the poor often resorted to home brews—sometimes made in bathtubs, leading to the term "bathtub gin"—some of which were poisonous enough to cause blindness or even death.

In WAR or PEACE

WHICH NEEDS IT MOST?

PAY ENVELOPE

SALOON KEEPER   HOME MAKER

For the Money Represented by

Three Ten Cent Drinks a Day For a Year

Even at "War Prices"

Any Grocer in Your Town Will Give You the Following Groceries:

10 Fifty-pound Sacks of Flour	25 Cans Tomatoes
10 Bushels Potatoes	10 Dozen Oranges
100 Pounds Granulated Sugar	10 Dozen Bananas
5 Pounds Salt	30 Cans Corn
20 Pounds Butter	10 Pounds Beans
10 Pounds Rice	100 Cakes Soap
10 Pounds Oat Flakes	1 Pound Pepper
10 Pounds Coffee	4 Gallons Molasses
5 Pounds Tea	20 Gallons Oil

And There Would Be ENOUGH MONEY LEFT To Buy a Good Present For Your Wife and Babies

A poster encouraging the Volstead Act. The poster says "In War or Peace Which Needs It Most?" and depicts a pay envelope, saloon keeper, homemaker, and list of groceries that could be purchased with the money used for alcoholic drinks. (Courtesy of The Library of Congress.)

A rise in organized crime

Organized crime existed even before Prohibition took effect. Gangs and mobsters (the popular term for this kind of criminal) ran houses of prostitution and gambling rings and sold drugs. But in the 1920s the big crime syndicates, or organizations, realized that there were huge profits to be made through making and selling alcoholic beverages to thirsty people willing to break the law. As the various gangs competed with one another, the rate of violence increased.

Chicago, Illinois, gained a reputation as one of the toughest towns, with almost four hundred gang-related deaths yearly toward the end of the decade. It was home to the most famous gangster of them all, Al Capone (1899–1947), the man whose name would become permanently linked with Prohibition and the darker side of the 1920s.

"Scarface" makes his mark

Alphonse Capone was born in New York City, and he was familiar with the life of the streets from an early age. During his younger years, he earned the nickname "Scarface" after a bar fight left him with a prominent scar down one cheek. Involved with a notorious New York gang, he moved to Chicago in 1919, both to join the thriving crime scene there and to avoid a murder charge. Capone gradually gained prominence among the underworld figures in Chicago, and by 1925 he had taken control of the city's illegal liquor operations. Although other gangsters were also active, Capone was the most successful: by 1929 he had amassed a fortune of fifty million dollars, had more than seven hundred men working for him, and controlled more than ten thousand speakeasies (places where illegal liquor was sold).

Capone was also known as the most ruthless and brutal of organized crime figures. He is suspected of involvement in the deaths of as many as two hundred members of rival gangs. In fact, it is widely believed that he masterminded one of the bloodiest and most dramatic events of the 1920s: the St. Valentine's Day Massacre. On February 14, 1929, seven members of the gang headed by Capone's leading rival, George "Bugs" Moran, were lured into a Chicago garage. They were then lined up against a wall and shot to death by men dressed in police uniforms, who were thought to be Capone gang members. The identities of the killers were never discovered, however, and it was never proved that Capone was involved.

It was not until 1931 that prosecutors were able to press charges against Capone that would actually hold up in court. Prosecuted for income-tax evasion (failing to pay income taxes on the many millions of dollars he had gained from his illegal activities), Capone was sentenced to eleven years in prison. Capone was surprised by this sentence since he expected a much shorter prison term. After his release, his criminal career was over. Suffering from the effects of syphilis (a serious sexually transmitted disease that may result, as in Capone's case, in brain damage), he lived in Florida until his death in 1947.

Drinkers ignore the law

The most popular setting for illegal drinking in the 1920s was the speakeasy, an unofficial drinking establishment that could be either glamorous or seedy, depending on its location and customers. (The New York City police commissioner claimed that there were about thirty thousand speakeasies in the city.) There were also places called "blind pigs," which were disguised to look like legal businesses but featured bars in back rooms. To gain access to either a speakeasy or a blind pig, a visitor usually had to provide a special password, which was meant to prove that the person was not a law enforcement official planning to raid the establishment and put it out of business.

The liquor sold in these places was provided by bootleggers. They got their supplies from smugglers called rumrunners, who brought the liquor into the United States either by ship or across the Canadian border. The states of New York, New Jersey, Michigan, Washington, California, and Florida were particularly active hubs for the illegal alcohol trade. One of the most famous rumrunners was Bill McCoy, who had been a Florida boat builder before the 1920s. He bought a boat that could hold three thousand cases of liquor, and he became famous for bringing high-quality Scotch whisky to the East Coast. This story possibly lead to the use of the term "the real McCoy" to refer to something authentic.

Eliot Ness was leader of the special force know as the Untouchables that was charged with making sure people did not manufacture, buy, or consume alcohol during Prohibition. *(© Bettmann/Corbis. Reproduced by permission.)*

Local police forces were underfunded, understaffed, and underpaid, all of which made them ineffective in enforcing the Prohibition laws. The federal government provided only fifteen hundred agents to implement Prohibition across the entire United States. And even when violators were brought to trial, judges seemed reluctant to convict them. People were still quite able to make, sell, and buy alcoholic beverages, and some maintained that the number of drinkers and the rate of public intoxication had even increased since the beginning of Prohibition. Even a special new force created by the U.S. Justice Department, known as the Untouchables because they were said to be incorruptible, and led by agent Eliot Ness (1902–1957), who had a flawless reputation for honesty and integrity, was only marginally effective.

Resistance grows

The atmosphere of lawlessness, violence, and suspicion that Prohibition created made people more and more uncomfortable. In her book *The Modern Temper: American Culture and Society in the 1920s,* historian Lynn Dumenil states that Prohibition "had created a nation of spies, of nosy busybodies, empowered by the state to infringe on personal liberties." Increasingly, people were finding the cost of Prohibition too high, and the fact was that most did not see drinking, moderate drinking, at least, as sinful.

Resistance to the Eighteenth Amendment became an issue in the presidential elections of the last half of the 1920s, particularly in 1928. The Democratic candidate in that election was New York governor Al Smith (1873–1944), who happened to represent everything that Prohibition's supporters distrusted. In addition to being a Wet, he was Catholic and the child of Irish immigrants. He was also closely associated with

The original "G-Man": J. Edgar Hoover

Director of the Federal Bureau of Investigation (FBI) for almost fifty years, J. Edgar Hoover rose to prominence in the 1920s. Under his leadership, the FBI grew from a young, inexperienced agency to a large, highly trained law enforcement organization.

Hoover was born in 1895 in Washington, D.C. He was forced to delay his university education because of his father's illness, but by 1916 had received a bachelor's degree in law, and the next year a master's degree, from George Washington University.

During World War I, Hoover worked for the Justice Department, determining how to handle those suspected of disloyalty to the United States. The war and the rise of the Communist Party in Russia had created an atmosphere of suspicion and fear about radical or unfamiliar political views.

When, in 1919, the U.S. attorney general conducted raids on those suspected of ties to the Communist Party or of holding anti-American views, Hoover was asked to prepare legal cases against twenty-five-hundred arrested suspects. Through his work, he acquired a reputation as an expert on radical groups and as a capable administrator.

In 1921 Hoover became assistant director of the FBI, at a time when the fairly young agency was riddled with corruption. One of his first investigative efforts was against the Ku Klux Klan. Hoover worked with the governor of Louisiana on a case that resulted in the arrest and conviction of several Klan members.

By 1924 he was appointed director of the FBI. In this position he was able to root out corrupt agents and appoint better-qualified men. He opened the first centralized finger-printing division in the United States and created an advanced crime laboratory and an academy to train FBI agents. Hoover also developed detailed files on people, including U.S. government officials and popular leaders.

Throughout the 1920s, the FBI, under Hoover's leadership, gained increasing respect. FBI agents, popularly referred to as "G-Men" (the G stands for government) during the 1930s, captured or killed notorious gangsters such as Charles Arthur "Pretty Boy" Floyd, George "Machine Gun" Kelly, and John Dillinger.

Hoover continued to lead the FBI into the 1960s. The documentation he had begun keeping on people in the 1920s had grown, and fear arose that this secret information gave Hoover too much power. The FBI began to focus its attentions on those involved in the civil rights movement and those opposed to the Vietnam War. Civil rights leader Martin Luther King Jr., Attorney General Robert Kennedy, and President John F. Kennedy were among those Hoover investigated. As word of such investigations got out, some worried that the FBI was less focused on crime and more intent on discrediting people for political purposes.

By the time of Hoover's death in 1972, it was widely agreed that the FBI had infringed on individual rights. Reforms and standards were developed to limit the FBI's power and ability to carry out certain tasks, but the debate about the FBI's role in U.S. government continues into the twenty-first century.

Tammany Hall, the political organization that was said to wield total power over New York City. Although Smith was defeated in the election (Commerce Secretary Herbert Hoover [1874–1964] was elected), the support he attracted highlighted a shift in the nation's mood. Prohibition was finally overturned with the passage of the Twenty-first Amendment in 1933.

The effects of nativism

During the late nineteenth and early twentieth centuries, immigrants had been welcomed into the United States, as the country was growing and industrializing rapidly and laborers were needed. In addition, the United States had always prided itself on being a refuge for people fleeing from hardship or mistreatment in their own countries, or seeking expanded opportunities for themselves and their children. Before 1890, most of these newcomers had arrived from the countries of northern and western Europe, just like the people who had first settled the United States. Generally, they shared the same social, political, and religious values of the original settlers, and most of them had spread out to the western parts of the nation.

A new kind of immigrant

By contrast, most of the immigrants who arrived in the first few decades of the twentieth century came from such southern and eastern European countries as Italy, Greece, Armenia, Slovakia, Russia, and Poland; in addition, some arrived from Puerto Rico, the West Indies, and Mexico. Unlike the Protestant majority, these people were often Catholics or Jews, and their cultural habits and beliefs were different. They tended to stay in the cities, settling in neighborhoods with others from the same backgrounds, and they usually had little experience with life in a democratic society. By World War I, immigrants were arriving at the rate of nearly one million per year, and about 80 percent of these were of the new variety.

This trend caused alarm among "old stock" citizens of the United States, those whose ancestors had come long ago from northern and western Europe. They felt that their way of life was threatened by the different ways and ideas of the new-comers. Some used a new pseudoscience (not a genuine science) called eugenics to warn of the dangers of what they called "mongrelization" (the mixing of superior white blood with that of the inferior immigrants). Whereas the people of the United States had once proudly called their society a "melting pot," in which people of many different backgrounds were welcomed and blended together, many of them now feared that such a blending would destroy the world they knew.

It was not just that immigrants were economic competitors (since they were generally willing to work for very low wages) or that their strange cultural practices (particularly the consumption of alcohol) threatened traditional values, although these were both significant factors. It was also that the newcomers were thought to hold dangerous, radical ideas about politics and social order. They believed, it was said, in ideologies like socialism (the theory that the means of production, distribution, and exchange of goods should be owned or run by the community as a whole) and anarchy (having no government at all). These suspicions had been inflamed by the success of the Bolshevik Revolution in Russia in 1917, when Communists (followers of a system in which all property is jointly owned by the community, rather than by individuals) took control of the country from the czar, its traditional ruler. In fact, though, most immigrants were too preoccupied with basic survival to worry about politics. They faced poverty, mistreatment, and prejudice and struggled daily with the challenges of learning a new language and fitting into an unfamiliar society.

Attorney General A. Mitchell Palmer was one of the leaders of the 1920 Red Scare that targeted anyone thought to have the wrong ideas about America.

(© Bettmann/Corbis. Reproduced by permission.)

A "scare" and a trial

In early 1920 nativism sentiment sparked a series of events known as the Red Scare (red was a color closely associated with Communism). The year before, several well-known government leaders and political figures had been the victims of bomb attacks, and printed materials calling for a worker revolution had been found at the attack sites. One of the leaders was Attorney General A. Mitchell Palmer (1872–1936), who had previously been a strong defender of individual rights. Mitchell now became the leading figure in a movement promoting what its members called "100 percent Americanism." Palmer organized a campaign against not only admitted Communists and other radicals but also people who were only suspected of having the wrong ideas about America.

On January 2, 1920, federal agents raided homes and businesses in thirty-three cities, arresting more than 4,000 suspects. Those who did not have the proper citizenship papers were threatened with deportation, and 249 were eventually sent to the Soviet Union. By the end of the year, however, the Red Scare was over, as the majority of U.S. citizens realized that the threat posed by suspected radicals was overblown. Perhaps many also recognized that the cherished, and constitutionally protected, right of freedom of speech had been in more danger from the federal government itself than from any outsiders.

Another event that highlighted the suspicion that native inhabitants felt toward the foreign-born was the trial of Nicola Sacco and Bartolomeo Vanzetti. Italian immigrants who had been trying to organize workers into labor unions, Sacco and Vanzetti were charged with the murder of two men during a 1920 robbery at a shoe factory in Braintree, Massachusetts. Despite flimsy evidence and obvious prejudice shown toward the defendants during the trial, Sacco and Vanzetti were convicted and sentenced to death.

Their lawyers managed to delay their execution for several years, and during this period a number of activists worked to have the sentence overturned. More and more voices were raised in their defense, and demonstrations of support were held at locations around the world. Nevertheless, the two men were executed on August 23, 1927. The case is still cited as an example of a miscarriage of justice resulting from public paranoia.

Anti-immigration laws

For several years, the United States government had put restrictions on the number of people who were allowed to immigrate from Asia, but an open-door policy on European immigrants had always prevailed. That changed in the 1920s, when new anti-immigration legislation was introduced.

It started with an emergency act, passed by Congress in 1921, that set a 355,000-per-year limit on European immigrants. Each nation was allowed a quota (a fixed number allowed to immigrate) of 3 percent of the number of foreign-born residents from that country who had been in the United States at the time of the 1910 Census (the official population count, taken every ten years). Even more restrictive was the National Origins Act of 1924, which set the yearly limit at 150,000 and made the quota 2 percent of those present at the time of the 1890 Census (this part was aimed directly at immigrants from southern and eastern Europe, not many of whom had lived in the United States at that time). No Asian immigrants were allowed at all.

All of these measures reflected the desire for racial and cultural homogeneity, or sameness, that now dominated U.S. society. Their immediate result was to prevent about two million Greeks, Italians, and others who were waiting to come to the United States from immigrating. The number of Italian immigrants, for example, dropped from forty thousand per year to less than four thousand, while the number of people arriving from Poland dropped from thirty thousand to about six thousand. Further steps were taken by individual states, where, for example, foreign-born people were sometimes banned from owning land. California's Alien Land Law was targeted at the large number of Japanese immigrants in that state, many of whom had become successful farmers.

The return of the Klan

Nativism also led to the resurgence of an organization that had wreaked havoc within the borders of the United States in the previous century. During the Reconstruction Era, a period stretching from the end of the Civil War to 1877, representatives of the U.S. government and military joined with white and black southerners to reorganize the political and social structure of the South,

The grand goblin of the Ku Klux Klan presiding over a 1922 meeting. By the 1920s suspicions of anyone different than the white majority lead to the resurrection of the Klan. (© *Underwood & Underwood/Corbis. Reproduced by permission.*)

which had emerged defeated and devastated from the bloody conflict that had just ended. Resistance to these efforts by white southerners, who mourned the loss of a system and way of life they had cherished, took many forms. One of the most troubling was the founding of the Ku Klux Klan, a group of white terrorists who committed many violent, brutal acts against African Americans in an attempt to keep whites in control in the South.

New suspicions and hatreds

By the end of the nineteenth century, the Jim Crow laws were firmly in place in the South, trapping black southerners in a system that made discrimination and inequality legal. The idea that blacks might someday enjoy the rights that the

Constitution supposedly guaranteed to all citizens of the United States seemed remote. Blacks were prevented from voting, for example, by obstructions like property and literacy tests (which whites were not required to pass), poll taxes, and grandfather clauses that allowed only those who had voted before 1865 and their descendants to cast votes (which disqualified virtually all blacks, who had not been allowed to vote at that time). In this repressive environment, there was not much need for the Ku Klux Klan, and they faded away. But in the 1920s, the increasing suspicion and hatred of anyone different from the white Protestant majority resurrected the Klan.

Society had undergone an important and, for some people, unsettling shift. In addition to the immigrants who had crowded into the cities, about four million people had moved from rural to urban areas. A significant portion of these were African Americans, who had migrated to the northern cities in search of greater opportunity and to escape from the political and social inequality they faced in the South. Of course, even in the North they would be allowed to hold only the lowest-paid jobs, and they would continue to struggle with discrimination and prejudice. Living as they did in their own communities, on the south side of Chicago, for example, and in New York City's Harlem neighborhood, and willing to work for low wages, African Americans seemed to pose both a social and an economic threat.

The Klan broadens its focus

In 1915 a white, thirty-five-year-old former minister named William J. Simmons (1880–1945) reorganized the Ku Klux Klan, beginning with a meeting held on top of Stone Mountain, just outside Atlanta, Georgia. Although the new Klan would employ many of the same violent tactics and intimidation (use of the threat or fear of attack or harassment) as the old, it was different in one significant way. The old Klan had targeted the newly freed African Americans of the South, as well as a few people who supported them. The new Klan broadened its scope to focus on anyone who was not white or Protestant, especially Catholics and Jews, and on every region of the nation, not just the southeastern states. That meant, for example, that in Texas they attacked people of Mexican heritage, while in California they focused on Japanese people and in New York on Jews.

The Klan referred to itself as the "Invisible Empire" and employed an elaborate system of secret rituals and costumes (with ordinary members wearing the traditional white robe and hood and leaders donning more colorful clothing) and fancy titles like "Imperial Wizard" and "Grand Goblin." It seems that many followers were attracted as much by these frills as by the chance to impose white supremacy (the view that people of northern and western European descent are superior to all others) on society. In his 1931 book *Only Yesterday: An Informal History of the 1920s,* Frederick Lewis Allen noted that the Klan allowed those who lived in "drab places" an escape from boredom and from their feelings of insignificance, "a chance to dress up the village bigot [someone who is prejudiced against and intolerant of others] and let him be a Knight of the Invisible Empire."

According to its constitution, as quoted in Erica Hanson's *The 1920s,* the Klan's objectives were to

> *"unite white male persons, native-born Gentile [Christian] citizens of the United States of America, . . . to shield the sanctity of the home and the chastity [purity] of womanhood; to maintain forever white supremacy, . . . and maintain the distinctive institutions, rights, privileges, principles, traditions and ideals of a pure Americanism."*

Klan membership grows . . . then declines

With help from two clever but somewhat shady promoters, Edward Young Clarke and Elizabeth Tyler, Simmons mounted what proved to be a very successful campaign to recruit members. Although it is difficult to gauge exact numbers, most historians agree that at the height of its popularity the Klan had as many as five million members, who included not only the group's traditional base of southerners but also midwestern farmers and factory workers in places like Detroit, Michigan, and Cleveland, Ohio. They used many of the same tactics the group had employed in the nineteenth century, including beatings, lynchings (unofficial, brutal, mob executions of people who may or may not have been charged with any crime), and a pattern of intimidation that included vandalizing homes and burning crosses on lawns.

In 1921 an article in *New York World* magazine about the violent acts committed by Klan members spurred an investigation by the U.S. House of Representatives. Witnesses spoke out both against and in defense of the Klan. Simmons himself testified, distancing himself from the violence and claiming that the Klan was actually a public service organization. Rather than exposing the Klan for the terrorist organization it was, the investigation served as free publicity for the group, which actually gained more members as a result.

The next year, Hiram Evans (1881–1940) took over leadership of the Klan. He set about giving the group a more political focus, and gradually the Klan gained more influence as politicians sought its endorsement. It is known that the Klan helped to elect seventy-five members of the House of Representatives, as well as governors in Georgia, Alabama, California, and Oregon; Klansman Earl Mayfield became a U.S. senator from Texas. Those who opposed the Klan were, of course, alarmed at the progress the group was making in the political realm. At the Democratic Party's 1924 convention, some wanted to include a condemnation of the Klan in the party's platform (a statement of positions on various issues), but the majority overruled this for fear that it would hurt the Democrats' popularity. However, both the Democratic presidential candidate, John Davis (1873–1955), and the nominee of the Progressive Party, Robert LaFollette (1855–1925), did speak out against the Klan.

By 1924 the Klan's membership and influence were in decline. It is probable that some supporters felt that, with Prohibition firmly in place, immigrants posed less of a threat. In addition, a few states had taken very aggressive measures to curb Klan violence. For example, in Oklahoma, a three-week period of martial law (when military or law enforcement officers take charge of society) resulted in a roundup of four thousand Klan suspects. Also contributing to the Klan's loss of popularity was the exposure of some of its leaders as being corrupt. In 1925, for instance, Grand Dragon David Stephenson (1891–1966) was found guilty of second-degree murder. Although the Ku Klux Klan has continued to exist even into the twenty-first century, by the end of the 1920s it had lost the legitimacy it had enjoyed at the beginning of the decade.

Crimes of the century

The Roaring Twenties was a decade of sensational crimes, dramatic trials, and executions, all of which were reported in colorful detail in the new tabloid press (newspapers that were half the size of ordinary newspapers and targeted to a mass audience). The public's attention seemed riveted to murder, rape, and other violent crimes. Some people were convinced that these cases provided evidence of social disorder caused by modern developments and influences.

Several of these famous crimes were labeled "the crime of the century." Among the most prominent was the 1924 murder trial of Nathan Leopold (1904–1971) and Richard Loeb (1905–1936), two nineteen-year-olds from wealthy Chicago families. These young men had shocked their families and the rest of the nation by confessing to the killing of Bobby Franks, a fourteen-year-old acquaintance. Leopold and Loeb revealed that they had planned for weeks to commit "the perfect crime," and they expressed no remorse for what they had done. Fearing that their children would receive the death penalty, their parents hired Clarence Darrow (1857–1938), a famous Chicago defense lawyer who had saved many clients from execution.

Darrow quickly determined that the boys, though very intelligent, had never developed a sense of right and wrong. Instead of trying to win their acquittal (a judgment of innocence) on the basis of insanity (in other words, they were not guilty because they had not been aware of what they were doing), Darrow directed his clients to enter a guilty plea. That meant that a judge, not a jury, would decide their fate, which Darrow believed was the young men's only chance to avoid execution. At the trial Darrow emphasized his clients' mental instability and lack of any moral compass. In his lengthy closing statement (see Closing Argument in the Leopold and Loeb Trial Primary Sources entry), he appealed to the judge to look toward the future, when the death penalty would certainly be viewed as a brutal relic of the past. The judge ruled in favor of a life sentence in prison rather than execution.

Darrow defends Sweet

Darrow also won a victory in his defense of Dr. Ossian Sweet, an African American physician charged with murder. After moving into a white neighborhood in Detroit, Sweet used

A historical marker in the yard of Ossian Sweet's house. Sweet's 1925 trial garnered national attention by focusing on whether a man, regardless of race, had the right to defend his property. *(AP/Wide World Photos. Reproduced by permission.)*

bodyguards to defend his family from the hostile whites who had been vandalizing his home. After a confrontation, a white mob surrounded Sweet's house and broke several windows. Shots were fired from inside (Sweet claimed that a warning had been shouted first), resulting in the death of one man in the crowd and the wounding of another. Sweet and eleven others who had been in the house were arrested and charged with murder.

The National Association for the Advancement of Colored People (NAACP) paid Darrow to defend Sweet. Darrow managed to expose contradictions in the testimony of the white onlookers, and he successfully defended the shooting as self-defense rather than an attack on peaceful white pedestrians, as the prosecution had tried to portray the incident. The case resulted in a mistrial due to a hung jury (the jury was unable to reach a verdict, so the trial came to an end), and the charges against Sweet were dropped. The Sweet case was viewed as a happy exception to the usual kind of justice that African Americans could expect from the court system.

Other sensational trials

Other famous court cases of the 1920s included the Halls-Mill murder trial, involving the wife of a minister accused of killing her husband and a married female member of the church choir with whom 'he had been having an affair. Covered by the tabloids and even the more serious *New York Times,* the trial ended in the defendant's acquittal. Not so lucky was Ruth Snyder, a Long Island, New York, homemaker who was convicted of killing her husband. Snyder's married lover, Henry Judd Gray, was also found guilty, and both went to the electric chair. A particularly sensational element of this case was the wide circulation of a photograph taken at the moment of Snyder's death, in defiance of prison rules, by a reporter with a camera strapped to his leg.

The young, lively motion picture industry centered in Hollywood, California, also had its share of scandalous crimes and dramatic trials. In 1921 the popular comic actor Roscoe "Fatty" Arbuckle (1887–1933) was accused of raping and murdering a young actress named Virginia Rappe (1895–1921). Arbuckle was eventually cleared (Rappe's death was due to a botched abortion), but his reputation was ruined, and he was never able to work in movies again. A case that was never solved involved the murder of director William Desmond Taylor (1872–1922), who reputedly had links to a drug ring.

For More Information

Books

Allen, Frederick Lewis. *Only Yesterday: An Informal History of the 1920s.* New York: Perennial, 1964.

Allsop, Kenneth. *The Bootleggers and Their Era.* Garden City, NY: Doubleday, 1961.

Altman, Linda Jacobs. *The Decade That Roared: America During Prohibition.* New York: Twenty-First Century Books, 1997.

Andryszewski, Tricia. *Immigration: Newcomers and Their Impact on the United States.* Brookfield, CT: Millbrook Press, 1995.

Barry, James P. *The Noble Experiment: 1919–33.* New York: Franklin Watts, 1972.

Bergreen, Laurence. *Capone: The Man and the Era.* New York: Simon & Schuster, 1992.

Chalmers, David. *Hooded Americanism: The History of the Ku Klux Klan.* Durham, NC: Duke University Press, 1987.

Clark, Norman H. *Deliver Us from Evil: An Interpretation of American Prohibition.* New York: W.W. Norton, 1976.

Dray, Philip. *At the Hands of Persons Unknown: The Lynching of Black America.* New York: Random House, 2002.

Dumenil, Lynn. *The Modern Temper: American Culture and Society in the 1920s.* New York: Hill and Wang, 1995.

Feuerlicht, Roberta Strauss. *America's Reign of Terror: World War I, the Red Scare, and the Palmer Raids.* New York: Random House, 1971.

Hanson, Erica. *The 1920s.* San Diego, CA: Lucent Books, 1999.

Higdon, Hal. *Crime of the Century: The Leopold & Loeb Case.* New York: Putnam, 1975.

Higham, John. *Strangers in the Land: Patterns of American Nativism.* New York: Atheneum, 1965.

Kobler, John. *Capone: The Life and World of Al Capone.* New York: Putnam, 1971.

Lucas, Eileen. *The Eighteenth and Twenty-First Amendments: Alcohol-Prohibition and Repeal.* Springfield, NJ: Enslow Publishers, 2000.

Miller, Nathan. *New World Coming: The 1920s and the Making of Modern America.* New York: Scribner, 2003.

Perret, Geoffrey. *America in the Twenties.* New York: Touchstone, 1982.

Sinclair, Andrew. *Prohibition: The Era of Excess.* New York: Harper Colophon, 1964.

Web Sites

"Al Capone." *Chicago Historical Society.* Available online at http://www.chicagohs.org/history/capone.html. Accessed on June 17, 2005.

"American Cultural History, Decade 1920–1929." *Kingwood College Library.* Available online at http://kclibrary.nhmccd.edu/decade20.html. Accessed on June 17, 2005.

Best of History Websites. Available online at http://www.besthistorysites.net/USHistory_Roaring20s.shtml. Accessed on June 17, 2005.

Clash of Cultures in the 1910s and 1920s. Available online at http://history.osu.edu/Projects/Clash/default.htm. Accessed on June 17, 2005.

Interpreting Primary Sources. Digital History. Available online at http://www.digitalhistory.uh.edu/historyonline/us16.cfm. Accessed on June 17, 2005.

Linder, Douglas. "Tennessee vs. John Scopes, The Monkey Trial, 1925." *Famous Trials in American History.* Available online at http://www.law.umkc.edu/faculty/projects/ftrials/scopes/scopes.htm. Accessed on June 17, 2005.

7

Surging Creativity: The Literary, Visual, and Performing Arts of the 1920s

For the people of the United States as well as much of the rest of the world, the 1920s were in many ways a decade of change. Technological advances brought both conveniences and worries, while shifts in population and in values made some people feel freer and others more threatened. The field of arts—whether they were of the written, visual, or performing variety—was no different. Major changes came as writers, artists, and musicians explored new forms and made new kinds of statements. Their efforts created the huge surge of creativity that marks this period.

Some important themes of the 1920s stand out, including the development of modernism (a movement that broke with traditional methods and ideas); the work of the expatriates, who often explored U.S. society and themes even as they lived abroad; and the Harlem Renaissance, the cultural explosion centered in New York City's African American community. Popular music was transformed when jazz and blues, born in the southern United States in the late nineteenth and early twentieth centuries, emerged as unique art forms. Modern dancers like Martha Graham (1893–1991) explored new,

The modern dance movement was just one of the culturally significant changes that occurred during the 1920s. (*Courtesy George Eastman House. Reproduced by permission.*)

nontraditional kinds of movement, while painters influenced by European trends—such as Cubism, which features the use of simple geometric shapes and interlocking planes to represent all kinds of objects, including the human form—portrayed distinctly local scenes and images in new ways. There is no doubt that the 1920s provided a treasure trove of art that is still much enjoyed and appreciated.

The literature of the 1920s

Many of the literary works considered masterpieces of twentieth-century literature were produced during the 1920s. It was a decade dominated on the one hand by large themes, especially the modernist techniques that many artists were employing, and on the other by larger-than-life characters who would forever after be linked to the 1920s.

Fitzgerald and Lewis capture the mood

Perhaps it is not surprising that works produced during such a colorful time would be created by colorful personalities. One of the most fascinating, and the most representative of 1920s style and concerns, is novelist and short story writer F. Scott Fitzgerald (1896–1940). Along with his beautiful wife, Zelda, who embodied the mystique of the flapper (a young woman of the 1920s who dressed and behaved in a carefree, bold manner), Fitzgerald is closely associated with the decade. Born in St. Paul, Minnesota, Fitzgerald achieved fame and success with his first novel, *This Side of Paradise* (1920). The book's protagonist, Amory Blaine, typifies the young people who came of age after World War I (1914–18) and who seemed to view things very differently than their parents had. Disillusioned by the world around them, they sought fun and pleasure and rejected the morality of their elders.

The 1920s is often called the "Jazz Age," a term first coined by Fitzgerald in the title of a 1922 short story collection. These *Tales of the Jazz Age* chronicle various trends of the decade; for example, in "Bernice Bobs Her Hair," a young woman makes the bold decision to cut off her long hair for a nontraditional but very stylish short "bob." In his finest work, the novel *The Great Gatsby* (see *The Great Gatsby* Primary Sources entry), Fitzgerald tells the story of a young man from the midwestern

United States who, having become wealthy as a bootlegger (a seller of illegal liquor), transforms himself in pursuit of the girl of his dreams. In the end, Jay Gatsby is betrayed by his illusions. Fitzgerald masterfully explores such themes as the ironic contrast between the material prosperity of U.S. society and its moral decay, and the persistence of dreams in the face of grim reality.

Another important literary figure of the 1920s was Sinclair Lewis (1885–1951), who showed in realistic detail many themes and trends of the period. Although his novels were intended to expose and condemn the shallowness of an increasingly materialistic society, they appealed to a wide audience. Most readers seemed to recognize the truth, without acknowledging the criticism, in Lewis's books. Lewis highlighted the limitations of small-town life in *Main Street* (1920) and satirized (used humor or exaggeration to expose weakness) popular evangelists (those who try to convert others to Christianity) in *Elmer Gantry* (1927). His best-received work, though, was *Babbitt* (1922; see *Babbitt* Primary Sources entry).

The title character of this novel is a middle-class businessman and resident of the up-and-coming town of Zenith. Through *Babbitt,* Lewis explores such important 1920s trends as the worship of business, the rise of consumerism, and the conflict between the older and younger generations. Despite this character's spiritual emptiness and complacency (going along with things as they are), he was enthusiastically embraced by readers, and his name came to stand for a particular kind of person in U.S. society: an uncultured, unthinking conformist (someone who behaves in the manner accepted and expected by his society).

The expatriates

A considerable number of U.S. painters, sculptors, writers, and musicians, both the truly talented and those who wished to become or be seen as talented, flocked to Europe in the 1920s. They found Paris, France, with its easygoing lifestyle and low cost of living, particularly welcoming. There they could drink alcohol without fearing arrest, and they could escape from what they saw as the bigotry (the attitude of not accepting other opinions, races, or religions) and hypocrisy (the practice of acting the opposite way of one's beliefs) of

U.S. society. They tended to look down on the small-town residents of the United States, whom they considered ignorant and intolerant. At the same time, however, their work often displays a deep longing and appreciation for home. Among the best known and most successful of the literary expatriates were novelist F. Scott Fitzgerald, who wrote *The Great Gatsby* while living in France, unconventional poets Ezra Pound (1885–1972) and e.e. cummings (1894–1962), and especially Ernest Hemingway (1899–1961).

A veteran of World War I, Hemingway was a dynamic figure who captured the admiration of his colleagues both for his bold, brave personality and for the new style he developed. Hemingway wrote in simple language and short sentences stripped of unnecessary description and emotion. His books are full of protagonists who lack the positive or heroic aspects of characters in traditional fiction. Hemingway's work *The Sun Also Rises* (1926; see *The Sun Also Rises* Primary Sources entry) concerns a veteran of World War I who has been rendered both physically and emotionally helpless by a combat wound and who wanders aimlessly around France and Spain with his similarly troubled friends. At the beginning of this novel, Hemingway included a comment made by Gertrude Stein (1872–1946), a U.S. writer who lived in Paris and served as a friend, adviser, and host to many younger artists. The quote, "You are all a lost generation, " led to the use of the term "Lost Generation" to refer to the young people of the post-World War I generation, even though Hemingway claimed that he had never intended the phrase to define anything or anyone.

In *For Whom the Bell Tolls,* Hemingway tells the story of a U.S. citizen who drives an ambulance in Italy during World War I (reflecting the author's own experience). After being wounded, he falls in love with a British nurse, who becomes pregnant but later dies. In both *The Sun Also Rises* and *For Whom the Bell Tolls,* the characters are disappointed by events and circumstances thrust upon them by the world or by life. They are forced to retreat into themselves and struggle to achieve the self-respect that is their only compensation. Hemingway was praised early in his career, but his reputation suffered somewhat as the twentieth century continued. Nevertheless, most critics agree with historian Geoffrey Perret, who notes in *America in the Twenties* that Hemingway's prose style, "combined with an attitude of stoicism [ability to endure hardship] in the face of life's cruelty...captured perfectly the disillusioned spirit of the times"

The influence of modernism

During the 1920s many U.S. writers experimented with techniques linked to modernism. This worldwide movement involved an intentional rejection of tradition in terms of style, content, and values, and frequently, a focus on the concerns of the individual in a world that was increasingly and confusingly mechanized and commercial. Influenced by the pioneering psychiatric studies of men like Sigmund Freud (1856–1939) and Carl Jung (1875–1961), the modernists engaged in intense self-examination. They sought freedom and originality of both ideas and methods of expression.

The most influential of the early modernists was probably the Irish novelist and short story writer James Joyce (1882–1941), whose masterpiece was *Ulysses* (1922). This chronicle of one day in the life of a resident of Dublin, Ireland, is written in a stream-of-consciousness style; that is, the narrative mimics the jerks, leaps, and disconnections of the human thought process. Joyce's technique was imitated by many writers, including U.S. novelist John Dos Passos (1890–1970), who wrote his novel *Manhattan Transfer* as a series of short portraits that come together to create a collage-like picture of New York City.

Other notable modernists include the poets William Carlos Williams (1883–1963), Hart Crane (1899–1932), and e.e. cummings, who purposely abandoned or played with many conventions of grammar and punctuation, including the uppercase letters of his own name. The most prominent of the modernist poets, though, was the U.S.-born T.S. Eliot (1888–1965), who moved to Great Britain as a young man and stayed there for the rest of his life. Eliot's complex long poem "The Wasteland" may have been too difficult to be widely understood, but it had a major influence on other writers. In his book *New World Coming: The 1920s and the Making of Modern America*, historian Nathan Miller writes that in "The Wasteland" Eliot "converted the spiritual emptiness following the war into a metaphor for the entire modern era."

An especially famous and popular cultural figure during the Roaring Twenties was Edna St. Vincent Millay (1892–1950), who would eventually be recognized as one of the most accomplished poets of the twentieth century. Her work was widely admired not only by critics, but also by a diverse audience of readers. Millay served as a voice of the post-World War I generation of young people who were rebelling against tradition and insisting on freedom of thought and behavior. An embodiment of the new, sexually liberated woman of the period, she lived in New York City's Bohemian (socially unconventional) neighborhood of Greenwich Village among artists and writers who expressed their beliefs in non-conformity, equality, and free love.

The poems included in Millay's second volume of poetry, *A Few Figs from Thistles* (1920) were written in traditional poetic forms rather than the free verse employed by modernists like T.S. Eliot and e.e. cummings. Yet they featured a breezy, carefree tone that captured the mood of the 1920s. Perhaps most representative of this perspective is the often-quoted "First Fig," which is probably Millay's most famous poem: "My candle burns at both ends;/It will not last the night;/But ah, my foes, and oh, my friends—/It gives a lovely light."

Following the publication of her fourth volume, *The Harp-Weaver and Other Poems* Millay won the Pulitzer Prize for Literature in 1923 (a prestigious yearly literary award). The next year she embarked on a tour of the Midwest, reading her poetry to audiences who seemed as entranced by her physical appearance, which included flaming red hair, slim figure, and elegant clothing, as by her accomplished poetry. In 1927, Millay's public life took a political turn when she marched in protests against the impending execution of Nicola Sacco and Bartolomeo Vanzetti, Italian immigrants who had been convicted of murder despite a lack of evidence. This incident inspired a poem "Justice Denied in Massachusetts," that appeared in *The Buck in the Snow and Other Poems* (1928). Millay continued to write until her death in 1950, but many critics felt that she had reached the peak of her ability and popularity during the 1920s.

The Southern Renaissance

Another author who often employed the modernist technique of stream-of-consciousness writing was William Faulkner (1897–1962), who is closely associated with a movement known as the Southern Renaissance. Like others involved in this movement, Faulkner, a native of the southern state of Mississippi, explored such uniquely southern topics as the lingering effects of the American Civil War (1861–65) and the legacy of slavery. Over the course of several novels, Faulkner created a fictional place called Yoknapatawpha County that was closely modeled after his own Lafayette County, Mississippi. The first of these novels, *Sartoris,* appeared in 1929.

Other novelists of the Southern Renaissance include Thomas Wolfe (1900–1938), who re-created his hometown of Asheville, North Carolina, in *Look Homeward, Angel,* and Ellen Glasgow (1873–1975), whose best works include *Barren Ground* (1924) and *The Romantic Comedians* (1926). Julia Peterkin (1880–1961) won the Pulitzer Prize for *Scarlet Sister Mary* (1928), a novel about African Americans living on a South Carolina plantation. Also writing from a southern perspective were the Nashville-based authors known as the Fugitives, or Agrarians, headed by poet and critic John Crowe Ransom (1888–1974).

Taking aim at society

Although this decade is often remembered as a time of enthusiasm and optimism, it was also a period in which some of the most biting satires of the twentieth century appeared. A number of highly skilled writers aimed their wit at the political and business leaders, reformers, and popular trends of the day. They made fun of everything and everybody, but especially of those they considered obnoxiously self-important. One of the most successful writers of humor and satire was Ring Lardner (1885–1933), whose stories about the funny aspects of ordinary U.S. citizens appeared in such collections as *How to Write Short Stories* (1924) and *The Love Nest* (1926).

A group of the nation's wittiest writers, and harshest social critics, held regular gatherings at a round table at the Algonquin Hotel in New York City. They called themselves the Vicious Circle, but they are more popularly referred to as the Algonquin Round Table. The group included newspaper and magazine columnists and editors as well as literary critics, dramatists, and fiction writers. Perhaps the most famous was Dorothy Parker (1893–1967), who wrote short stories but also served as an editor at *Vogue* and as the *New Yorker* magazine's columnist, writing under the nickname Constant Reader. In Baltimore, Maryland, the renowned journalist H.L. Mencken (1880–1956) held court, providing searing commentary on many events and trends of the 1920s.

The masterful humorist James Thurber (1894–1961), who would achieve his greatest fame in later decades, published his first book during the 1920s. He collaborated with the great essayist and fiction writer E.B. White (1899–1995; also the author of *Charlotte's Web*) on *Is Sex Necessary? Or, Why You Feel the Way You Do* (1929), a parody of the psychology books popular during the period. Screenwriter Anita Loos (c. 1893–1981) scored a big hit with her novel *Gentlemen Prefer Blondes*, which was later made into a movie starring screen goddess Marilyn Monroe (1926–1962). Many of the people who admired Loos's books apparently did not realize that its sweet-talking, falsely innocent heroine was actually a prostitute.

Writing for a mass audience

While the literary giants of the 1920s gained fame and praise in certain circles, the authors who geared their work to a mass audience were much more popular with the ordinary people of the period. For example, Fitzgerald's most successful novel, *This Side of Paradise,* sold fifty thousand copies, while Harold Bell Wright's one-dimensional, purely escapist, moralistic novel *The Re-Creation of Brian Kent* (1919) sold almost one million. Also popular were the western stories of Zane Grey (1875–1939); an example is *Riders of the Purple Sage,* published in 1912. In fact, between 1915 and 1924, Grey had books on the list of the top ten bestsellers every year but 1916. Similarly, more people read and enjoyed the poetry of Edgar A. Guest (1881–1959), with its simple themes and traditional rhyme schemes, than the very difficult, unconventional verse of Eliot or cummings.

Also extremely popular and influential was fiction that involved mysteries, detectives, and crime. Written in what has been termed the "hard-boiled" style, which features an emphasis on frequently violent action, slang, and tough

Anita Loos scored a big hit during the 1920s with her novel *Gentlemen Prefer Blondes.* *(Hulton Archive/Getty Images. Reproduced by permission.)*

characters, these stories often appeared in magazines that were printed on cheap paper made of wood pulp. Thus they came to be called "pulp fiction." One of the most popular magazines was *Black Mask,* in which several authors who later gained critical acclaim first published their work. Among them were Dashiell Hammett (1894–1961), whose novels include *Red Harvest* (1929) and *The Maltese Falcon* (1930) and Raymond Chandler (1888–1959), who would later write the classic detective novels *The Big Sleep* (1939) and *Farewell My Lovely* (1940).

Many stage productions

The theater fans of the 1920s had their pick of high-quality stage productions, from serious dramas to satirical comedies to musical revues that combined singing, dancing, and comedy routines. The center for much of this activity was New York City, both in its Broadway theater district and beyond, including a thriving scene in the African American community of Harlem. Leading playwrights of the period included Maxwell Anderson (188–1959), George S. Kaufman (1889–1961), Edna Ferber (1887–1968), and Ben Hecht (1894–1964). All took part in a major shift away from the melodramas of the Victorian Era (roughly referring to the years 1837 to 1901, when Queen Victoria ruled Great Britain), which had featured romance or adventure plots and exaggerated characters and dialog, toward plays offering social commentary and protest. These playwrights also explored family relationships and personal values.

O'Neill experiments with expressionism

Most prominent among the new, modern playwrights was Eugene O'Neill (1888–1953), who would reach his peak in the 1930s and 1940s as a master of realism and naturalism (genres that attempted to convey authentic characters, scenes, and themes). During the 1920s, though, O'Neill produced nineteen plays, many of them featuring such experimental techniques as symbolism (the use of objects or symbols to represent ideas or emotions) and expressionism. The latter method, which had originated in Europe, involved the use of distorted speech, action, and settings to portray the characters' innermost emotions. O'Neill's 1920 play *The Emperor Jones* drew rave reviews and big crowds when it premiered at a small playhouse in Providence, Rhode Island.

Considered the first expressionistic play to achieve success in the United States, *The Emperor Jones* was unique and controversial not only because its main character was African American but also because O'Neill chose a black actor to play the role (such roles in white theaters had previously been played by white actors in makeup designed to make them look black). The play centers on the character of Brutus Jones, a strong-willed African American who, after fleeing a murder charge in the United States, has taken control of a Caribbean island. Eventually the islanders realize he is not as all-powerful as he has claimed, and they revolt. Jones escapes into the jungle, where his own terror overcomes him. He is finally killed by his former subjects.

The Harlem Renaissance

During the first two decades of the twentieth century, African Americans were migrating in large numbers from the southern states to the northern cities. They left in search of better lives, including both an escape from the economic hardships and racial oppression (harsh treatment) they had experienced in the South and the promise of better opportunities in the North. African American communities sprang up in several northern cities, but the most famous was undoubtedly New York City's Harlem. There people of African descent, drawn not just from the southern United States but from all over the world, came together to create and celebrate a rich, thriving culture. They explored their heritage and expressed their ideas and emotions, and they took part in a cultural blossoming that would later be named the Harlem Renaissance.

Paul Robeson: Actor, Singer, and Political Activist

One of the most dynamic African American figures of the Harlem Renaissance era was multi-talented Paul Robeson. Acclaimed as an actor for his appearances in both Broadway musicals and serious dramas, Robeson was also an accomplished singer and a committed social activist.

Born in 1898 the son of a minister in Princeton, New Jersey, Robeson broke the barriers of racial prejudice and discrimination to become an outstanding student and athlete at Rutgers University. He later earned a law degree at New York City's Columbia University, but only worked in the field for a short time after realizing that racism would make this a difficult profession (for example, a white secretary refused to take dictation from him because he was black). Robeson was soon drawn into a very different kind of work.

Even before he graduated from law school, Robeson had appeared in the smash Broadway hit *Shuffle Along,* which drew rave reviews. His reputation as an actor grew when, in 1924, he was cast in the lead role in *All God's Chillun Got Wings* by the up-and-coming white playwright Eugene O'Neill, who had written the role with Robeson in mind. This play was controversial at the time because of its mixed-race cast and focus on an interracial couple.

In 1925 Robeson appeared in the title role in O'Neill's play *The Emperor Jones.* In the play, the African American title character has run away from the law in the United States and become the dictator of a small West Indian island; he is eventually driven insane by his own doubts and fears and is executed by his subjects. Robeson also drew critical praise for

his appearances in *Black Boy* (1926) and in the London version of the musical *Showboat* (1928). It was in *Showboat* that Robeson sang "Ol' Man River," a song that many would forever closely associate with his deep, bass voice.

Robeson's appearance in the title role of Shakespeare's *Othello* was enthusiastically received when performed at London's Savoy Theatre in May 1930. It was not until more than a decade later that U.S. audiences were ready to accept an African American actor in a Shakespearean play, even though the character of Othello was supposed to be black. Opening in New York City in 1943, the play ran for 296 performances, making it the longest-running of any Shakespeare play in Broadway history.

Although Robeson's acting skills were considerable, they may have been overshadowed by his talent as a singer. In April 1925 Robeson showcased his voice in a concert featuring African American spirituals and other songs by black composers. His popularity as a singer grew to the point that, in 1929, he sold out a concert at New York's Carnegie Hall, as well as several European concert venues.

During the next several decades, Robeson made hundreds of recordings, not only of the blues songs and spirituals, but of classical and popular songs. He also appeared in a number of movies, including the film versions of *The Emperor Jones* (1933) and *Showboat* (1936).

Robeson was strongly committed to the struggle for African American civil rights. His outspoken support for the Soviet Union's communist government, however, made him a controversial figure during the 1950s. By the time of his death in 1976, his reputation had recovered. In 1998 he received a posthumous Grammy lifetime achievement award.

This explosion of talent and achievement included an important element of political consciousness and mobilization (to assemble or coordinate). It was in the field of the arts, however, for which the Harlem Renaissance is most noted. Under the guidance of some prominent older figures, including African American professor and essayist Alain Locke (1886–1954) and white critic and arts patron Carl Van Vechten (1880–1964), a number of young writers emerged. The creativity and dedication they displayed added excitement to a community and movement that seemed endlessly promising.

Voices of the Harlem Renaissance

Foremost among these young writers was poet Langston Hughes (1902–1967), whose name has always been the one most closely linked to the Harlem Renaissance. Raised in the Midwest, Hughes arrived in Harlem as a young man and almost immediately established himself as a star with his innovative poetry. Inspired by the jazz and blues he was hearing in Harlem nightclubs and speakeasies (places where illegal liquor was sold), Hughes used the rhythms and themes of this bold new music in his writing. Like other writers of this period, he sought to convey the realities of African American life, however harsh those realities might be. In poems like "The Negro Speaks of Rivers," "The Weary Blues" (see "The Weary Blues" Primary Sources entry), and "Mother to Son," Hughes used simple but memorable language and images, creating a rich collage of black lives and concerns.

Other important writers of the Harlem Renaissance include poet Countee Cullen (1903–1946), whose work addressed many racial and social issues, and Claude McKay (1890–1948), a Jamaican immigrant who earned the disapproval of the Talented Tenth (the leading intellectuals of the African American community, who were supposed to provide a model of accomplishment for others to follow) with his novel *Home to Harlem*, a gritty, unflinching glimpse into urban African American lives. Another significant novelist was Jean Toomer (1894–1967), whose *Cane* (1923) brought together several short pieces noted for their modernist technique and poetic language. Novelist and editor Wallace Thurman (1902–1934) explored divisions based on skin tone in *The Blacker the Berry* (1929) and also founded a short-lived but influential journal called *Fire* (1926) that showcased the work of Harlem Renaissance writers.

Also involved in the production of *Fire* was Zora Neale Hurston (1891–1960), one of several notable women writers of the Harlem Renaissance (and the one who probably had the most influence on later authors). Although best known for her novel *Their Eyes Were Watching God* (1937), which was published well after the end of the Harlem Renaissance, Hurston was active during the 1920s as a folklorist (someone who collects and records the traditional beliefs and stories of a community) and short story writer. The stories she produced during this period include "Drenched in Light" and "Spunk."

Other women achieved recognition during the Harlem Renaissance as well. Jessie Redmon Fauset (1882–1961) authored the novels *This Is Confusion* (1924) and *Plum Bun* (1928) and served as literary editor of *Crisis,* the journal of the National Association for the Advancement of Colored People (NAACP). Nella Larson (1891–1964), who was herself the daughter of a white father and a black mother, chronicled the struggles of people of mixed racial heritage in *Quicksand* (1928) and *Passing* (1929).

A worldwide passion for jazz

The unique new musical form called jazz was so important to the 1920s that the period is sometimes termed the "Jazz Age." A product of African American influences blended with elements from other cultures, jazz provided the background music for this period. It was played in nightclubs, on the Broadway stage, and at teenagers' parties, and it drew New Yorkers by the thousands to Harlem, the center of African American culture during the 1920s. There, people listened to jazz and the blues, a related, equally exciting and influential musical form. Jazz and blues were quickly gaining popularity, in fact, all around the world.

A blend of influences

The deepest roots of both jazz and blues are found much earlier than the 1920s. They date back several centuries, to the arrival of the first African American slaves in the United States. Rhythms and instruments brought from Africa combined with the tunes and fiddle strains of the British Isles, the origin of the nation's earliest settlers. These blended traditions evolved slowly until the 1890s, when a new kind of popular music called ragtime emerged. These tunes featured strong, syncopated melodies (created when the weak beat is stressed in place of the usual strong one). Ragtime piano playing eventually began to be called jazz, a term that may have originated as African American slang for "sex."

The birthplace of jazz is often identified as New Orleans, Louisiana, where musicians from a rich racial mix—including African, European, and Native American—began to play instruments discarded by the military bands of the Civil War era. In a style known as Dixieland, they formed groups like marching bands, but incorporating offbeat rhythms and improvised solos in which individual players take off from the main melody with their own interpretations of the music. Early figures in the New Orleans scene included piano player Ferdinand "Jelly Roll" Morton (1885–1941), who is considered the first jazz composer, and cornet player Joe "King" Oliver (1885–1938). The latter moved to Chicago, Illinois, the next hotbed for jazz and blues, and formed the Creole Jazz Band. Hoping to improve the band's sound, Oliver hired another cornet player, a talented young man named Louis Armstrong (1901–1971), who would become one of the most revered of all jazz musicians.

Armstrong and Ellington lead the way

Born in New Orleans, Armstrong learned to play the cornet at the Colored Waifs Home, where, as a young teenager, he was sent as punishment for a prank. He went on to become a highly accomplished player and to perfect his own distinct style, which featured an incredible ability to improvise. During the 1920s, Armstrong performed in both Chicago and New York, eventually landing a long-term engagement at Connie's Inn, one of Harlem's most popular and glamorous nightclubs. He also performed on Broadway in the renowned show *Hot Chocolates,* playing as well as singing in his gravelly, unforgettable voice. Armstrong's career stretched well beyond the 1920s, and he continues to be lauded as a key figure in the development of jazz.

While Armstrong was playing at Connie's Inn, Edward "Duke" Ellington (1899–1974) was winning rave reviews at the Cotton Club, the nightspot most often associated with the hot music and glamour of the Roaring Twenties and with

Harlem at its peak. Along with bandleader Fletcher Henderson (1898–1952), Ellington created the Big Band sound, which featured a jazz orchestra with more than one player on each instrument. During their long engagement at the Cotton Club, Ellington and his band performed their trademark "jungle" sound, using mutes and growl techniques in the horns. Even though most of Ellington's greatest achievements came later, he wrote some of his most famous compositions during the 1920s, including "Creole Love Call" and "Mood Indigo."

Other notable jazz musicians of the 1920s include Thomas "Fats" Waller (1904–1943), the leader among the Harlem Renaissance-era piano players who performed in fancy clubs and respectable musical revues as well as seedy dives and rent parties (late-night gatherings held to raise money for tenants). Waller's best songs include "Honeysuckle Rose" and "Ain't Misbehavin'," which Armstrong sang in *Hot Chocolates*.

The popular music of the 1920s was heavily infused with jazz, as white bandleaders, especially the very popular Paul Whiteman (1891–1967), promoted as the "Jazz King," brought "symphonic" versions of this innovative new music to white audiences. The finest and longest-lasting contribution made by Whiteman was the 1924 concert at which his orchestra introduced a jazz-tinged composition called *Rhapsody in Blue* by George Gershwin. Along with his brother Ira, Gershwin was among the most popular songwriters of the 1920s. He successfully incorporated into music written for Broadway elements from jazz, classical music, and even opera. The Gershwins wrote the scores for such hit Broadway shows as *Oh, Kay!*, and *Funny Face*.

Singing and playing the blues

A close relative of jazz, blues music originated in the work songs and spirituals (religious songs) of African American slaves in the southern United States. Blue was the color of emotional pain, and the blues provided a way both to express that pain and to rise above the sorrow, sadness, and troubles of everyday life. The influence of the blues stretches to the present, for it played a major role in the development of rock music.

Some of the earliest blues musicians include W.C. Handy (1873–1958), a cornet player who established a standardized notation pattern for this new musical form, becoming one of the first to write down and publish blues songs. Another early, great figure was Gertrude "Ma" Rainey (1885–1939), who helped to establish a prominent role for women in this musical genre. Rainey toured with various bands, appeared in revues, and made many records. Her music was well known to the blues singers of the 1920s, many of whom performed in Harlem.

Perhaps the greatest blues singer of all time, however, was Bessie Smith (c. 1894–1937). Smith was a rough, tough, and physically large woman with a soulful, mournful voice. Her first record, "Downhearted Blues," was a huge success, earning her the title "Empress of the Blues." Smith generally performed only in the South, but her records were popular throughout the nation, and she influenced many blues singers who followed her.

Bessie Smith is perhaps one of the greatest blues singers of all time. (© *Bettmann/Corbis. Reproduced by permission.*)

Dance, both popular and serious

During the 1920s almost everybody was crazy about dancing, especially young people, who now made dancing, rather than games like charades, the main activity of their parties. Many popular dances originated in the African American community. It was in Harlem, for example, that the world got its first taste of the Charleston in the all-black show *Runnin' Wild*. This fast-paced, jerky dance of flying arms and knocking knees would become symbolic of the Roaring Twenties. Flappers and their boyfriends, as well as more ordinary people, performed it with abandon in all kinds of settings. Other popular dances included the fox-trot, the camel walk, the tango, the toddle, the varsity drag, and the shimmy.

Serious dance also made major progress during the 1920s. Students of the Denishawn School in Los Angeles, California, helped to popularize the still-young art form of modern dance, which, like other artistic pursuits of the period, involved a rejection of tradition. Modern dance differed from the much older form of ballet in its greater emotional expressiveness and its more earth-bound movements. Modern dancers often used elements from exotic or ancient cultures as inspiration for their pieces. Perhaps the most famous of the Denishawn alumnae is Martha Graham, who began performing in the 1920s and formed her own company in 1929. She has since been acknowledged as one of the greatest choreographers (people who compose the sequences of steps and moves for dance performances) of the twentieth century.

The visual arts

Before the twentieth century, many painters and sculptors had portrayed subjects far removed from ordinary life, such as scenes or characters from the Bible or from classical mythology. As the twentieth century dawned, however, artists began to incorporate new kinds of subjects and more modernistic techniques. During the 1920s a number of artists moved to Europe, joining the writers and musicians who formed the expatriate scene, especially in the city of Paris. They drew inspiration, and even took lessons, from European artists, but they continued to look toward home for ideas.

Not all painters of the 1920s were associated with schools (groups of artists who followed a particular philosophy or style), but some of the most famous ones were. The so-called "Ashcan" school was made up of artists who favored informal subjects, including many urban scenes, which they portrayed in a realistic style. One of these Ashcan artists was John Sloan (1871–1951), whose painting "Sixth Avenue Elevated at Third Street" is a good example of this style. Although he was not a member of the Ashcan school, Edward Hopper (1882–1967) also painted scenes of urban life. In paintings such as *Drugstore,* he conveyed the stark loneliness of life in a modern city.

Georgia O'Keeffe (1887–1986), who was married to photographer and gallery owner Alfred Stieglitz (1864–1946), created close-up paintings of flowers and plants in a style known as precisionism. O'Keeffe skillfully combined realistic detail with an overall abstract effect. This style of painting was not meant to represent reality. In sculpture, meanwhile, artists were incorporating modern styles and techniques. Jo Davidson (1883–1952) used simplified forms for his portrait bust of Gertrude Stein, while Alexander Calder (1898–1976) put playfulness, light, and motion into his mobiles. Other artists were inspired by images both of Africa and of African American life, such as Harlem Renaissance painter Aaron Douglas (1899–1979) and sculptor Richmond Barthe (1901–1989).

Many of the artists who were part of the expatriate scene in France during the 1920s were interested in the Art Deco movement, which was featured in an exposition in Paris in 1925. This approach to commercial art and design was enthusiastically adopted in the United States, and it helped to create the sleek, modern look of the Roaring Twenties. The Art Deco look replaced the ornate decoration and clutter of the Victorian Era with a streamlined, balanced style. Simple lines created a stark, modern effect set off by bold colors and the use of such new materials as plastic and concrete. Art Deco would exert a major influence on architecture, interior design, furniture, and even fashion for many years.

The main contribution of the 1920s to architecture was the skyscraper, which changed the skylines of cities across the United States. The most famous skyscraper was the Empire State Building in New York City. Begun in 1929 and finished two years later, this building's elegant lines and sharp angles made it a tall, imposing symbol of the modern age.

For More Information

Books

Allen, Frederick Lewis. *Only Yesterday: An Informal History of the 1920s*. New York: Perennial, 1964.

Applebaum, Stanley, ed. *The New York Stage: Famous Productions in Photographs*. New York: Dover Publications, 1976.

Berry, Michael. *Georgia O'Keeffe*. New York: Chelsea House, 1988.

Candael, Kerry. *Bound for Glory 1910–1930: From the Great Migration to the Harlem Renaissance*. New York: Chelsea House, 1996.

Cowley, Malcolm, ed. *The Stories of F. Scott Fitzgerald*. New York: Charles Scribner's Sons, 1952.

Dumenil, Lynn. *The Modern Temper: American Culture and Society in the 1920s*. New York: Hill and Wang, 1995.

Freedman, Russell. *Martha Graham: A Dancer's Life*. New York: Clarion, 1998.

Hanson, Erica. *The 1920s*. San Diego, CA: Lucent Books, 1999.

Hardy, P. Steven, and Sheila Jackson Hardy. *Extraordinary People of the Harlem Renaissance*. New York: Children's Press, 2000.

Huggins, Nathan I. *The Harlem Renaissance*. New York: Oxford University Press, 1971.

Jacques, Geoffrey. *Free within Ourselves: The Harlem Renaissance*. New York: Franklin Watts, 1996.

Meltzer, Milton. *Langston Hughes*. Brookfield, CT: Millbrook Press, 1997.

Miller, Nathan. *New World Coming: The 1920s and the Making of Modern America*. New York: Scribner, 2003.

Ogren, Kathy J. *The Jazz Revolution: Twenties America and the Meaning of Jazz*. New York: Oxford University Press, 1989.

Orgill, Roxanne. *If I Only Had a Horn: Young Louis Armstrong*. Boston: Houghton Mifflin, 1997.

Orgill, Roxanne. *Shout, Sister, Shout! Ten Girl Singers Who Shaped a Century*. New York: Margaret McElderry, 2001.

Perret, Geoffrey. *America in the Twenties*. New York: Touchstone, 1982.

Reef, Catherine. *George Gershwin: American Composer*. Greensboro, NC: Morgan Reynolds, 2000.

Tessitore, John. *F. Scott Fitzgerald: The American Dreamer*. New York: Franklin Watts, 2001.

Turnbull, Andrew. *Scott Fitzgerald*. New York: Scribner, 1962.

Ward, Geoffrey, and Ken Burns. *Jazz: A History of America's Music*. New York: Knopf, 2000.

Yanuzzi, Della A. *Ernest Hemingway: Writer and Adventurer*. Springfield, NJ: Enslow Publishers, 1998.

Yanuzzi, Della A. *Zora Neale Hurston: Southern Story Teller*. Springfield, NJ: Enslow Publishers, 1996.

Web Sites

"American Cultural History, Decade 1920–1929." *Kingwood College Library*. Available online at http://kclibrary.nhmccd.edu/decade20.html. Accessed on June 17, 2005.

Best of History Websites. Available online at http://www.besthistorysites. net/USHistory_Roaring20s.shtml. Accessed on June 17, 2005.

Clash of Cultures in the 1910s and 1920s. Available online at http://history.osu.edu/Projects/Clash/default.htm. Accessed on June 17, 2005.

"Edna St. Vincent Millay." *The Academy of American Poets.* Available online at http://www.poets.org/poet.php/prmPID/160. Accessed on June 17, 2005.

The F. Scott Fitzgerald Society. Available online at http://www.fitzgerald society.org/. Accessed on June 17, 2005.

Harlem: Mecca of the New Negro. Available online at http://etext.lib. virginia.edu/harlem/. Accessed on June 17, 2005.

Interpreting Primary Sources. Digital History. Available online at http://www. digitalhistory.uh.edu/historyonline/us16.cfm. Accessed on June 17, 2005.

Jazz Age Culture. Available online at http://faculty.pittstate.edu/knichols/ jazzage.html. Accessed on June 17, 2005.

8

"Ain't We Got Fun?!"

The title of one of the hit songs of 1921, "Ain't We Got Fun?!," puts into words the mood that dominated much of the decade called the Roaring Twenties. Although some citizens of the United States did not share in the good times, most benefited from the country's general economic prosperity. By and large, people had at least a little extra money in their pockets, and they also had a little more time to relax. These two factors combined to allow for an energetic pursuit of leisure that had never been seen before in the United States.

For the first two centuries of the nation's existence, the majority of people had to work very hard at the backbreaking, time-consuming tasks involved in building a new country. Hard work was, in fact, one of the core values of this white Protestant society, along with religion, restraint, and frugality (not spending much money). With the twentieth century came both different kinds of work and different attitudes about work. Mass production had resulted in consumerism: people wanted very much to buy a variety of things that in earlier days they might have done without. They bought

During the 1920s Americans purchased many things, especially radios, to enhance their newly increased leisure time. *(Courtesy of The Library of Congress.)*

automobiles and household appliances, for example, to make their lives more convenient. But they also bought things to enhance their newly increased leisure time, especially radios, around which millions of families gathered each evening to hear shows like *Amos and Andy*, and tickets to movies and sporting events.

This new pursuit of leisure, along with the growth of the mass media, led to the emergence of popular idols, heroes drawn from the realms of motion pictures and sports. Movie fans adored actresses Clara Bow (1905–1965) and Louise Brooks (1906–1985), who seemed to embody the fun and freedom of the flapper (young women who dressed and behaved in a bold, modern way and who came to symbolize the free-wheeling spirit of the 1920s). Women swooned over the impossibly handsome, exotic Rudolph Valentino (1895–1926) and the dashing Douglas Fairbanks (1883–1939). They flocked to see Al Jolson (1886–1950) in the first "talkie" (movie with sound). It has been estimated that in the mid-1920s fifty million people in the United States went to the movies every week.

The heroes of the playing fields, boxing rings, golf courses, tennis courts, and swimming pools were many. They included baseball players like George Herman "Babe" Ruth (1895–1948), quite possibly the most popular and beloved sports figure of all time, football players like Red Grange (1903–1991), boxers like Jack Dempsey (1895–1983), golfers like Bobby Jones (1902–1971) and Walter Hagen (1892–1969), and tennis players like Bill Tilden (1893–1953) and Helen Wills (1905–1998). They also included a young swimmer named Gertrude Ederle (1906–), the first woman to swim across the English Channel (the body of water that lies between England and France), and an African American baseball player named Leroy "Satchel" Paige (1906–1982), who embodied the skill and determination of black athletes in the face of discrimination and limited opportunity.

New attitudes toward work and leisure

Advances in technology that occurred in the latter half of the nineteenth century led to the industrialization of much of the United States. As the twentieth century dawned, what had been a predominantly rural nation was changing. Farm laborers were moving to the city to work in factories. This new kind of job meant boring, impersonal, and sometimes unpleasant or even dangerous working conditions, but it paid fairly well. Because new labor laws had resulted in shorter work hours, people had both more money and more time in which to spend it.

Attitudes toward work and leisure had shifted too. During the Victorian Era (roughly the period from 1837 to 1901, when Queen Victoria ruled England), people had concentrated on working hard, behaving properly, and saving money. As the twentieth century unfolded, however, a new awareness of psychological theories, especially those of Sigmund Freud (1859–1939), whose ideas were very popular during the 1920s, began to encourage a more inward focus. Books about self-exploration and self-improvement became popular. The idea that individuals, many of whom suffered from impersonal workplaces and the sense that their work was meaningless, deserved to relax, have fun, and be entertained was gradually becoming the norm.

At the same time, mass production of relatively inexpensive consumer goods, such as cosmetics, records and record players, books, and household appliances, was taking place. Among the most essential items, in the eyes of many people, was a radio.

Millions tune in to radio

Basic radio technology had been around for several decades (see Chapter 4), but until the 1920s, only hobbyists had radios in their homes. That changed in 1920, after Dr. Frank Conrad (1874–1941), an engineer at the Westinghouse company in East Pittsburgh, Pennsylvania, started broadcasting musical recordings from his home radio. The attention and listeners he attracted resulted in the founding of the country's first radio station, KDKA. More radio stations quickly sprang up, so that by the end of 1922 more than five hundred were operating. Whereas about $1 million had been spent on radios in 1920, in 1925 consumers spent $400 million on them.

By the end of the decade, more than twelve million families (or one-third of the population) would be listening to radios. In the words of historian Geoffrey Perret in *America in the Twenties,* "Nothing had ever succeeded on so vast a scale in so short a time."

As more listeners tuned in, radio stations quickly expanded their programs to offer information, music, and sports coverage. Sporting events became especially popular, with announcers bringing fans on-the-spot accounts of boxing matches and baseball games.

The popularity of music and sports broadcasts was increasingly matched by the public's growing passion for variety and comedy shows, such as *The Chase and Sanborn Hour* and *The Eveready Hour* (sponsored by the Eveready battery company). Typical segments would feature the latest jazz music, opera selections, drama, lectures, and comedy. Some shows, like *The Happiness Boys* and *Amos and Andy,* focused exclusively on comedy. *Amos and Andy* was especially popular. Its title characters were African Americans who displayed stereotypical black qualities, such as foolish innocence; the show, however, was actually written and performed by two white men.

Evangelist Aimee Semple McPherson and radio expert Kenneth G. Ormiston. McPherson took advantage of the radio as a means to address her followers and to attract more converts. (© *Bettmann/Corbis. Reproduced by permission.*)

Entertainers were not the only voices heard on the radio in the 1920s. Politicians also recognized the potential of this medium for reaching a large segment of the population. Calvin Coolidge (1872–1933; served 1923–29) became the first U.S. president heard on the radio, making sixteen very effective, well-received broadcasts while in office. Popular evangelists (those who try to persuade others to become Christians) like Aimee Semple McPherson (1890–1944) also took advantage of radio as a means to address their followers and attract more converts.

A golden age for motion pictures

The technology for making motion pictures, like that of radio, existed before the 1920s. It was not until the end of the decade, however, that movies were made with sound.

Before that, the actors in the so-called "silent movies" spoke only through printed text that appeared on the screen; sometimes film viewings would be accompanied by music played live in the movie theater. In the first two decades of the twentieth century, going to the movies, in tiny neighborhood viewing places called nickelodeons, was considered a lower-class entertainment, indulged in only by factory workers and other laborers.

During the 1920s, though, motion pictures became part of mass culture in the United States, something almost everybody enjoyed. Some have even called this decade the "Golden Age" of movies, while others reserve that title for the 1930s and 1940s, when the sound and color technologies introduced at the end of the 1920s were better developed.

A multimillion-dollar industry

The fact that people now had more money and time did not go unnoticed by the producers of motion pictures, and they made the most of the new pursuit of leisure. Interestingly, many of the top producers of the period were immigrants or the children of immigrants, such example is Louis B. Mayer (1885–1957), the head of the Metro-Goldwyn-Mayer studio, who had started life as a junk collector, who would achieve their own spectacular version of the American dream of success. Other leading producers included the four Warner Brothers and Cecil B. DeMille (1881–1959).

These men built up a multimillion-dollar industry based in Hollywood, California, where there was space to create large movie sets. Their motion pictures were shown in the thousands of movie theaters that were being built across the country; in fact, by 1926 there were twenty thousand movie theaters in the United States. Unlike the small, shabby nickelodeons of the old days, some of these were made to look like ornate palaces, with chandeliers and huge staircases. Every big and even medium-sized city prided itself on one or more fancy movie theaters, such as New York's Roxy, which seated five thousand viewers.

Swashbucklers, flappers, and exotic locales

This was the age of big epics and swashbucklers, stories of adventure with lots of action that often took place in the context of war, ancient history, or the untamed West. They always featured a romantic hero, played by someone like Douglas Fairbanks or John Barrymore (1882–1942), the great-grandfather of actress Drew Barrymore, who saved the day and won the pretty girl by the end of the movie. Also hugely popular with moviegoers was Rudolph Valentino, an Italian immigrant who made women swoon with his devastating handsomeness. Valentino was closely identified with the Middle Eastern character he played in *The Sheik* (1921), which took place in an exotic locale of the kind favored by audiences.

The leading female star of the 1920s was Clara Bow, whose bobbed hair, love of dancing, and carefree manner made her the essence of the flapper. In fact, she was called the "It Girl" because she was thought to possess a special, indefinable kind of attractiveness. Other popular actresses included Louise Brooks, Joan Crawford (1906–1977), and Gloria Swanson (1897–1983). A number of actresses who had not been born in the United States were appreciated by U.S. audiences for their exotic, mysterious beauty and glamour; examples include Greta Garbo (1905–1990) and Marlene Dietrich (1901–1992).

Delighting audiences with comedy

The classic comedies, most of them silent, of the 1920s are still treasured by movie fans. Films featuring the slapstick antics of the Keystone Kops, the duo of Stan Laurel (1890–1965) and Oliver Hardy (1892–1957), the deadpan humor of Buster Keaton (1895–1966), and the zany adventures of Harold Lloyd (1893–1971), delighted audiences. In *Safety Last* (1925), Lloyd wins the girl he loves by carrying off the dangerous stunt of climbing up a tall building.

Most gifted of all the comic actors, though, was Charlie Chaplin (1889–1997). He had performed on the English stage before coming to the United States, and he had a remarkable ability to pantomime (acting that consists of gestures instead of words) and a masterful sense of comic timing. Chaplin's endearing character of the Little Tramp, always dressed in baggy pants and a bowler hat, made him universally recognized and loved. The Tramp was shy, and his shabby clothes reflected his poverty, but he was neat and polite. He was perpetually yearning for a beautiful girl who seemed far out of reach. In such movies as *City Lights* (1931) and *The Gold Rush* (1925),

Fads of the Roaring Twenties

The Roaring Twenties was an era in which people sought more ways to entertain themselves. Whether it was to improve the mind, make money, or break records, numerous fads rose to popularity quickly, and some were gone just as fast. Here are some of the top fads that captured the imagination of the 1920s public.

Crossword Puzzles

The world's first collection of crossword puzzles was *The Cross Word Puzzle Book,* published by Richard Simon and Max Schuster. Sold with a pencil attached to each copy, *The Cross Word Puzzle Book* was a bestseller and sparked a nationwide craze. The Baltimore and Ohio Railroad equipped its trains with dictionaries for its crossword-crazy customers. College students were especially enthusiastic, and college campuses hosted competitions and even courses focused on crosswords.

Dance Marathons

One of the lasting popular images of the Roaring Twenties is that of an exhausted couple leaning against each other on a dance floor, desperately trying to keep dancing longer than anyone else and thus win a prize. Dance marathons were wildly popular during the decade. Across the nation, dancers competing for cash prizes devised ways to keep each other awake, from smelling salts to kicks and punches. Many records were set, the first on April 1, 1923, by

thirty-two-year-old dance teacher Alma Cummings, who went through six male partners in her twenty-seven hours on a dance floor.

Flagpole sitting

This bizarre fad was started by a former boxer named Alvin "Shipwreck" Kelly. To attract publicity, a Hollywood theater paid Kelly to sit on top of a flagpole (equipped with a disk-seat and stirrups for his feet, to help him balance). He spent twenty-three days and seven hours on top of the pole, consuming little and sleeping for five minutes every hour. Kelly repeated his feat many times, spending a total of one hundred forty five days on flagpoles in 1929. He inspired many imitators, including several women and a teenager named Avon Freeman, who set the so-called "juvenile record" by sitting on a Baltimore flagpole for ten hours and ten minutes.

Mah-Jongg

The ancient Chinese game of mah-jongg, which resembles both dominoes and dice and is played with a set of 144 tiles of carved bone, grew extremely popular after it was introduced to the United States in 1922. Many women's mah-jongg clubs formed during the 1920s, and college students also took to the game, which became almost as common on college campuses as the card game of bridge. In 1923 more U.S. citizens bought mah-jongg sets than radios. More than twenty rule books helped players sort through the game's complex rules.

the Tramp won the girl through his cleverness and good heart, making audiences laugh and sympathize along the way. Many saw Chaplin's character as embodying the triumph of human dignity in an increasingly dehumanized, unfair world.

The talkies are introduced

From the earliest days of the motion picture, inventors had tried to devise a way to incorporate music and speech into movies. Finally, backed by research money from the Warner Brothers movie studio, engineers at Western Electric invented a system called Vitaphone that worked fairly well, even though the sound and picture were run separately and had to be synchronized. Later technology would place the sound directly on the film carrying the images, and by the end of the 1930s, the silent movie would be a thing of the past. The only people who were disappointed by the new technology were those actors whose careers ended because their voices or accents were considered unsuitable for the talkies.

In 1926 Warner Brothers introduced the first motion picture with sound, a swashbuckling epic called *Don Juan.* This was not, however, a full-length movie, and it featured only synchronized music and sound effects, such as clashing swords, not speech. The next year, Warner Brothers achieved a milestone in motion picture technology when it released *The Jazz Singer,* the first full-length movie with synchronized dialog as well as music and singing. The movie featured actor and singer Al Jolson, who was already famous from his work on the Broadway stage. Considering the hostility that was directed toward immigrants during the 1920s, it is amazing that this film with not only a Jewish star but also a Jewish theme was so popular.

The Jazz Singer tells the story of Jack Robin, a second-generation Jew and the son of a cantor (an official who sings religious music and leads prayers in a synagogue, a Jewish place of worship). The father wants his son to become a cantor too, but Jack has other ideas. He wants to be a jazz singer. Jack rejects the old ways and is estranged from his parents, but at the end of the movie he sings Kaddish (the Jewish prayer of mourning) for his father's funeral. The next night, Jack performs his own music at Madison Square Garden (a large arena in New York City). Thus tradition and modernity are reconciled. *The Jazz Singer,* which begins with Jolson's famous utterance, "You ain't heard nothin' yet!," was the top moneymaking film of the year, even though only five hundred theaters were equipped to show talkies.

Broadway musical comedies charm audiences

While those looking for intellectual stimulation could attend the plays of Eugene O'Neill or other dramatists (see Chapter 7), people interested in lighter entertainment on the live stage were going to the musical variety shows being produced on Broadway and elsewhere. Every year, producer Florenz Ziegfeld (1869–1932) introduced a new version of his *Follies,* which featured catchy songs and dancers doing the latest steps. Also produced annually was George White's *Scandals,* with songs by the talented brothers George (1898–1937) and Ira (1896–1981) Gershwin, and Irving Berlin's *Music Box Review.* Berlin (1888–1989) wrote many of the decade's most memorable songs, including "White Christmas," "There's No Business Like Show Business," and "Puttin' on the Ritz."

An elaborate scene from the *Ziegfeld Follies,* a popular stage production during the 1920s. *(© Bettmann/Corbis. Reproduced by permission.)*

Also popular were musical comedies such as "I'll Say She Is!" with the comedy team the Marx Brothers and others with such stars as Fred Astaire (1899–1987), Jolson, Ethel Merman (1908–1984), and W.C. Fields (1879–1946). One of the most popular musicals of the decade was *Showboat,* based on a novel by Edna Ferber (1887–1968). Centered on a romance between a riverboat gambler and an entertainer, *Showboat*'s interracial subplots and cast made it somewhat controversial.

People go wild for sports

The 1920s was definitely a decade of idols, from aviator Charles Lindbergh (1902–1974), who crossed the Atlantic alone in a small airplane (see Chapter 4), to movie stars like

Fairbanks and Bow. The mass media had the power to bring people close to figures who seemed larger than life and whom everybody admired. Some of the most beloved of these heroes came from the world of sports. At the same time, people were themselves participating in sports in ever-greater numbers.

The increase in leisure time and spending money that occurred during the 1920s gave people the opportunity to enjoy both watching and playing sports. In fact, they spent about $200 million per year on sporting goods such as tennis rackets and golf clubs during the decade. Much interest was spurred by the achievements of the great athletes who seemed to emerge in every imaginable sport, especially baseball, football, boxing, golf, and tennis.

At the same time, however, not everyone who excelled in athletics was treated with the same admiration. Due to the Jim Crow laws (the system of legalized segregation that, beginning in the 1890s, mandated separate schools and public facilities for blacks and whites and put restrictions on voting rights) in the South and the discrimination common throughout the nation, African Americans were prevented from achieving the same heights as white athletes. Nevertheless, many are now remembered and revered, especially those who played baseball in the Negro leagues formed in and around the 1920s.

Baseball gains popularity

The game of baseball had existed for several decades, but in the 1920s the sport underwent a major change that made it much more fun to watch and much more popular with the public. Instead of the short hits and base running that had been employed in its early years, baseball now became a game of long balls hit by talented, powerful batters. The sport had formerly been calm and somewhat slow, but now attentive spectators waited in the stands for the thrill of the home run. Their reaction led to the invention of a new kind of ball (easier to hit for long distances), new and larger stadiums, and new rules (such as one preventing pitchers from applying substances to balls). The result was larger crowds and bigger salaries for players.

A decade that would prove to be full of exciting, marvelous moments in sports began on a sour note, however. In September 1920 eight members of the Chicago White Sox team were charged with conspiring to lose the 1919 World Series, which they had played against the St. Louis Cardinals, in exchange for bribes totaling $80,000. Among the accused were two of the most promising young players in baseball, pitcher Eddie Cicotte (1894–1969) and left fielder "Shoeless Joe" Jackson (1887–1951). The White Sox had been heavily favored to beat the Cardinals, so a group of gamblers came up with the idea of getting the team to intentionally lose, so that anybody who had bet on the Cardinals would win a lot of money.

Because important evidence disappeared before the trial, the White Sox players were acquitted (found innocent) by the court. However, the newly appointed commissioner of baseball, Kenesaw Mountain Landis (1866–1944), who was also a judge and a passionate baseball fan, disregarded that verdict and banned the eight players from baseball for life. Landis was determined to protect the sport he loved from being tainted by gambling.

"The Babe" to the rescue

Any discussion of the brightest sports stars of the 1920s has to begin with George Herman "Babe" Ruth, who is still revered by many as the greatest of them all. In addition to all of his other accomplishments, Ruth is credited with restoring the public's faith in baseball after the shameful scandal involving the Chicago White Sox. Born into a poor Baltimore family, Ruth was sent at the age of ten to St. Mary's Industrial School, a home for misbehaving boys whose parents could not or would not control them. There Ruth learned to play baseball, and there he was discovered by Jack Dunn, a scout for the Baltimore Orioles baseball team. Ruth became one of the young players known as Dunn's "babes" (which is how he got his nickname) when he was signed to the Orioles in 1914.

Later that year, Ruth was sold to the Boston Red Sox. He quickly became a star pitcher and hitter and began to draw crowds to every game. His rowdy behavior off the field, however, caused problems for the team managers. In early 1920 Ruth was sold to the New York Yankees, the team he would stay with for the rest of his career. The first year he had a batting average of .376, he stole 14 bases, and he hit 54 home runs.

Meanwhile, the second and third best hitters in baseball scored less than 20 home runs each!

Remarkably, Ruth did better and better every year. Ruth's spectacular feats meant equally impressive ticket sales for the Yankees as fans flocked to see the Babe in action. In 1923 he asked for and got the then-astronomical salary of $52,000 per year (he said that he had always dreamed of making a thousand dollars a week). The same year, the Yankees opened a new stadium, which had cost $2.5 million to build and which was known as "The House That Ruth Built."

Meanwhile, the men who played alongside Ruth were also extremely talented. The legendary Yankees squad of the 1920s featured first baseman Lou Gehrig , also a power hitter, as well as Bob Muesel, Earl Combs, and Tony Lazzeri. The Yankees won the World Series in 1923, 1927, and 1928. In 1926 they lost to another great team, the Cardinals, led by slugger Rogers Hornsby (1896–1963), whose .424 average in 1924 has never been beaten.

In 1927 Ruth had his most spectacular year ever, hitting a record 60 home runs and achieving a batting average of .356. Over his entire career, he would hit 714 home runs. He was a big, bulky, uneducated man who ate, drank, and smoked to excess; swore; got in fights; and chased women. But all this seemed to make him even more popular with ordinary people. Ruth had brought excitement and suspense to baseball, and he would never be forgotten.

The Negro leagues

During the early decades of the twentieth century, the mixing of black and white athletes in sports, as in other aspects of society, was either discouraged or prohibited by law. Major league baseball would not be integrated until 1946, when Jackie Robinson (1919–1974) was hired to play for the Brooklyn Dodgers. Beginning in the 1890s, though, African American baseball players played on their own, loosely organized teams. A big organizational boost came in 1920 with the formation of the National Negro Baseball League (NNBL) and the Eastern Colored League. Although these leagues underwent various stages of disbanding and reforming through the early 1930s, sixty-three black baseball teams played between 1920 and 1949. Some of the most famous include the Kansas

Lou Gehrig (left), Babe Ruth (center), and Tony Lazzeri (right) who were part of the legendary New York Yankees squad which won the World Series three times during the 1920s. *(AP/Wide World Photos. Reproduced by permission.)*

City Monarchs, the Philadelphia Hilldales, the Crawford Colored Giants, and the Homestead Grays.

Baseball was, of course, as popular with African American spectators as it was with whites. The NNBL, for example, drew more than 400,000 spectators to its games in 1923 (earning $200,000 in ticket sales). Players made a wide range of salaries and did not enjoy much job security, as teams formed and disbanded quickly, sometimes with little or no notice. Statistics were unreliable, and most games were not covered by the press, so it was difficult to establish records. But in the 1970s, Major League Baseball (the organization that oversees baseball in the United States) made a serious attempt to collect the records of black baseball players from this period.

In an effort to make up for some of the injustices of the past, several of these players were inducted into the Baseball Hall of Fame in Cooperstown, New York. The first was Satchel Paige, a pitcher who played for twenty-one years in the NNBL, followed by six years in the major leagues (with the Cleveland Indians, the St. Louis Browns, and the Kansas City Athletics). Others include catcher Josh Gibson, outfielder John Thomas "Cool Papa" Bell, and third baseman William Julius "Judy" Johnson.

Summarizing the achievement of the African American players of the Negro leagues, historian Mark Ribowsky notes in his book *Don't Look Back: Satchel Paige in the Shadows of Baseball:*

> Despite tremendous hardships, the Negro leagues played on schedule. They kept their buses rolling through the East, the South, and the Midwest, lodged their players in hotels and rooming houses, rented stadiums, printed and sold tickets, even traveled with portable lights a decade before the first big league night game. Above all, the men of the Negro leagues played serious ball.

Excitement in the boxing ring

Before World War I (1914–18), most people considered boxing a violent, low-class sport, and it was even illegal in some places. After the war, however, many of the laws banning boxing were overturned, and commissions were set up to regulate the sport and prevent criminals and gamblers from influencing it. During the 1920s, boxing gained respectability and became one of the most popular spectator sports for people from all levels of society.

Among the stars of boxing, the most brilliant was Jack Dempsey, who reigned as heavyweight champion, the most prestigious of the weight categories, from 1919 to 1926. Raised in a mining camp in Colorado, Dempsey came from a rough-and-tumble, working-class background, which made him appealing to many ordinary people. In the ring, he was known for his ferocious style, which featured fast, short punches and quick knockouts of his opponents.

One of the decade's other most famous fighters was the more refined Gene Tunney (1898–1978), a New York City native who had started boxing as a soldier in World War I. The tall, blonde, handsome boxer was from a middle-class background, and he was said to enjoy such high-class pursuits as reading and tea drinking. His fighting style was less aggressive than Dempsey's, as he tended to wait for his opponent to tire before moving in for the winning punch.

In 1926 Dempsey and Tunney met in a boxing match in Philadelphia that was billed as the "Fight of the Century." There were more than 120,000 spectators on hand, while another 50 million or so listened in on the radio as announcers provided ringside coverage. About 1,200 reporters were also present, as well as a number of Hollywood stars, business leaders, and other famous people. Tunney won the match and became the new heavyweight champion, but he was never as popular with the public as Dempsey had been.

Other boxing stars of the 1920s include the undefeated lightweight (under 135 pounds) Benny Leonard (1896–1947) and Tiger Flowers (1895–1927), who in 1926 became the first African American to win the middleweight (under 160 pounds) champion title.

College football catches fire

During the 1920s college enrollment doubled as young people who in earlier years might have gone straight to work on farms or as skilled laborers, instead sought further education. With this growth in college attendance came increased interest in college sports, especially football. Attending Saturday football games during the fall and early winter became the thing to do for sheiks and shebas (popular nicknames for the fashionable young men and women of the Roaring Twenties) as well as many people who had never even been to college. The teams worked to increase spectator interest by developing more interesting strategies and plays. This effort was so successful that college football became a big business, with schools building huge stadiums to accommodate the crowds and maximize ticket sales.

In the East, some of the greatest teams of the decade played for Princeton and Yale universities and for the Army's West Point Academy. In the South, schools with powerhouse teams included Tennessee, Alabama, Vanderbilt, Georgia Tech, Southern Methodist, and Texas A&M. In the Midwest, the leaders were Notre Dame and the universities of Illinois, Iowa, Michigan, and Chicago, among others.

Midwestern stars included George Gippe at Notre Dame and especially Red Grange at Illinois. In the twenty games he played as a college star, Grange averaged 182 yards per game. In a 1924 game against Michigan, Grange carried the ball four times in the first twelve minutes and scored four touchdowns. Grange became the first athlete to appear on the cover of *Time* magazine, and one hundred thousand spectators were on hand to watch him play his final game for Illinois.

College football games were broadcast over the radio, and filmed highlights were shown in movie theaters, lending to the game's mass appeal. Football blended strength, skill, and strategy in a way that made it seem, as phrased by John R. Tunis in a 1926 *Harper's Weekly* article, "The Great American Game." Thus it is not surprising that a professional football organization was created. In 1920 the American Professional Football League was founded with eleven franchise teams. Two years later, it was reorganized as the National Football League. The league went about recruiting some of the most successful college players, such as Grange, who would play for the Chicago Bears.

Golf and tennis attract fans

Another sport that made great leaps in popularity during the 1920s was golf. What had once been a pursuit only for the upper class now became wildly popular with middle-class weekend athletes. The number of players doubled between 1916 and 1920, leading to a big increase in the construction of private and public courses. By 1928 eighty-nine U.S. cities had public courses.

As in other sports, the popularity of golf was sparked by the public's admiration for the star athletes of the age. In previous years, the leading figures in golf had come from Europe, where the sport originated. But in the 1920s a number of U.S. players took the lead. For example, U.S. golfers won the British Open, a tournament of long tradition that is always held at St. Andrews, Scotland, nine times out of ten between 1921 and 1930.

The greatest of these American golfers was Bobby Jones, who won the U.S. Open tournament in 1923 and spent the next seven years dominating every competition he entered. He was admired for his technical mastery of the game and his tolerant attitude toward fans. Although he suffered from nerves behind the scenes, Jones always appeared calm and in control on the course. Other great golfers included Walter Hagen (1892–1969) and Gene Sarazen (1901–1999), who, along with Jones, made up the Three Musketeers of U.S. golf.

Just as many amateur athletes across the United States were heading for golf courses each weekend, others were flocking to tennis courts to take part in a sport that, like golf, had once been only for the rich but was now enjoyed by a wide variety of people. Followers of this sport previously dominated by British, French, and Australian players were now inspired by a number of spectacular U.S. athletes, especially Bill Tilden and Helen Wills. Tilden won Great Britain's prestigious Wimbledon singles title in 1920 and dominated the sport until 1926, when he was felled by a knee injury. Supremely athletic and daring, Tilden was credited with turning tennis into a popular, moneymaking spectator sport. Over the course of her

Bobby Jones, one of the greatest American golfers during the 1920s, dominated every competition he entered during the decade. *(AP/Wide World Photos. Reproduced by permission.)*

career, Wills won thirty-one major international tennis championships, including eight singles titles at Wimbledon; she also won a gold medal at the 1924 Olympics.

The 1920s saw the establishment of several well-known international tennis competitions, including the Whiteman Cup, which featured women's team play, and the Davis Cup.

Gertrude Ederle

Another sports star of the 1920s gained fame not on the baseball diamond, golf course, or tennis court, but in the water. Gertrude Ederle had been swimming since childhood and won her first world record at the age of twelve. Between 1921 and 1925, she held twenty-nine national and world swimming records, and she won three medals at the 1924 Olympics.

In the summer of 1926, Ederle became the first woman to swim the English Channel. At 7 AM on August 6, Ederle plunged into the choppy waters off Cap Gris-Nez, France. After a grueling struggle against changing tides, she arrived on the English shore at 10 PM. The crossing had beaten the record of the fastest man by nearly two hours, bringing the young woman affectionately known as "Our Trudy" even more acclaim.

For More Information

Books

Bacho, Peter. *Boxing in Black and White.* New York: Henry Holt, 1999.

Dumenil, Lynn. *The Modern Temper: American Culture and Society in the 1920s.* New York: Hill and Wang, 1995.

Finkelstein, Norman H. *Sounds of the Air: The Golden Age of Radio.* New York: Charles Scribner's, 1993.

Flink, Steven. *The Greatest Tennis Matches of the Twentieth Century.* Danbury, CT: Rutledge Books, 1999.

Gilbert, Thomas. *The Soaring Twenties: Babe Ruth and the Home Run Decade.* New York: Franklin Watts, 1996.

Hanson, Erica. *The 1920s.* San Diego, CA: Lucent Books, 1999.

Herald, Jacqueline. *Fashions of a Decade: 1920s.* New York: Facts on File, 1991.

Kahn, Roger. *A Flame of Pure Fire: Jack Dempsey and the Roaring 20s.* New York: Harcourt Brace, 1999.

Katz, Ephraim. *The Film Encyclopedia.* 4th ed. New York: HarperResource, 2001.

Kavanaugh, Jack. *Shoeless Joe Jackson.* New York: Chelsea House, 1995.

MacCann, Richard Dyer. *The Silent Comedians.* Metuchen, NJ: Scarecrow Press, 1993.

McKissack, Patricia, and Frederick McKissack Jr. *Black Diamond: The Story of the Negro Baseball Leagues.* New York: Scholastic Trade, 1994.

Miller, Nathan. *New World Coming: The 1920s and the Making of Modern America.* New York: Scribner, 2003.

Perret, Geoffrey. *America in the Twenties.* New York: Touchstone, 1982.

Ribowsky, Mark. *Don't Look Back: Satchel Paige in the Shadows of Baseball.* New York: Simon & Schuster, 1994.

Seymour, Harold. *Baseball: The Golden Age.* New York: Oxford University Press, 1971.

Wagenheim, Karl. *Babe Ruth: His Life and Legend.* Chicago: Olmstead Press, 2001.

Whittingham, Richard. *Rites of Autumn: The Story of College Football.* New York: Free Press, 2001.

Web Sites

"American Cultural History, Decade 1920–1929." *Kingwood College Library.* Available online at http://kclibrary.nhmccd.edu/decade20.html. Accessed on June 17, 2005.

Best of History Websites. Available online at http://www.besthistorysites. net/USHistory_Roaring20s.shtml. Accessed on June 17, 2005.

"Charlie Chaplin." *American Masters (PBS).* Available online at http:// www.pbs.org/wnet/americanmasters/database/keaton_b.html. Accessed on June 17, 2005.

Clash of Cultures in the 1910s and 1920s. Available online at http://history. osu.edu/Projects/Clash/default.htm. Accessed on June 17, 2005.

Christy's Fashion Pages: Flapper Fashion. Available online at http:// www.rambova.com/fashion/fash4.html. Accessed on June 17, 2005.

Interpreting Primary Sources. Digital History. Available online at http://www. digitalhistory.uh.edu/historyonline/us16.cfm. Accessed on June 17, 2005.

The Jazz Age: Flapper Culture & Style. Available online at http://www. geocities.com/flapper_culture/. Accessed on June 17, 2005.

9

The Crash . . . and Beyond

It is common to think of the Roaring Twenties as a distinct period in history, bounded on one end by World War I (1914–18) and on the other by the stock market crash and the Great Depression (1929–41), the period of economic downturn and hardship when millions lost their life savings, their jobs, and the sense of security they had once known. The special nature of the 1920s, with its colorful characters, exciting developments and events, and entertaining fads and trends, makes it tempting to frame the decade in that way. It is more accurate, however, to recognize that many of the changes and circumstances of the 1920s were rooted in previous decades. Similarly, the shift to the grim days of the Depression was neither as unexpected, nor as sudden as it may seem. However few people saw the change coming and of those who did, most ignored it.

Even as enthusiastic investors were trading stocks at unprecedented rates, and a majority of the population assumed that the good times would go on forever, there were warning signs that this was not the case. Examples include the out-of-control speculation on the stock market, overproduction of goods, and

Headline of Broadway *Variety* stating "Wall St. Lays An Egg," referring to the 1929 stock market crash. (© Bettmann/Corbis. Reproduced by permission.)

declines in construction. Of course, some parts of the economy, and some people, had been left out of the general prosperity of the 1920s from the beginning. But as the decade wore on, there were indications that even those who had benefited most from the strong economy would soon be in trouble. Many decades later, it is easy to say that these warnings should have been heeded. At the time, however, they were not so clear.

Optimism and bright predictions

Throughout the 1920s a pro-business atmosphere had dominated the United States, and the economy had flourished, with companies expanding, foreign trade thriving, and the stock market on the rise. When President Herbert Hoover (1874–1964; served 1929–33) took office in early 1929, he declared in his inaugural address, "I have no fears for the future of our country. It is bright with hope." By the end of the year, these words would ring hollow.

But Hoover was not the only one who felt optimistic. Others also predicted a continuation of business as usual. Alfred Sloan (1875–1966), president of General Motors, made his own pronouncement, as quoted in Nathan Miller's *New World Coming: The 1920s and the Making of Modern America*: "Personally, I believe it is going to be a very good year—I don't see how it could be otherwise."

The stock market craze

Before the 1920s few ordinary U.S. citizens had invested in the stock market, which was considered a pursuit for the wealthy. But the decade brought not only extra cash to many but also a get-rich-quick mentality, along with a close alliance between business and government that made all kinds of business activities seem more acceptable. Many more people, including some of modest income, were buying and selling stocks. There were not as many, though, as some accounts of the 1920s have suggested: of a total U.S. population of 120 million, only about 1.5 million were involved with the stock market. More significant was the way that the stock boom became a popular, well-received part of U.S. culture.

When an investor buys stock (also called shares) in a company, he or she provides it with money with which to operate. If the company does well and makes a profit, the investor receives a share of that money in the form of a dividend, and the stock he owns becomes more valuable. He can sell it for more than the purchase price. A rise in the price of a stock means that it has become more valuable, usually because the company has been successful or seems promising. If the stock price goes down, however, the investor may lose money if he sells (he may, of course, choose to hold on to the stock in the hope that its value will rise again). Many of the investors of the 1920s were indulging in speculation, which means that they were buying and selling stocks quickly to make fast profits.

Some of the people who were now investing in the stock market used their own savings, while others bought stocks through a kind of credit system called "on the margin." This meant that they paid a small amount, usually about 10 percent, of the price of the stock while the stockbroker (a person who is authorized to conduct stock sales) paid the rest. If stock prices rose, the investor could pay back the debt while also making a profit. If prices fell, however, he or she would have to pay back the full amount to the stockbroker right away. By late 1929 broker loans totaled close to $7 billion.

The prospect of easy money and instant wealth had great appeal during the 1920s. By the end of the decade, the New York Stock Exchange—the center for stock trading, located on Wall Street in New York City—was trading six to seven million shares (or stocks) per day, compared to a more normal rate of three to four million. The prices of stocks were far higher than their real value and out of proportion to the profit-making ability of the companies. Yet people continued to invest enthusiastically, believing that prices could rise indefinitely to make them richer and richer.

Most ignore warning signs

Even as stock prices and investor enthusiasm were rising at a frantic pace, there were indications that not all was well with the economy. According to Miller, "Despite the continuation of the era of wonderful nonsense, cracks in the nation's economic foundation were evident to those who looked closely."

Ever since the end of World War I, when the demand for farm products that the European conflict had brought came to an end, farmers had been suffering from hard times. There was a huge oversupply of food in the United States, and prices were dropping dramatically. For example, a bushel of wheat that had cost $2.57 in 1920 cost only $1.00 a year later. As the decade progressed, wheat prices fell even more, and the coal mining and textile (cloth) industries were also in trouble. Construction on new houses slowed drastically; in the short period between 1928 and 1929, the construction industry declined by $1 billion.

Wages were also in decline, which meant that more and more people were unable to keep up with their former pace of consumerism (the preoccupation with acquiring goods that had dominated much of the decade). Radios and other items stayed on store shelves, and cars gathered dust on dealership lots, while new production slowed down. Unemployment was on the rise, an especially troubling sign during a decade in which most people had been able to find work. In Europe, changes in monetary policies and political unrest created instability that sent ripples across the sea to the United States.

A few sharp observers were calling attention to these trends, such as financial adviser Roger Babson, who predicted, as quoted in Miller's book, that "sooner or later a crash is coming." A few big investors, including the very wealthy Joseph Kennedy (1888–1969), father of future president John F. Kennedy (1917–1963; served 1960–63), started selling off stocks. Even President Hoover knew the danger of the kind of out-of-control speculation that was taking place. His belief that government should allow business to manage its own affairs as much as possible, however, was so strong that he did little to interfere.

Two black days in October

From September to October of 1929, the stock market rose to incredible heights. The widespread belief that things could continue this way came to a screeching halt on October 24, a day that would always be known as Black Thursday. The day before, stock trading had been especially heavy. But even before the bell that traditionally opened the New York Stock Exchange stopped ringing that Thursday morning, prices

People gather on Wall Street on Black Thursday, the day the New York stock market crashed, and the day that led to the Great Depression.

(© Bettmann/Corbis. Reproduced by permission.)

began to fall with stunning swiftness. The ticker tape (the ribbon-like paper in the telegraphic machine that printed information about stock prices) could not keep up with the pace of transactions as traders frantically bought and sold.

Brokers began calling in their loans, and investors who had bought on the margin could not pay back their debts. Disaster, or the fear that disaster was just around the corner, was in the air. Crowds gathered in New York City's financial district, and extra police were sent in to control them. Rumors flew, especially those claiming that bankrupt investors and desperate brokers were killing themselves by jumping off buildings. In fact, a workman seen on top of a Wall Street building was wrongly assumed to be on the verge of suicide.

A measure of calm was introduced in the early afternoon, when a group of prominent bankers pooled their resources and bought $40 million worth of blue-chip shares (reliably valuable shares in leading companies like General Motors and U.S. Steel). This helped to restore people's confidence in the market and to reduce the panic somewhat. The relief proved short-lived, though. On the following Tuesday, October 29, Black Tuesday, came an even worse crash. Orders to sell stocks flooded the stock market, but hardly anyone was buying. Not even the blue-chip stocks were being bought.

The Federal Reserve (the government agency that makes rules for the banking industry) called a hasty meeting but could not decide what to do. In only a few hours, stocks had lost about $10 million in value. More than sixteen million shares were sold during the day. Chaos reigned in and around the New York Stock Exchange as well as in 'brokers' offices and banks across the country. Banks had lent speculators money that they had in turn borrowed from corporations. The corporations were now demanding that the banks repay their loans, and the banks were quickly running out of the funds needed to do so. Those funds included the savings that people had entrusted to the banks, which were now being wiped out.

A downward spiral

Despite the drama, surprise, and shock of the October crash, the idea that it caused an instant plunge into the harsh conditions of the Great Depression is faulty. For a few months it was not at all clear how much impact the disaster would have on the wider economy. Meanwhile, financial and government leaders tried to figure out what to do. President Hoover called for calm and then stuck to his usual policy of politely requesting cooperation and voluntary action from the business world. He asked manufacturers to cut into their profits before making pay cuts or trimming jobs, and he urged state and local governments to start public works projects (such as the building of roads and parks) to put people to work. In a remark often attributed to Hoover, Vice President Charles Curtis (1860–1936), as quoted in Miller, declared that "Prosperity is just around the corner."

By the spring of 1930, however, there were more bad signs. A full-fledged economic depression had begun as wages were cut, workers were laid off from their jobs, and factories closed. This led to a drop in consumer spending. Farm prices fell, and a terrible drought in the midwestern and southern states ruined crops and livelihoods. More and more banks closed, with depositors losing all of their savings. By the end of the year, sixteen hundred banks had closed. According to Frederick Lewis Allen in his book *Only Yesterday: An Informal History of the 1920s,* "The grocer, the window-cleaner, and the seamstress had lost their capital. In every town there were families which had suddenly dropped from showy affluence into debt."

Following a slight, temporary improvement in the economy in early 1931, the economic decline continued. Influences from abroad were also having an impact. The 1930 passage of the Hawley-Smoot Tariff (a tax that foreign countries had to pay on goods they wanted to sell in the United States) led to a decline in products coming into the country, while the demand for U.S. goods and food overseas also slowed. The European economies were in trouble too. In fact they had been since the end of World War I. The European countries had borrowed money from the United States to pay for the war effort, but now they could not pay back those loans. These factors made the U.S. economic situation even worse. Although Hoover put most of the blame for the nation's troubles on outside influences, most analysts cite the weak links in the U.S. economy itself as the main cause.

The devastating impact of the Depression

As the Depression continued, it took a heavy toll on every aspect of the nation's life. Before it was over, unemployment would reach as high as seventeen million, or more than one-quarter of the workforce; in some places, it would hit especially hard (such as Toledo, Ohio, where 80 percent were out of work). The overall national income would be slashed in half.

Worst of all, perhaps, was the impact of the Depression at the most personal level. Previously prosperous or comfortably well-off families were now broke. Men in business suits sold apples from carts on street corners. In contrast to the consumerism practiced during the Roaring Twenties, people had to save their pennies and do without not only luxuries, but also without necessities.

The Democrats choose New York governor Franklin D. Roosevelt as their presidential candidate in 1932 because of his "New Deal" plan. *(Courtesy of The Library of Congress.)*

Lost-looking, weary faces were seen on the breadlines and in the soup kitchens (set up to provide the poor with food) in every city, and thousands of men and boys, as well as a few women, hopped freight trains to look for work or simply escape from the shame and harsh realities they faced at home. Farmers who were unable to pay back their debts watched their land, houses, and possessions being auctioned off.

Despite some gains made in the first decades of the twentieth century, African Americans had always been subject to discrimination and had always been at the bottom level of society. They suffered even more now. Their unemployment rate was four to six times higher than that of whites, as even the least desirable jobs were now often taken by white people.

Even with so many suffering, Hoover continued to do little to help. The United States did not yet have unemployment insurance, which provides income to those laid off from their jobs, and the president did not approve of giving direct aid to people who were out of work. He did, however, increase spending on public works, and he directed the Federal Farm Board to buy and store surplus food from farmers in order to keep prices stable. Hoover also gave a certain amount of government money to endangered banks, railroads, and insurance companies. He was hesitant, though, to put too much money into these efforts or to give them much time to take effect.

The Democrats choose Roosevelt

Members of the Democratic Party were in a relatively happy mood as they gathered in Chicago in June 1932 to choose a candidate for the November presidential election.

After a whole decade of Republican dominance of the U.S. government, the Democrats now seemed to stand a very good chance of gaining power. They knew that the people of the United States were eager for change, and that much of the blame for the nation's woes was being cast on Hoover and his fellow Republicans.

Nine candidates vied for the nomination, which was eventually won by New York governor Franklin Delano Roosevelt (1882–1945; served 1933–45). He was a dynamic person who was widely respected for having used some effective measures to deal with the Depression in his own state. In accepting the nomination of his party, Roosevelt said, "I pledge you, I pledge myself to a new deal for the American people." (The phrase "new deal" would later be used as the name of the economic program that Roosevelt would put in place.) During the campaign, the Democrats avoided the issues that had divided people in previous years, especially that of Prohibition, the controversial ban on alcoholic beverages that had gone into effect at the beginning of the 1920s, and focused on the economy.

That summer, Hoover's reputation was damaged even more by his harsh treatment of World War I veterans who had marched to Washington, D.C., to demand early payment of a bonus promised for 1945. As many as twenty thousand men had gathered in the nation's capital. After Congress turned down their request, most of them left, but Hoover sent in the army to chase out the rest. There were many injuries, and two of the veterans were killed, creating much bad feeling.

The November 1932 election resulted in a resounding victory for Roosevelt. At his inauguration, broadcast into an estimated sixty million U.S. homes by radio, the new president assured U.S. citizens that "the only thing we have to fear is fear itself." He promised that his New Deal plan would put the nation back on track through such measures as public works projects for the unemployed, the stimulation of farm prices, loans to prevent foreclosures (when banks take possession of property due to failure to repay the debt), and new regulations to control banking and credit practices. The 1935 Social Security Act would ensure income for retired or disabled workers.

Franklin Delano Roosevelt: A Guiding Light through the Great Depression

Considered one of the greatest leaders in U.S. history, Franklin Delano Roosevelt became president at a time of extreme hardship and fear. Roosevelt's New Deal program and his own personal optimism gave many U.S. citizens renewed hope for the future.

Born in 1882, Roosevelt was educated in law but soon followed in the footsteps of his distant cousin, former president Theodore Roosevelt, and entered politics. In 1910 Franklin Roosevelt was elected to the New York state senate. Two years later, President Woodrow Wilson appointed Roosevelt assistant secretary to the navy. His success in the position led to his nomination as a vice presidential candidate in the 1920 election. Although the Democrats lost that election, Roosevelt gained much experience during the campaign.

One year later, Roosevelt contracted polio, a serious disease that causes paralysis. He lost the ability to move his legs and spent most of the rest of his life in a wheelchair, but he maintained a positive outlook and continued his political career, serving as governor of New York in 1929. The stock market crashed that year, and the Great Depression began. To counter New York's high unemployment rate, Roosevelt established a program of direct financial aid for workers who had lost their jobs.

In 1932 Democrats selected Roosevelt as their presidential candidate. Promising to introduce a "New Deal" to help those suffering from the depression, Roosevelt won a landslide victory over Herbert Hoover and entered office in spring 1933. He immediately started addressing the nation's most pressing concerns. He established many federal jobs programs, including the Civilian Conservation Corps, the National Youth Administration, and the Works Progress Administration, to put more than twelve million people to work. He also introduced measures to help the banking and agricultural industries, to provide low-cost electricity, and to protect bank deposits.

Roosevelt's second term, begun in 1936, faced growing criticism over some of his programs. Despite this opposition, the National Labor Relations Act and the Social Security Act were passed and had far-reaching impacts on business and public welfare.

Roosevelt was elected to a third term (the presidency was later restricted to two terms). Now recovering from the Great Depression, the United States offered indirect support to Great Britain as it defended itself against German attack in World War II. The United States did not fully enter the war until December 1941, when Japan attacked the U.S. naval base at Pearl Harbor, Hawaii. Roosevelt led the successful U.S. war effort.

In November 1944 Roosevelt was elected to a fourth term in office, becoming the only U.S. president to serve four terms. The following February, he met with British and Soviet leaders at Yalta in the Soviet Union to plan for the war's aftermath. Returning to the United States, Roosevelt traveled to his vacation home in Warm Springs, Georgia. He died there on April 12, 1945, of a cerebral hemorrhage.

"A swell time while it lasted"

Now it seemed that the Roaring Twenties were really over. In addition to the shift in economic fortunes, other changes were in the air. Labor unions, for example, which had lost influence and members during the 1920s, now found management listening to their demands. At the same time, the unions were including more immigrants, African Americans, and women in their ranks as they recognized for the first time the reality of a diverse workforce. Another big change had to do with Prohibition. Resistance to this amendment, which had come to be seen as both an unwelcome attempt to intrude on people's private lives and a stimulus to crime, finally led to its downfall. The Twenty-First Amendment, passed in 1933, repealed (overturned) Prohibition.

Meanwhile, writers and other artists began to look back on the Roaring Twenties with new eyes. The pursuits that F. Scott Fitzgerald (1896–1940) had chronicled in his "Jazz Age" short stories and novels now seemed frivolous and shallow. From the perspective of the Depression, the 1920s appeared as a time of wasteful excess. Writing in his autobiography, *The Big Sea,* African American poet Langston Hughes (1902–1967) looked back at the end of the Harlem Renaissance, the blossoming of African American arts and culture that had taken place in the 1920s, and sighed, "I had a swell time while it lasted." The writers of the 1930s would turn increasingly to social issues, adopting a more serious tone and a style of social realism to reflect the harsh conditions and downcast mood of the Great Depression.

Students of the Roaring Twenties have been left with many colorful images, from flappers dancing the Charleston to gangsters toting guns to Charles Lindbergh (1902–1974) flying solo across the Atlantic Ocean. But these pictures do not tell the whole story. The 1920s were a period of great fun as well as major advancements in technology, science, medicine, and the arts. It was also a time of sometimes painful change in values and ideas as the modern world bumped up against traditional beliefs.

It was the period in which the modern U.S. culture—for example, women participate fully in society, improvements in technology and transportation bring color and convenience to life, and people are fascinated with celebrities—first emerged. The Roaring Twenties will no doubt always interest anyone who seeks the story of U.S. history in the twentieth century. It was truly an unforgettable decade, an era both of serious conflict and, in Nathan Miller's words, of "wonderful nonsense."

For More Information

Books

Allen, Frederick Lewis. *Only Yesterday: An Informal History of the 1920s*. New York: Perennial, 1964.

Dumenil, Lynn. *The Modern Temper: American Culture and Society in the 1920s*. New York: Hill and Wang, 1995.

Fremon, David K. *The Great Depression in American History*. Springfield, NJ: Enslow Publishers, Inc., 1996.

Goldston, Robert. *The Great Depression: The United States in the Thirties*. Greenwich, CT: Fawcett, 1968.

Hughes, Langston. *The Big Sea: An Autobiography*. New York: Knopf, 1940.

Katz, William Loren. *The New Freedom to the New Deal 1913–1939*. Austin, TX: Raintree Steck-Vaughn, 1993.

Klein, Maury. *Rainbow's End: The Crash of 1929*. New York: Oxford University Press, 2001.

Miller, Nathan. *New World Coming: The 1920s and the Making of Modern America*. New York: Scribner, 2003.

Parrish, Michael E. *Anxious Decades: America in Prosperity and Depression*. New York: Norton, 1992.

Perret, Geoffrey. *America in the Twenties*. New York: Touchstone, 1982.

Sobel, Robert. *The Great Bull Market: Wall Street in the 1920s*. New York: Norton, 1968.

Wilson, Joan Hoff. *American Business and Foreign Policy, 1920–1933*. Boston: Beacon, 1973.

Web Sites

"America from the Great Depression to World War II: Photos from the FSA-OWI, 1935–1945." *Library of Congress*. Available online at http://memory.loc.gov/ammem/fsowhome.html. Accessed on June 17, 2005.

"American Cultural History, Decade 1920–1929." *Kingwood College Library*. Available online at http://kclibrary.nhmccd.edu/decade20.html. Accessed on June 17, 2005.

Best of History Websites. Available online at http://www.besthistorysites.net/USHistory_Roaring20s.shtml. Accessed on June 17, 2005.

Clash of Cultures in the 1910s and 1920s. Available online at http://history. osu.edu/Projects/Clash/default.htm. Accessed on June 17, 2005.

"Herbert Clark Hoover (1929–1933)." *American President.* Available online at http://www.americanpresident.org/history/herberthoover/. Accessed on June 17, 2005.

Interpreting Primary Sources. Digital History. Available online at http://www. digitalhistory.uh.edu/historyonline/us16.cfm. Accessed on June 17, 2005.

New Deal Network. Available online at http://newdeal.feri.org/. Accessed on June 17, 2005.

Primary Sources

Warren G. Harding

The "Return to Normalcy" Speech
Published in 1920

The 1920 election marked a major shift in the mood and direction of U.S. society. During the Progressive Era (roughly 1900 to 1914), elected officials and other leaders sought to achieve social reforms by expanding the federal government's power to protect the vulnerable, especially workers, children, and consumers. Under the lead of the idealistic Democratic president Woodrow Wilson (1856–1924; served 1913–21), the nation had stood by the Allies (Great Britain, France, and Italy) against German aggression in a war that was meant, in a phrase common during the period, to "make the world safe for democracy." But in the aftermath of that bloody conflict, U.S. citizens faced not only the knowledge of its horrors but also an economic recession at home. They began to retreat from the outward-looking stance of progressivism toward isolationism (staying separate from other countries' affairs). When it came time to elect a new president, Wilson's Democratic Party was weak and divided. It chose as its candidate Ohio's progressive-leaning governor, James M. Cox (1870–1957). The Republicans also chose an Ohioan: a popular

"America's present need is not heroics, but healing; not nostrums, but normalcy; not revolution, but restoration; not agitation, but adjustment; not surgery, but serenity...."

Warren G. Harding delivering a campaign speech much like the "return to normalcy" speech. (*© Bettmann/Corbis. Reproduced by permission.*)

newspaper publisher and senator named Warren G. Harding (1865–1923; served 1921–23).

The speech excerpted here contains what is probably Harding's best-known phrase: "return to normalcy." The phrase and the speech, delivered in Boston in May 1920, express Harding's view of the direction the nation should take. Harding promised voters that if he was elected, the United States would stay out of other nations' troubles and concentrate on its own affairs. Further, Harding vowed to support business interests and to steer the federal government away from the protective, activist role it had taken, while also making it more efficient. One of Harding's campaign slogans, in fact, was "Less government in business and more business in government."

Things to remember while reading this excerpt from Harding's "Return to Normalcy" speech ...

To understand Harding's calming effect on the nation, it is important to take into account the devastating impact of World War I (1914–18; the United States entered the war in 1917). More than 15,000,000 people died in this conflict, which was waged with new, more effective weapons, airplanes, and trench warfare. While the United States suffered a comparatively low 320,000 casualties (including 130,000 killed), its citizens joined the rest of the world in horror at the high cost of war and disillusionment with its results.

Harding is often considered one of the worst presidents in U.S. history. Although he was personally honest, many of the men he chose to serve in his administration proved corrupt. His short presidency (he died before the end of his first term) was marred by several bribery scandals that shocked the U.S. public in the years following Harding's death.

Harding's speeches were usually peppered with grandiose words and phrases, some of which he made up himself. One of these is the word "normalcy," which Harding later defined, as quoted in Geoffrey Perret's book *America in the Twenties,* as

World War I: A Devastating Conflict

The "Great War," later known as World War I, was fought from 1914 to 1918, and had a major impact on the Roaring Twenties. Although the decade was noted for its carefree spirit, it was also the same period of what Ernest Hemingway called "The Lost Generation," referring to the young people whose outlooks were greatly affected by the war.

In the decades preceding World War I, Europe was a continent divided by tense alliances. Both Germany and Austria-Hungary, called the Central Powers, wanted to expand their territories. They aligned with each other, while Great Britain, France, Russia, and Italy had their own agreement. If one was attacked, all would defend. In June 1914 a Serbian student who was unhappy with Austria-Hungary's rule of his country assassinated Austro-Hungarian archduke Franz Ferdinand and his wife. This event sparked greater violence as Austria-Hungary declared war against Serbia, and Germany soon followed with a declaration of war against Russia and France. Britain, Italy, and a number of smaller European nations came to France and Russia's defense. Collectively, this group was known as the Allies.

New technologies greatly influenced how the war was fought. U-boats, or submarines, could now hide beneath the seas to attack ships above, and the automatic rifle, machine gun, and hand grenade changed the battlefield on land. The traditional combat style of marching onto a field to fight with gun and sword was replaced with trench warfare. Soldiers dug ditches into the ground, shooting and bombing the enemy from a distance. The ground in between the trenches was a deadly "no man's land," nearly impossible to cross. The use of chemical weapons, such as mustard gas, and airplanes to drop bombs also dramatically increased the number of those injured and killed during what was the bloodiest conflict the world had seen. An estimated ten million soldiers were killed and twenty million wounded, while millions of civilians also died from hunger and rapidly spreading diseases like influenza.

The United States finally entered the war on the side of the Allies in April 1917, after intercepting a telegram indicating Germany wanted to make Mexico its ally. U.S. troops bolstered the weary European soldiers and provided the momentum to victory. The Central Powers surrendered, signing a peace agreement on November 11, 1918. As Europe turned its attention to rebuilding, the United States retreated into a policy of isolationism. Though it had suffered far fewer casualties than its European allies, American soldiers were deeply affected by the conflict and returned home to a public that could not understand the destruction they had witnessed, which made it difficult for many veterans to adjust.

"a regular steady order of things normal procedure, the natural way, without excess."

Excerpt from the "Return to Normalcy" speech

*There isn't anything the matter with world civilization, except that humanity is viewing it through a vision impaired in a **cataclysmal** war. **Poise** has been disturbed, and nerves have been racked, and fever has rendered men irrational; sometimes there have been **draughts** upon the dangerous cup of **barbarity**, and men have wandered far from safe paths, but the human procession still marches in the right direction.*

*America's present need is not heroics, but healing; not **nostrums**, but normalcy; not revolution, but restoration; not agitation, but adjustment; not surgery, but serenity; not the dramatic, but the **dispassionate**; not experiment, but **equipoise**; not submergence in internationality, but sustainment in triumphant nationality.*

*It is one thing to battle successfully against world domination by military **autocracy**, because the infinite God never intended such a program, but it is quite another thing to revise human nature and suspend the fundamental laws of life and all of life's acquirements. . . .*

This republic has its ample tasks. If we put an end to false economics which lure humanity to utter chaos, ours will be the commanding example of world leadership today. If we can prove a representative popular government under which a citizenship seeks what it may do for the government rather than what the government may do for individuals, we shall do more to make democracy safe for the world than all armed conflict ever recorded.

*The world needs to be reminded that all human ills are not curable by legislation, and that quantity of **statutory enactment** and excess of government offer no substitute for quality of citizenship.*

*The problems of maintained civilization are not to be solved by a transfer of responsibility from citizenship to government, and no **eminent** page in history was ever drafted by the standards of mediocrity. More, no government is worthy of the name which is directed by influence on the one hand, or moved by **intimidation** on the other. . . .*

Cataclysmal: Devastating.

Poise: Calmness.

Draughts: Drinks.

Barbarity: Wildness, cruelty.

Nostrums: An unreliable remedy or medicine.

Dispassionate: Unemotional.

Equipoise: Balance.

Autocracy: Government run by one person with unlimited power.

Statutory enactment: Putting laws into effect.

Eminent: Well-respected.

Intimidation: Threatening.

*My best judgment of America's needs is to steady down, to get squarely on our feet, to make sure of the right path. Let's get out of the fevered **delirium** of war, with the hallucination that all the money in the world is to be made in the madness of war and the wildness of its aftermath. Let us stop to consider that tranquillity at home is more precious than peace abroad, and that both our good fortune and our eminence are dependent on the normal forward stride of all the American people. . . .*

What happened next . . .

Harding won the 1920 election, gaining 60.4 percent of the popular vote (the largest margin of votes a presidential candidate ever received). The Republicans also won majorities in both the House of Representatives and the Senate, making it easy for them to push through their program of cutting taxes, loosening government control of industry, and restricting immigration. The economy began to grow steadily stronger, and many U.S. citizens gave Harding's administration the credit. Yet behind the scenes, a web of corruption was being woven. It seems likely that at the time of his death, which occurred while he was on a speaking tour of the western states, Harding was worried about the misdeeds committed by the friends he had elevated to high government offices. One of these, Secretary of the Interior Albert Fall (1861–1944), was involved in the Teapot Dome scandal. In 1931 Fall became the first cabinet member to go to jail after he was convicted of renting public oil fields to private companies in exchange for personal loans.

Did you know . . .

- Harding's wife Florence, or Flossie (called Duchess by her husband in reference to her dominant personality), was a strong and in many ways positive presence in her husband's administration. She opened the White House, which had been shut up tight during Wilson's long illness, to visitors and helped to create a lighter, more welcoming

Delirium: State of confusion or craziness.

Florence Harding was a strong and positive presence in her husband's administration. *(Courtesy of The Library of Congress.)*

atmosphere there. Even though their marriage seems to have been unhappy, she is credited with having supported and encouraged her husband throughout his political career.

- Despite his weaknesses as a president, Harding was a friendly, outgoing person who was much loved by the ordinary people of the United States. While serving as president, he played golf and poker twice a week, kept his private quarters well stocked with illegal liquor, and was rumored to indulge in extramarital affairs. He loved dogs, went frequently to baseball games, and actually enjoyed standing in long reception lines, shaking people's hands and exchanging small talk.

Consider the following ...

- Under President Wilson, the federal government had taken an *activist* role in people's lives. Harding promised a *laissez-faire* approach to government. Investigate the meaning of these terms and relate them to the 1920s.

- World War I was supposed to make the world safe for democracy. In this speech, Harding introduced a twist on that phrase. What do you think he means?

For More Information

Books

Dean, John, and Arthur M. Schlesinger. *Warren G. Harding.* New York: Times Books, 2004.

Downes, Randolph C. *The Rise of Warren Gamaliel Harding: 1865–1920.* Columbus: Ohio State University Press, 1970.

Kent, Deborah. *Warren G. Harding: America's 29th President.* New York: Children's Press, 2004.

Landau, Elaine. *Warren G. Harding.* Minneapolis, MN: Lerner Publications, 2005.

Murray, Robert K. *The Harding Era: Warren G. Harding and His Administration.* Minneapolis: University of Minnesota Press, 1969.

Perret, Geoffrey. *America in the Twenties.* New York: Touchstone, 1982.

Trani, Eugene P., and David L. Wilson. *The Presidency of Warren G. Harding.* Lawrence: Regents Press of Kansas, 1977.

Web Sites

Warren G. Harding. Available online at http://www.whitehouse.gov/history/presidents/wh29.html. Accessed on June 17, 2005.

Sinclair Lewis

Excerpt from Babbitt
Published in 1922

A native of the midwestern United States, Sinclair Lewis (1885–1951) chronicled through novels and short stories the changes brought by the shift from a mainly rural, agricultural society to one that was increasingly urban and industrial. The middle-class businessman and resident of the up-and-coming town of Zenith who is the title character of *Babbitt* is probably Lewis's best-known creation. The novel captures in realistic detail many of the major trends of the 1920s, including the worship of business, rising materialism and consumerism, boosterism (enthusiastic promotion), and the conflict between the older and younger generations. Lewis exposes a spiritual emptiness and complacency (being uncritically satisfied with oneself or one's society) at the core of his characters' lives.

Lewis was born in 1885 in Sauk Centre, a tiny village on the Minnesota prairie. He entered Yale University in 1903, pursuing his interest in writing and publishing his work in student magazines. After traveling to Europe and Central America, Lewis graduated in 1908. He lived in Iowa, New York, California, and Washington, D.C., working as a journalist while also writing short stories and novels. Lewis's first big

"He entered a place curiously like the saloons of ante-prohibition days, with a long greasy bar with sawdust in front and streaky mirror behind. . . . The bartender . . . stared at Babbitt as he stalked plumply up to the bar and whispered, "I'd, uh— Friend of Hanson's sent me here. Like to get some gin."

Sinclair Lewis's novel *Babbitt* captures many of the trends of the 1920s. *(AP/Wide World Photos. Reproduced by permission.)*

success came with the publication of his novel *Main Street* (1920), in which the central character, Carol Kennicott, is an idealistic city dweller who moves to a small town with her new husband. There she struggles with and finally accepts the narrow-mindedness and limitations of her environment.

In *Babbitt,* which appeared two years later, real estate salesman George Follansbee Babbitt suspects that something is lacking in his well-ordered, up-to-date lifestyle, but by the end of the novel he has embraced it again. In this excerpt from Chapter 8, Babbitt and his wife have planned a dinner party at which they hope to entertain and impress their guests. They intend to treat their friends to alcoholic beverages, which are illegal due to the passage of the Eighteenth Amendment in 1919, which forbade the sale and purchase of liquor, but nevertheless accepted and expected. This passage chronicles Babbitt's journey into a seedy part of town to buy gin.

Things to remember while reading this excerpt from *Babbitt* . . .

The character of George Babbitt has come to symbolize the 1920s, particularly its glorification of business values and of the businessman as a natural leader. In fact, the name "Babbitt" has since been used to describe a type of person who, like the novel's title character, is not very cultured, does not think very deeply, and conforms strictly to his society's expectations.

Some critics have found Babbitt's moments of deeper awareness and doubt unconvincing. They contend that such self-questioning reflects the distaste that intellectuals like Lewis, and certainly not the average person, felt for the common materialism and mindless boosterism of the United States during the 1920s.

The fact that the Babbitts purchase their ice cream from Vecchia's suggests the presence of Italian immigrants in their town. During the 1920s, newcomers from southern and eastern Europe were objects of scorn and suspicion due to their religious and cultural differences (for example, most Italians were Catholic, while most U.S. residents were Protestants). Although the Babbitts frequent an Italian-owned store, there are no recent immigrants among their social crowd.

Excerpt from Babbitt

On the morning of the dinner, Mrs. Babbitt was **restive**.

"Now, George, I want you to be sure and be home early tonight. Remember, you have to dress."

"Uh-huh. I see by the Advocate *that the Presbyterian General Assembly has voted to quit the Interchurch World Movement. That—"*

"George! Did you hear what I said? You must be home in time to dress to-night."

"Dress? . . . I'm dressed now! Think I'm going down to the office in my **B.V.D.'s**?*"*

"I will not have you talking indecently before the children! And you do have to put on your dinner-jacket!"

"I guess you mean my Tux. I tell you, of all the doggone nonsensical nuisances that was ever invented—"

Three minutes later, after Babbitt had wailed, "Well, I don't know whether I'm going to dress or NOT" in a manner which showed that he was going to dress, the discussion moved on.

"Now, George, you mustn't forget to call in at Vecchia's on the way home and get the ice cream. Their delivery-wagon is broken down, and I don't want to trust them to send it by—"

"All right! You told me that before breakfast!"

Restive: Unable to keep silent.

B.V.D.s: Underwear.

"Well, I don't want you to forget. I'll be working my head off all day long, training the girl that's to help with the dinner—"

"All nonsense, anyway, hiring an extra girl for the feed. Matilda could perfectly well—"

"—and I have to go out and buy the flowers, and fix them, and set the table, and order the salted almonds, and look at the chickens, and arrange for the children to have their supper upstairs and—And I simply must depend on you to go to Vecchia's for the ice cream."

"All riiiiiight! Gosh, I'm going to get it!"

"All you have to do is to go in and say you want the ice cream that Mrs. Babbitt ordered yesterday by phone, and it will be all ready for you."

At ten-thirty she telephoned to him not to forget the ice cream from Vecchia's.

He was surprised and blasted then by a thought. He wondered whether Floral Heights dinners were worth the hideous toil involved. But he repented the **sacrilege** in the excitement of buying the materials for cocktails.

Now this was the manner of obtaining alcohol under the reign of righteousness and prohibition:

He drove from the severe rectangular streets of the modern business center into the tangled byways of Old Town—jagged blocks filled with sooty warehouses and lofts; on into The Arbor, once a pleasant orchard but now a **morass** of lodging-houses, **tenements**, and **brothels**. Exquisite shivers chilled his spine and stomach, and he looked at every policeman with intense innocence, as one who loved the law, and admired the Force, and longed to stop and play with them. He parked his car a block from Healey Hanson's saloon, worrying, "Well, rats, if anybody did see me, they'd think I was here on business."

He entered a place curiously like the saloons of ante-prohibition days, with a long greasy bar with sawdust in front and streaky mirror behind, a pine table at which a dirty old man dreamed over a glass of something which resembled whisky, and with two men at the bar, drinking something which resembled beer, and giving that impression of forming a large crowd which two men always give in a saloon. The bartender, a tall pale Swede with a diamond in his lilac scarf, stared at Babbitt as he stalked plumply up to the bar and whispered, "I'd, uh— Friend of Hanson's sent me here. Like to get some gin."

Sacrilege: Violation of something cherished.

Morass: Complicated or confused area.

Tenement: House divided into several separate residences.

Brothels: Places where prostitutes worked.

The bartender gazed down on him in the manner of an outraged bishop. "I guess you got the wrong place, my friend. We sell nothing but soft drinks here." He cleaned the bar with a rag which would itself have done with a little cleaning, and glared across his mechanically moving elbow.

The old dreamer at the table petitioned the bartender, "Say, Oscar, listen."

Oscar did not listen.

"Aw, say, Oscar, listen, will yuh? Say, lis-sen!"

The decayed and drowsy voice of the loafer, the agreeable stink of beer-dregs, threw a spell of **inanition** over Babbitt. The bartender moved grimly toward the crowd of two men. Babbitt followed him as delicately as a cat, and **wheedled**, "Say, Oscar, I want to speak to Mr. Hanson."

"Whajuh wanta see him for?"

"I just want to talk to him. Here's my card."

It was a beautiful card, an engraved card, a card in the blackest black and the sharpest red, announcing that Mr. George F. Babbitt was Estates, Insurance, Rents. The bartender held it as though it weighed ten pounds, and read it as though it were a hundred words long. He did not bend from his **episcopal dignity**, but he growled, "I'll see if he's around."

From the back room he brought an immensely old young man, a quiet sharp-eyed man, in tan silk shirt, checked vest hanging open, and burning brown trousers—Mr. Healey Hanson. Mr. Hanson said only "Yuh?" but his **implacable** and **contemptuous** eyes queried Babbitt's soul, and he seemed not at all impressed by the new dark-gray suit for which (as he had admitted to every acquaintance at the Athletic Club) Babbitt had paid a hundred and twenty-five dollars.

"Glad meet you, Mr. Hanson. Say, uh—I'm George Babbitt of the Babbitt-Thompson Realty Company. I'm a great friend of Jake Offutt's."

"Well, what of it?"

"Say, uh, I'm going to have a party, and Jake told me you'd be able to fix me up with a little gin." In alarm, in **obsequiousness**, as Hanson's eyes grew more bored, "You telephone to Jake about me, if you want to."

Hanson answered by jerking his head to indicate the entrance to the back room, and strolled away. Babbitt melodramatically crept into an apartment containing four round tables, eleven chairs, a brewery calendar, and a smell. He waited. Thrice he saw Healey Hanson **saunter** through, humming, hands in pockets, ignoring him.

Inanition: Mindlessness.

Wheedled: Used endearments or flattery to get someone to do something.

Episcopal dignity: Like that of a high church official.

Implacable: Incapable of being pleased.

Contemptuous: Reflecting that belief that someone is worthless.

Obsequiousness: Showing obedience or servility.

Saunter: Walk leisurely.

A Decade of Colorful Language

Sinclair Lewis was particularly praised for his ability to mimic the everyday speech of U.S. citizens. During the Roaring Twenties, the language spoken by ordinary Americans became increasingly colorful. Many of the slang words that entered the U.S. vocabulary during this period are still used today. Some came from the world of Prohibition, and many from African American culture. Here are some examples.

All wet: Incorrect.

Attaboy!: Well done.

Baby: Sweetheart.

Baloney: Nonsense.

Beat it: Get lost, get out of here.

Bee's knees: Terrific.

Big Apple, the: New York City.

Big cheese: Important person.

Blind pig: A drinking establishment with a false front.

Blowing your top: Getting angry.

Boogie Woogie: A kind of dancing.

Cat's meow: Great, wonderful.

Clam: A dollar.

Coffin varnish: Homemade alcohol.

Crush: An infatuation.

Dig: To understand.

Dogs: Feet.

Doll: An attractive woman.

Don't take any wooden nickels: Don't do anything foolish.

Dough: Money.

Fella: Fellow (used like dude or guy are today).

Flivver: First a Ford Model T, and later any old, broken-down car.

Glad rags: Party or going-out clothes.

Goods, the: The right material, or the facts, the truth.

Goofy: In love.

Hauling: Running away.

Heavy sugar: A lot of money.

Hip to the jive: Cool.

Hooey: Nonsense.

Euphemistically: Substituting a milder word for one that is unpleasant or embarrassing.

Disdainful: Reflecting the belief that someone is unworthy of respect.

*By this time Babbitt had modified his valiant morning vow, "I won't pay one cent over seven dollars a quart" to "I might pay ten." On Hanson's next weary entrance he besought "Could you fix that up?" Hanson scowled, and grated, "Just a minute—Pete's sake—just a minute!" In growing meekness Babbitt went on waiting till Hanson casually reappeared with a quart of gin—what is **euphemistically** known as a quart—in his **disdainful** long white hands.*

"Twelve bucks," he snapped.

"I have to see a man about a dog.": I have to go buy (illegal) liquor.

Java: Coffee.

Joe: Coffee.

John: Toilet.

Joint: Establishment, place of business.

Keen: Appealing.

Level with me: Be honest.

Live wire: An energetic person.

Mind your potatoes: Mind your own business.

Moonshine: Homemade alcohol.

Neck: To kiss passionately.

Nifty: Great, excellent.

On the level: Legitimate, honest.

Petting: Necking, making out.

Pinch: To arrest.

Pipe down: Stop talking.

Rag-a-muffin: Dirty, messy child or person.

Razz: To make fun of.

Real McCoy: A genuine thing, authentic.

Sap: A fool, an idiot.

Says you!: Expression of disbelief.

Sheba: A young woman.

Sheik: A young man.

Shin dig: A party that is so crowded that one is in danger of getting kicked while dancing.

So's your old man: An irritated reply.

Soused: Drunk.

Speakeasy: An undercover saloon where people could buy and consume illegal liquor.

Stuck on: In love.

Tin Lizzie: A Model T Ford.

Wet blanket: A solemn, joyless person.

What's eating you?: What's wrong?

Whoopee: Wild fun.

For many more examples of Roaring Twenties slang, see *The Harlem Renaissance: A Historical Dictionary for the Era*, edited by Bruce Kellner (Greenwood Press, 1984); *The Writer's Guide to Everyday Life from Prohibition through World War II*, by Mark McCutcheon (Writer's Digest Books, 1995), or *The Internet Guide to Jazz Age Slang*, compiled by David Larkins (http://www.home.earthlink.net/dlarkins/slang-pg.htm).

"Say, uh, but say, cap'n, Jake thought you'd be able to fix me up for eight or nine a bottle."

*"Nup. Twelve. This is the real stuff, smuggled from Canada. This is none o' your **neutral spirits with a drop of juniper extract**," the honest merchant said virtuously. "Twelve bones—if you want it. Course y' understand I'm just doing this anyway as a friend of Jake's."*

"Sure! Sure! I understand!" Babbitt gratefully held out twelve dollars. He felt honored by contact with greatness as Hanson

Neutral spirits with a drop of juniper extract: Ingredients in the gin made by people in their own homes during Prohibition.

yawned, stuffed the bills, uncounted, into his radiant vest, and swaggered away.

*He had a number of **titillations** out of concealing the gin-bottle under his coat and out of hiding it in his desk. All afternoon he snorted and chuckled and gurgled over his ability to "give the Boys a real shot in the arm to-night."*

What happened next . . .

After the publication of *Babbitt,* Lewis continued his exploration of the new culture of the United States with several acclaimed novels. In *Arrowsmith* (1925), an idealistic scientist sees his dreams overwhelmed by commercial concerns. *Elmer Gantry* (1927) satirizes the evangelical religious leaders who were so popular in the 1920s, while in *Dodsworth* (1929) an American businessman traveling in Europe finds his values tested and changed.

Lewis's popularity and influence were confirmed when, in 1930, he became the first U.S. author to win the Nobel Prize for Literature. However, most commentators agree that after the end of the 1920s the quality of his work began a steady decline. His short stories lacked the satire and realism that had enlivened his earlier novels, and they actually reflected the sentimentality that Lewis had once scorned. His last years were marked by restless travel, failed relationships, and alcoholism. He died in Rome in 1951.

Did you know . . .

- In addition to being the first American writer to win the Nobel Prize for Literature, Lewis was also the first to decline the Pulitzer Prize, which he won in 1926. Lewis objected to the idea that the prize championed everything that was supposedly wholesome in U.S. society, and he also claimed that prizes were corrupting to writers. Some critics, however, suggested that Lewis turned the prize down because he was angry that *Babbitt* had been snubbed.

Titillations: Arousing mild excitement.

- Despite his harsh criticism of U.S. society and culture, Lewis was much read and admired by a wide audience. His books remained consistently on bestseller lists throughout the 1920s.

Consider the following ...

- Prohibition was controversial, with some people (commonly known as the Drys) supporting it as a way to resolve social problems and some (known as the Wets) maintaining it was both unnecessary and harmful. How do you think Lewis felt about Prohibition? Provide evidence from this excerpt to support your conclusion.

- Read other chapters of *Babbitt* to learn how Lewis satirizes other aspects of the 1920s. For example, in Chapter 14 he describes the "representative businessman"; in Chapter 18, the Babbitt's teenaged son invites his friends to a party that highlights the differences between young people and their parents.

For More Information

Books

Dooley, D.J. *The Art of Sinclair Lewis*. Lincoln: University of Nebraska Press, 1967.

Fleming, Robert E., and Esther Fleming. *Sinclair Lewis: A Reference Guide*. Boston: G.K. Hall, 1980.

Grebstein, Sheldon N. *Sinclair Lewis*. New York: Twayne, 1962.

Hutchisson, James M. *The Rise of Sinclair Lewis, 1920–1930*. University Park: Pennsylvania State University Press, 1996.

Lingeman, Richard R. *Sinclair Lewis: Rebel from Main Street*. New York: Random House, 2002.

Love, Glen A. *Babbitt: An American Life*. New York: Twayne, 1993.

Schorer, Mark. *Sinclair Lewis: An American Life*. New York: McGraw Hill, 1961.

Stevenson, Elizabeth. *Babbitts and Bohemians: The American 1920s*. New York: Macmillan, 1967.

Web Sites

"Sinclair Lewis and His Life." *The Sinclair Lewis Society Web Page.* Available online at http://www.english.ilstu.edu/separry/sinclairlewis/. Accessed on June 17, 2005.

"Sinclair Lewis—Autobiography." *Nobelprize.org.* Available online at http://www.nobelprize.org/literature/laureates/1930/lewis-autobio.html. Accessed on June 17, 2005.

Ellen Welles Lewis

Excerpt from "A Flapper's Appeal to Parents"
Published on December 6, 1922

E ven before the 1920s began, a new kind of young woman was emerging in the world. As early as 1915, the celebrated journalist H.L. Mencken (1880–1956) was commenting on this woman's appearance in the pages of *The Smart Set,* a New York-based magazine that combined social satire with commentary on the arts. According to Mencken, this new young woman was characterized by her very different appearance, especially her shorter skirts and bobbed (short) hair. The use of the word "flapper" to describe her seems to have originated in England, in reference to the unbuckled, floppy galoshes (rain boots) that some young women there were wearing.

The women of the previous generation had been part of the Victorian era, which corresponds roughly to the years 1837 to 1901, when Queen Victoria (1819–1901) ruled Great Britain. Women of this period were expected to dress and behave modestly. They wore long skirts and high collars, with tight corsets (body-shaping undergarments) and layers of petticoats underneath, and their long hair was piled on top of their heads. They were the embodiments of innocence, protectors of morality, obedient to their husbands, and devoted to their children. By

"We are the Younger Generation. The war tore away our spiritual foundations and challenged our faith. We are struggling to regain our equilibrium. The times have made us older and more experienced than you were at our age."

The flapper symbolized the freedoms that women were being allowed during the 1920s. (© John Springer Collection/Corbis. Reproduced by permission.)

the 1920s, however, new ideas about women's roles were taking hold, a development that had something to do with World War I (1914–18), when many women had taken a more public role in society. More of them were now attending college and entering the workforce. Changes were also taking place in the behavior and habits of young people, who were taking advantage of the new freedoms and opportunities. All of these new trends combined to create the flapper.

Her appearance itself was a radical shift from the past. In addition to her short hair and skirts, the flapper wore dresses that gave her a boyish appearance. She wore silk stockings, makeup, and long strings of beads, and she projected an independent, free-spirited, and fun-loving manner. She often smoked and drank illegal liquor in public, and, like the young woman who wrote the article excerpted here, she adored dancing. Although she took a more relaxed approach to showing affection for her boyfriend in public and in "petting" (engaging in various forms of kissing and touching) than had previous generations, she was not generally as sexually free as some assumed.

In this article from a magazine published in 1922, a self-confessed flapper defends her behavior, suggesting that not all flappers are alike; she, for instance, does not smoke, drink, pet, or use makeup. The author reminds her older, parental audience that this is a modern era in which the sudden onslaught of war and technology has caused dislocation and confusion. She calls for more understanding between the older and younger generations, highlighting the fact that this was the first time in U.S. history when such a division was perceived to exist. Finally, this young woman recommends that parents become friends with their children, underlining the new trend toward what was called the "companionate" family, in which members openly express their feelings for and interest in each other.

Things to remember while reading this excerpt from "A Flapper's Appeal to Parents"...

The daring appearance and bold manners of the flapper were not appreciated by everybody. In fact, those who disapproved of the changes occurring in society saw in the emergence of, what they considered, this scantily clad,

John Held's illustration of a young flapper dancing the Charleston with an elderly gentleman that appeared on the cover of *Life* magazine. *(© Corbis. Reproduced by permission.)*

cocktail-drinking young woman more evidence of society's moral decline.

Motion picture stars like Louise Brooks (1906–1985) and Clara Bow (1905–1965), with their bobbed hair and fashionably boyish figures, helped to popularize the flapper image. Cartoonist John Held (1889–1958), whose drawings of flappers and their boyfriends appeared in such popular magazines as *The New Yorker* and *Life*, both satirized and glamorized this trend.

Suffragists (those who fought to win for women the right to vote) viewed the passage of the Nineteenth Amendment to the U.S. Constitution, which guaranteed women voting rights, in 1920 as a great victory. They hoped that the younger generation would now seize the chance to become politically active and improve the world around them, and they were disappointed when that generally failed to happen. Instead young women seemed to turn away from social concerns and focus their energies on fashion, fun, and attracting the opposite sex. Yet Lewis suggests here that young people of her generation were in a state of understandable confusion caused by the sudden changes brought about by World War I and new technologies.

Excerpt from "A Flapper's Appeal to Parents"

If one judges by appearances, I suppose I am a flapper. I am within the age limit. I wear bobbed hair, the badge of flapperhood. (And, oh, what a comfort it is!) I powder my nose. I wear fringed skirts and bright-colored sweaters, and scarfs, and waists with Peter Pan collars, and low- heeled "finale hopper" shoes. I adore to dance. I spend a large amount of time in automobiles. I attend **hops**, and proms, and ball-games, and **crew races**, and other affairs at men's colleges. But none the less some of the most thoroughbred superflappers might blush to claim sistership or even remote relationship with such as I. I don't use rouge, or lipstick, or pluck my eyebrows. I don't smoke (I've tried it, and don't like it), or drink, or tell "peppy stories." I don't pet. . . . But then—there are many degrees of flapper. There is the semi-flapper; the flapper; the superflapper. Each of these three main general divisions has its degrees of variation. I might possibly be placed somewhere in the middle of the first class. I think every one realizes by this time that there has been a marked change in our much-discussed tactics. Jazz has been modified, and probably will continue to be until it has become **obsolete**. Petting is gradually growing out of fashion through being overworked. Yes, undoubtedly our hopeless condition is improving. But it was not for discussing these aspects of the case that began this article.

I want to beg all you parents, and grandparents, and friends, and teachers, and preachers—you who constitute the "older generation"—to overlook our shortcomings, at least for the present, and to appreciate our virtues. I wonder if it ever occurred to any of you that it required brains to become and remain a successful flapper? Indeed it does! It requires an enormous amount of cleverness and energy to keep going at the proper pace. It requires self-knowledge and self-analysis. We must know our capabilities and limitations. We must be constantly on the alert. Attainment of flapperhood is a big and serious undertaking!

"Brains?" you repeat, **skeptically**. "Then why aren't they used to better advantage?" That is exactly it! And do you know who is largely responsible for all this energy's being spent in the wrong directions? You! You parents, and grandparents, and friends, and teachers, and preachers—all of you! "The war!" you cry. "It is the effect of the war!" And then you blame prohibition. Yes! Yet it is you who set the example there! But this is my point: Instead of helping us work out our problems with constructive, sympathetic thinking and acting, you have muddled them for us more hopelessly with destructive public condemnation and **denunciation**.

Think back to the time when you were struggling through the teens. Remember how spontaneous and deep were the joys, how serious and penetrating the sorrows. Most of us, under the present system of modern education, are further advanced and more thoroughly developed mentally, physically, and vocationally than were our parents at our age. We hold the infinite possibilities of the **myriads** of new inventions

Hops: Dances.

Crew races: Boat rowing races.

Obsolete: No longer needed or in existence.

Skeptically: Doubtfully.

Denunciation: Declaring wrong or evil.

Myriads: Wide variety.

The Fun, Free Fashions of the Roaring Twenties

The major changes that were affecting U.S. society during the Roaring Twenties were well reflected in the way that people, especially women, dressed. In earlier centuries and right up to the beginning of the 1920s, women wore long dresses, often with long sleeves and high collars, with layers of undergarments and stiff corsets underneath. Their long hair was piled atop their heads, and makeup was considered something that only so-called "loose" women or prostitutes wore.

But with the modern age came a real shift not only in the way women looked at themselves, but in how they lived. More women than ever before were attending college and working outside the home. They were driving cars and participating in sports like golf, tennis, and swimming. The clothing of earlier decades did not fit women's new pursuits.

Although flappers showed off the most up-to-date and daring fashions of the 1920s, many other women began to wear shorter skirts, bobbed hair, and makeup as well. Radio broadcasting, movies, and new magazines made communication easier, reducing geographic isolation, and allowing women to see what others were wearing. The styles of popular movie stars and sports heroes could be studied and copied.

Some of the most distinctive women's clothing styles of the 1920s came from European fashion designers such as Coco Chanel, Jean Patou, and Paul Poiret. They helped establish the sporty, boyish look that characterized the Roaring Twenties, and mass clothing manufacturers were quick to catch on. Cheaper versions of the European designs were made available in shops and in catalogs such as Sears Roebuck. The most popular style was short hemlines, dropped waists, and a flattened, "tubular" shape. Evening dresses often had low necklines or were backless, and were often adorned with lamé (fabric interwoven with gold or silver threads), beads, or sequins, and worn with capes.

Women accessorized their new fashions with long strings of beads and cloche, or bell, hats that fit snugly over short hair and rested just above the eyes. Chunky, high-heeled shoes, with pointed toes and t-straps across the top of the foot, became increasingly popular. After the spectacular 1922 find of the ancient Egyptian king Tutankhamen's tomb, Egyptian-themed scarves, earrings, necklaces, and other items were in high demand.

Women used makeup to finish off their look. They plucked and redrew their eyebrows, wore heavy face powder, rouge (blush), deep red lipstick, and dark kohl eyeliner, which created a smudged, smoky look. Tanned skin and designer perfumes also became trends to follow.

Men's fashions also changed. Modeled after Britain's young prince of Wales and the well-dressed students at Oxford University, college men began to sport knickers, flannel trousers, sweaters, blazers, and loose-fitting pants known as Oxford bags. Illegal liquor flasks could be easily hidden inside the popular long, raccoon-skin coats, but were harder to conceal in aviator jackets with fitted waists and wrists, like that worn by famed pilot Charles C. Lindbergh.

within our grasp. We have learned to take for granted conveniences, and many luxuries, which not so many years ago were as yet undreamed of. We are in touch with the whole universe. We have a tremendous problem on our hands. You must help us. Give us confidence—not distrust. Give us practical aid and advice—not criticism. Praise us when praise is **merited**. Be patient and understanding when we make mistakes.

We are the Younger Generation. The war tore away our spiritual foundations and challenged our faith. We are struggling to regain our **equilibrium**. The times have made us older and more experienced than you were at our age. It must be so with each succeeding generation if it is to keep pace with the rapidly advancing and mighty tide of civilization. Help us to put our knowledge to the best advantage. Work with us! That is the way! Outlets for this surplus knowledge and energy must be opened. Give us a helping hand.

Youth has many **disillusionments**. Spiritual forces begin to be felt. The emotions are frequently in a state of **upheaval**, struggling with one another for supremacy. And Youth does not understand. There is no one to turn to—no one but the rest of Youth, which is as perplexed and troubled with its problems as ourselves. Everywhere we read and hear the criticism and distrust of older people toward us. It forms an **insurmountable** barrier between us. How can we turn to them?

In every person there is a desire, an **innate** longing, toward some special goal or achievement. Each of us has his place to fill. Each of us has his talent—be it ever so humble. And our hidden longing is usually for that for which nature equipped us. Any one will do best and be happiest doing that which he really likes and for which he is fitted. In this "age of specialists," as it has been called, there is less excuse than ever for persons being shoved into **niches** in which they do not belong and cannot be made to fit. The lives of such people are great tragedies. That is why it is up to you who have the supervision of us of less ripe experience to guide us sympathetically, and to help us find, encourage, and develop our special abilities and talents. Study us. Make us realize that you respect us as fellow human beings, that you have confidence in us, and, above all, that you expect us to live up to the highest ideals, and to the best that is in us.

It must begin with individuals. Parents, study your children. Talk to them more intimately. Respect their right to a point of view. Be so understanding and sympathetic that they will turn to you naturally and trustfully with their glowing joys or with their heartaches and tragedies. Youth has many of the latter because Youth takes itself so

Merited: Deserved.

Equilibrium: Mental or emotional balance.

Disillusionments: Without faith or trust.

Upheaval: Upsetting changes.

Insurmountable: Impossible to overcome.

Innate: Natural.

Niches: Corners or positions.

seriously. And so often the wounds go unconfessed, and, instead of gradually healing, become more and more gnawing through suppression until of necessity relief is sought in some way which is not always for the best.

Mothers, become acquainted with your children. Be the understanding, loving, happy comrade of your daughter. Become her ideal. And strive to live up to the ideal you set for the woman who is to become your son's wife. Be his **chum**. *Be young with him. Oh, what a powerful and wonderful influence you are capable of exerting if you only will!*

Fathers, find out what is within the minds and hearts and souls of your children. There is a wonderful, an interesting, and a sacred treasure-house there if you will take the time and pain to explore. The key is yours in return for patient understanding, sympathetic encouragement, and kindly wisdom. **Make love** *to your daughter if necessary! Make her realize the depth of your love and make her feel that you have confidence in her ability to live up to your standards of upright womanhood. Be your son's best pal. Make his interests your interests. Encourage him to formulate a workable philosophy of life. And remember this: A little merited praise means so much! A little encouragement goes such a long way!*

Oh, parents, parents everywhere, point out to us the ideals of truly glorious and upright living! Believe in us, that we may learn to believe in ourselves, in humanity, in God! Be the living examples of your teachings, that you may inspire us with hope and courage, understanding and truth, love and faith. Remember that we are the parents of the future. Help us to be worthy of the sacred trust that will be ours. Make your lives such an inspiration to us that we in our turn will strive to become an inspiration to our children and to the ages! Is it too much to ask?

What happened next . . .

The flapper's moment in the spotlight was relatively brief. The 1920s ended in the shocking event known as "the Crash"—when, in October 1929, the stock market collapsed and the economy began a long decline, and soon the Great

The ideal flapper look involved a slim and boyish silhouette and lots of accessories, especially the tight-fitting, bell-shaped cloche hats.

(© Bettmann/Corbis. Reproduced with permission.)

Depression (the period of hardship that lasted until the beginning of World War II [1939–45]) was underway. During the grim 1930s, the carefree attitude and frivolous pursuit of fun that had characterized the flapper's way of life would seem shallow and self-indulgent. Yet the flapper's freer approach both to clothing styles and to public behaviors like smoking and drinking was adopted by a wide swath of society. And the flapper herself, her long beads swinging as she danced the Charleston, would remain a lasting and colorful symbol of the 1920s for generations to come.

Did you know . . .

- Flapper fashions featured simpler lines, fewer undergarments, and a new silhouette: whereas the previous generation had idealized the "hourglass" figure (small waist and wide hips), the flapper ideal was slim and boyish. The ideal look involved flattened breasts, a dropped waistline, shorter skirts, and lots of accessories (such as jewelry, scarves, cigarette holders, and especially the tight-fitting, bell-shaped cloche hats).

- Novelist and short story writer F. Scott Fitzgerald (1896–1940) both described and glamorized the flapper in such pieces as "Bernice Bobs Her Hair," a short story about a young woman who decides to adopt the popular 1920s trend of shorter hair. Fitzgerald's beautiful, lively, and mentally unstable wife Zelda typified the new woman in many ways, engaging with her husband in such intentionally outrageous behavior as splashing in public fountains and riding on the roofs of taxis.

- Despite resistance from some quarters, society's ideas about the ways women should behave were changing. One piece of evidence was the establishment of the Miss America Pageant, which featured the spectacle of young women parading in swimsuits before judges, in 1921.

Consider the following . . .

- Not every young woman in the 1920s became a flapper. Who do you think might have been left out of this trend?

- It has been said that the 1920s were a difficult period in which to be the parent of a teenager. Why was this the case?

- Can you relate to this author's plea for parents to treat the younger generation with more understanding? Write an article similar to this one, in which you express the perspective of your own generation.

For More Information

Books

Boer, Lawrence, and John D. Walther, eds. *Dancing Fools and Weary Blues: The Great Escape of the Twenties.* Bowling Green, OH: Bowling Green University Press, 1990.

Cowley, Malcolm, ed. *The Stories of F. Scott Fitzgerald.* New York: Charles Scribner's Sons, 1952.

Hanson, Erica. *The 1920s.* San Diego, CA: Lucent Books, 1999.

Herald, Jacqueline. *Fashions of a Decade: 1920s.* New York: Facts on File, 1991.

Latham, Angela J. *Posing a Threat: Flappers, Chorus Girls, and Other Brazen Performers of the 1920s.* Hanover, NH: University Press of New England, 2000.

Mowry, George E., ed. *The Twenties: Fords, Flappers, and Fanatics.* Gloucester, MA: Peter Smith/Prentice Hall, 1963.

Perret, Geoffrey. *America in the Twenties.* New York: Touchstone, 1982.

Web Sites

Christy's Fashion Pages: Flapper Fashion. Available online at http://www.rambova.com/fashion/fash4.html. Accessed on June 17, 2005.

The Jazz Age: Flapper Culture & Style. Available online at http://www.geocities.com/flapper_culture/. Accessed on June 17, 2005.

Langston Hughes

Excerpt from "The Weary Blues"
Published in 1923

"In a deep song voice with a melancholy tone I heard that Negro sing, that old piano moan—Ain't got nobody in all this world...."

Recognized as the best known and most celebrated of African American poets, Langston Hughes (1902–1967) began his career, which would span five decades, during the Harlem Renaissance. This period of creative and intellectual achievement took place during the 1920s and was centered in New York City's Harlem neighborhood, which had become a gathering place for African Americans. As a young, exciting, up-and-coming poet, Hughes played an important role in setting the tone and style of this era. His vivid, often earthy poems were written in language that echoed both the jazz and blues music that dominated the Harlem Renaissance and the language spoken by the ordinary people of that time and place.

Born in Joplin, Missouri, Hughes was raised by his mother after his father left for Mexico. They moved often, and Hughes sometimes lived with his grandmother. While attending high school in Cleveland, Ohio, where his mother had moved with her new husband, Hughes began writing poems that were published in his school's literary magazine. These poems were written in traditionally rhymed and metered verse modeled after the work of the African American poet Paul Laurence Dunbar (1872–1906). However, Hughes was also influenced by some less conventional poets, such as Carl Sandburg (1878–1967) and Walt Whitman (1819–1892).

After graduating from high school, Hughes traveled by train to Mexico to spend a year with his father. He wrote one of his most famous poems, "The Negro Speaks of Rivers," during that journey. Hughes persuaded his father to pay for a year at Columbia University in New York City, where he was supposed to study engineering. But once he reached Harlem, Hughes dove wholeheartedly into the creative life thriving there. In the spring of 1921 he dropped out of Columbia. The next winter, he penned "The Weary Blues" in a voice that imitates those of piano players in the Harlem nightclubs that Hughes frequented. Writing in free verse (poetry that does not employ regular rhyme, rhythm, or other traditional patterns), Hughes used the images and rhythms of the blues to convey the spirit, strength, and cultural richness of the poem's setting.

Eager to see the world, Hughes took a job as a cook on a freighter and traveled to Africa and Europe, finally landing in Paris. He was working as a busboy in a restaurant there when he received a visit from Alain Locke (1886–1954), an older, highly influential Harlem Renaissance leader. Locke was gathering work for an issue of *Survey Graphic* magazine that was to focus on the accomplishments of young African American writers and artists; Hughes gave Locke some poems. Meanwhile, "The Weary Blues" had been published in *Opportunity,* one of the leading new magazines targeted to a black audience. After returning to New York, Hughes won a prize for the poem in the magazine's annual poetry contest.

By this time Hughes had met Carl Van Vechten (1880–1964), a well-connected white writer and critic who was an enthusiastic supporter of African American artists. Van Vechten sent a manuscript of Hughes's poems to publisher Alfred A. Knopf, resulting in the appearance of a volume titled *The Weary Blues* in 1926. Although some commentators, especially the older, more conservative leaders of the Harlem Renaissance, accused Hughes of presenting a negative picture of African Americans, most critics had a high regard for his work. They praised Hughes for his authentic, colorful, and compassionate portrait of both the beautiful and ugly aspects of black life.

Langston Hughes penned "The Weary Blues" in a voice that imitates those of piano players like the one pictured here often found in the Harlem nightclubs of the 1920s. *(Getty Images. Reproduced by permission.)*

Things to remember while reading this excerpt from "The Weary Blues" . . .

Like other writers of the Harlem Renaissance, Hughes wanted to celebrate, but not sanitize, the African American heritage that he cherished. In his poetry he aimed to speak in a voice that was both personal and authentic, that expressed his own feelings but was spoken as people really talked and was thus accessible to a wide audience. He wanted to portray black people's lives in a way that was both realistic and dignified.

Hughes's gritty portrayal of the seedy side of African American culture (such as poverty and prostitution) was not appreciated by the Talented Tenth. This was the name given by black leader W.E.B. Du Bois (1868–1963) to the upper crust

Countee Cullen: Favorite of the Talented Tenth

Unlike Langston Hughes, Harlem Renaissance poet Countee Cullen was a favorite of the "Talented Tenth," which was black leader W.E.B. Du Bois's term for the most educated and accomplished segment of African American society. Whereas the poetry of Langston Hughes was written in jazz-inflected free verse and embraced the entire spectrum of black life, Cullen used traditional forms and focused on more universal subject matter.

Born around 1903, Cullen's early childhood was spent in the care of a woman thought to have been his grandmother. He was adopted in 1918 by Reverend Frederick Cullen and his wife. Cullen's adoptive parents were civil rights advocates and active in the National Association for the Advancement of Colored People (NAACP). Cullen absorbed their political values, but did not share their religious beliefs.

Cullen was an excellent student, and he began to write and publish his poetry while still in high school. Soon after graduating in 1922, he became involved with a group of writers who met regularly at the Harlem branch of the New York Public Library. Well-liked for his gentlemanly manners and sunny personality, Cullen, like Du Bois, believed in projecting a positive image to gain respect, both as an individual and as an African American in a predominantly white society.

While attending New York University, Cullen won a prominent poetry prize for "The Ballad of a Brown Girl," a poem that highlights his awareness of racial strife. In 1925 he won three more major awards, including one from *Opportunity*, a leading black magazine. That same year Cullen's first collection of poetry, *Color*, was published. This volume included some of his best known works, including "Yet Do I Marvel," in which the narrator wonders why God created him as a black poet in a world too racist to accept either him or his poetry.

Cullen received a master's degree from Harvard University in 1926, and then became an assistant editor at *Opportunity*. He also began writing a weekly column commenting on literature. One of the views he expressed was that African American poets should not expose the more unpleasant aspects of black life, but should focus more on universal subjects and themes. By the end of the 1920s, Cullen had published several more volumes of poetry, including *The Ballad of a Brown Girl* and *Copper Sun,* and an anthology of poems by African Americans.

In 1928 Cullen married Du Bois's daughter Nina, but the couple divorced two years later. Soon after the wedding Cullen traveled to France, where he authored a book of poetry and his one novel. Neither received much critical praise. Returning to the United States, Cullen taught French and English in a Harlem high school, a job he held throughout the rest of his life. He published several more books of poetry and two collections of children's stories. After Cullen's death in 1946, a branch of the New York Public Library was named for him.

of African American society, whose members, it was hoped, would help bring about racial progress through their abilities and achievements. Du Bois and others felt that exposing the less positive aspects of black life would merely confirm the racist assumptions of many whites.

"The Weary Blues" was one of several poems printed on the walls of the Dark Tower, a nightclub and literary gathering place on Striver's Row, where the richest residents of Harlem lived. The Dark Tower was located in the elegant home of A'lelia Walker, heir to the fortune of Madame C.J. Walker, who had made millions through the manufacture of black hair care products. During the Harlem Renaissance, the Dark Tower was *the* place for both black and white enthusiasts of African American culture to see and be seen.

Excerpt from "The Weary Blues"

*Droning a drowsy **syncopated** tune,*

*Rocking back and forth to a mellow **croon**,*

I heard a Negro play.

*Down on **Lenox Avenue** the other night*

*By the pale dull **pallor** of an old gas light*

He did a lazy sway . . .

He did a lazy sway . . .

To the tune o' those Weary Blues.

With his ebony hands on each ivory key

He made that poor piano moan with melody.

O Blues!

Swaying to and fro on his rickety stool

He played that sad raggy tune like a musical fool.

Sweet Blues!

Coming from a black man's soul.

Syncopated: A rhythmic pattern typical of jazz or blues, where the beats or accents are displaced so that the beats that would usually be strong become weak and vice versa.

Croon: A soft, low kind of singing.

Lenox Avenue: A well-known street in Harlem.

Pallor: An unhealthy paleness.

O Blues!

In a deep song voice with a melancholy tone

I heard that Negro sing, that old piano moan–

"Ain't got nobody in all this world,

Ain't got nobody but ma self.

*I's **gwine** to quit ma frownin'*

And put ma troubles on the shelf."

Thump, thump, thump, went his foot on the floor.

He played a few chords then he sang some more–

"I got the Weary Blues

And I can't be satisfied.

Got the Weary Blues

And can't be satisfied–

I ain't happy no mo'

And I wish that I had died."

And far into the night he crooned that tune.

The stars went out and so did the moon.

The singer stopped playing and went to bed

While the Weary Blues echoed through his head.

He slept like a rock or a man that's dead.

What happened next . . .

Hughes continued to create his detailed portraits of Harlem life in *Fine Clothes to the Jew* (1927), which features finely crafted poems written in the language of the streets. In 1930, a year after Hughes graduated from Lincoln University in Pennsylvania, his novel *Not Without Laughter* was published. Centered on a black family living in mostly white Kansas, the novel was not highly acclaimed. The next year Hughes began a successful poetry-reading tour of the

Gwine: African American dialect for "going."

Langston Hughes continued to write poetry and lecture on black history and culture until his death in 1967. *(Getty Images. Reproduced by permission.)*

South, during which he was warmly received at numerous black colleges. His interest in socialism (a political and economic system by which the means of production and distribution are owned by the community as a whole) inspired him to spend some time in the Soviet Union. Soon after his return, he wrote the short stories that appeared in *The Ways of White Folk* (1934).

During the Great Depression, the period of economic hardship that followed on the heels of the prosperous 1920s, Hughes's poetry became much darker, reflecting the suffering endured by blacks during these years. He remained busy over the next several decades, producing poetry and plays as well as a weekly column for the *Chicago Defender* newspaper. The volume titled *Montage of a Dream Deferred* (1951) contains some of Hughes's most powerful poems. For example, the poem titled "Harlem" asks "What happens to a dream deferred?" Up until his death in 1967, Hughes continued to write poetry and to lecture on black history and culture.

Did you know . . .

- As the Harlem Renaissance drew to a close, several important relationships in Hughes's life also ended. He made a break with Charlotte Mason (1854–1946), an elderly white supporter of African American culture who had given him both moral and financial support but who had become too controlling of his work. Hughes's friendship with Zora Neale Hurston also came to an end over a disagreement about a play called *Mule Bone* that the two had worked on together.

- At Hughes's funeral, a song by Duke Ellington (1899–1974), one of the most prominent jazz musicians of the Harlem Renaissance, called "Do Nothing Until You Hear from Me" was played. Then his friends gathered in a circle and recited Hughes's early poem "The Negro Speaks of Rivers" as his body was wheeled away to be cremated. This poem evokes the connections between black people and the great rivers of the world, including the Nile in Egypt, the Congo in southern Africa, and the Mississippi in the United States. It concludes with the words "My soul has grown deep like rivers."

Consider this . . .

- The popular image of the 1920s is that it was a time of prosperity, fun, and frivolity. How does Hughes's poem present a different view of life during this decade?

- Compare this poem with one written by an earlier African American poet, like Paul Laurence Dunbar. Describe the styles of the two writers, and explain why each may have written the way he did.

For More Information

Books

Berry, Faith. *Langston Hughes: Before and Beyond Harlem.* Westport, CT: Lawrence Hill, 1983.

Bloom, Harold, ed. *Langston Hughes: Comprehensive Research and Study Guide.* Broomall, PA: Chelsea House, 1999.

Emanuel, James. *Langston Hughes.* New York: Twayne, 1967.

Hill, Christine. *Langston Hughes: Poet of the Harlem Renaissance.* Hillside, NJ: Enslow Publishers, 1997.

Web Sites

"Langston Hughes." *Poetry Exhibits. Academy of American Poets.* Available online at http://www.poets.org/poets/poets.cfm?45442B7C000C0E01. Accessed on June 20, 2005.

"Langston Hughes (1902–1967)." *Modern American Poetry.* Available online at http://www.english.uiuc.edu/maps/poets/g_l/hughes/hughes.htm. Accessed on June 20, 2005.

5

Clarence Darrow

Closing Argument in the Leopold and Loeb Trial
Published in 1924

> "Your Honor stands between the past and the future. You may hang these boys; you may hang them by the neck until they are dead. But in doing it you will turn your face toward the past."

In the late spring of 1924 the nation was shocked by the news of a kidnapping and murder in Chicago, Illinois. Nathan Leopold and Richard Loeb, two nineteen-year-olds from wealthy families, had confessed to the brutal killing of fourteen-year-old Bobby Franks. The young men had shown no remorse, admitting that they had plotted for some time to commit the perfect crime. Their plan was spoiled when Leopold left his eyeglasses at the scene, which eventually led to their arrest. The public expressed outrage at the crime, with many declaring that the killers, popularly characterized as "spoiled brats," deserved the death penalty.

Hoping to spare their children from such a fate, the families of Leopold and Loeb hired the famous lawyer Clarence Darrow (1857–1938) to defend them. A Chicago attorney in his late sixties, Darrow had earned a reputation as a champion of the underdog through his defense of union leaders, antiwar activists, and others. He was also a strong opponent of capital punishment (the death penalty) and had already saved more than one hundred clients from execution.

Richard Loeb (right) and Nathan Leopold (left) during their murder trial.
(© Underwood & Underwood/Corbis. Reproduced by permission.)

Through interviews with Leopold and Loeb, Darrow concluded that the young men did not know the difference between right and wrong. But he did not want to pursue an insanity plea (that is, one based on the idea that the defendants were innocent because they had not known what they were doing), because that would force a jury trial. Darrow knew that public sentiment was against the young men, and that a jury would be likely to condemn them to death. Instead, he directed his clients to enter a guilty plea, which meant that a judge would determine their fate. Darrow planned to appeal to the judge to spare the young men's lives based on their youth and their deranged personalities.

The trial began in July, with Darrow arguing his case before Chief Justice John Caverly. Darrow produced three psychiatrists as expert witnesses who testified that, as Darrow stated as quoted in Nathan Miller's *New World Coming: The 1920s and the Making of Modern America,* the crime had been "the act of immature and diseased brains." In a powerful but lengthy closing statement, which lasted twelve hours and stretched out over two days, Darrow made no attempt to downplay the horror of the crime or his clients' guilt. Instead, he asked for mercy on the grounds of the young men's age, their mental condition, and the general inhumanity of capital punishment. In the last part of the statement, excerpted here, Darrow calls on Judge Caverly to look toward the future, when, he suggests, the execution of criminals will be viewed as a brutal practice of the past.

Things to remember while reading this excerpt from Darrow's closing argument . . .

The case of Leopold and Loeb was one of several that were popularly labeled "crimes of the century." Newspapers as well as the new medium of radio both helped to inform the public and to sensationalize (make exciting, often at the expense of accuracy, in order to attract public attention) the crime and the trial. Some observers saw this seemingly irrational crime as evidence of the moral breakdown of traditional U.S. society and as a sign of more senseless violence to come.

Part of the public's shock over the case was due to the background of the people involved. Leopold and Loeb were not only wealthy (as was their victim) but also intelligent young men, both had scored high on IQ tests and graduated from high school early, with promising futures. They were both graduate students at the University of Chicago, and Leopold was set to attend Harvard Law School in the fall. They had planned and executed the murder with precision and emotional detachment. As quoted in Miller's book, Leopold later said that he had felt nothing more than an entomologist (a scientist who studies insects) would when "impaling a butterfly on a pin."

Darrow's appearance in the courtroom was not particularly impressive. A tall man with a slouching posture, his face was craggy and tired-looking and his clothing rumpled. But

Freudianism Becomes a Fad

The Roaring Twenties were a time of major breakthroughs in science, technology, and medicine. The theories of groundbreaking Austrian psychiatrist Sigmund Freud (1856–1939), who is recognized as one of the most influential thinkers of the twentieth century, were especially popular during this period. Aspects of Freudianism, as his theories are called, found their way into the conversations of both highly educated and ordinary people, as well as magazine and journal articles, literary works, and some court cases.

Freud's ideas were developed during the two decades leading up to the 1920s. In such works as *Studies on Hysteria* (1895), *The Interpretation of Dreams* (1900), and *The Origin and Development of Psychoanalysis* (1910), Freud proposed that childhood experiences could determine a person's behavior as an adult, particularly in cases of mental illness, even if the actual memories of specific incidents had been forgotten or buried.

Previously, those involved in treating mental illness had relied on the conscious, or surface awareness, of people's thoughts and personalities. Freud focused on the subconscious (the part of the mind of which one is unaware) to explain neurotic (abnormally sensitive, anxious, or obsessive) behavior and psychological problems. He believed that through psychoanalysis (talking with a specially trained analyst) deeply hidden causes to psychological problems could be exposed and addressed.

Freud's theories were scientific and complex, and thus his work was not accessible to most readers. In the early 1920s, however, several summaries of his work became available, and a mass audience was exposed to simplified, and sometimes distorted, explanations of Freudianism. Words like *sublimate* (to divert an instinctual impulse into a more socially acceptable form) and *inferiority complex* were fashionable cocktail party talk, and it became a common pastime to psychoanalyze one's friends. A particularly popular game based on the work of Freud's student Carl Jung involved answering a series of forty questions to determine one's personality type.

All of this alarmed Freud, who worried that unqualified and poorly informed people were carelessly applying his theories. Other people agreed, but some of them blamed Freud himself rather than the mass popularity that Freudianism had achieved. Those who criticized Freud often pointed to his emphasis on the role of sexual repression in neurosis; they felt that Freud was encouraging people to be sexually free and irresponsible.

Darrow's passionate stance against the death penalty and his gift for public speaking made him a formidable force. It was rumored that his rich clients had paid Darrow $1,000,000, but in fact his fee was less than $100,000.

Excerpt from Darrow's closing argument

*Now, I must say a word more and then I will leave this with you where I should have left it long ago. None of us are **unmindful** of the public; courts are not, and juries are not. We placed our fate in the hands of a trained court, thinking that he would be more mindful and considerate than a jury. I cannot say how people feel. I have stood here for three months as one might stand at the ocean trying to sweep back the tide. I hope the seas are subsiding and the wind is falling and I believe they are, but I wish to make no false pretense to this court. The easy thing and the popular thing to do is to hang my clients. I know it. Men and women who do not think will applaud. The cruel and the thoughtless will approve. It will be easy today; but in Chicago, and reaching out over the length and breadth of the land, more and more fathers and mothers, the humane, the kind and the hopeful, who are gaining an understanding and asking questions not only about these poor boys, but about their own—these will join in no **acclaim** at the death of my clients. These would ask that the shedding of blood be stopped, and that the normal feelings of man **resume their sway**. And as the days and the months and the years go on, they will ask it more and more. But, your Honor, what they shall ask may not count. I know the easy way.*

*I know your Honor stands between the future and the past. I know the future is with me, and what I stand for here; not merely for the lives of these two unfortunate lads, but for all boys and all girls; for all of the young, and as far as possible, for all of the old. I am pleading for life, understanding, charity, kindness, and the infinite mercy that considers all. I am pleading that we overcome cruelty with kindness and hatred with love. I know the future is on my side. Your Honor stands between the past and the future. You may hang these boys; you may hang them by the neck until they are dead. But in doing it you will turn your face toward the past. In doing it you are making it harder for every other boy who in ignorance and darkness must **grope** his way through the mazes which only childhood knows. In doing it you will make it harder for unborn children. You may save them and make it easier for every child that some time may stand where these boys stand. You will make it easier for every human being with an **aspiration** and a vision and a hope and a fate. I am pleading for the future; I am*

Unmindful: Not paying attention to.

Acclaim: Praise.

Resume their sway: Return to normal.

Grope: Feel one's way with uncertainty.

Aspiration: Goal.

Defense attorney Clarence Darrow presenting his closing arguments in the Leopold and Loeb case. *(© Bettmann/Corbis. Reproduced by permission.)*

pleading for a time when hatred and cruelty will not control the hearts of men. When we can learn by reason and judgement and understanding and faith that all life is worth saving, and that mercy is the highest **attribute** of man.

I feel that I should apologize for the length of time I have taken. This case may not be as important as I think it is, and I am sure I do not need to tell this court, or to tell my friends that I would fight just as hard for the poor as for the rich. If I should succeed in saving these boys' lives and do nothing for the progress of the law, I should feel sad, indeed. If I can succeed, my greatest reward and my greatest hope will be that I have done something for the tens of thousands of other boys, for the countless unfortunates who must tread the same road in blind childhood that these poor boys have trod—that I have done something to help human understanding, to **temper** justice with mercy, to overcome hate with

Attribute: Quality, characteristic.

Temper: Balance.

love. I was reading last night of the aspiration of the old Persian poet, Omar Khayyam. It appealed to me as the highest that I can vision. I wish it was in my heart, and I wish it was in the hearts of all:

"So I be written in the Book of Love

I do not care about that Book above.

Erase my name or write it as you will,

So I be written in the book of Love."

What happened next . . .

On September 10, 1924, Judge Caverly (who had received threats against both his own and his wife's life from people on both sides of the issue) announced his decision. Given the defendants' youth, the judge said, he had decided to sentence them to life in prison rather than execution.

After his involvement in one of the "crimes of the century," Darrow went on to participate in what would be called "the trial of the century." In 1925 he went to the small town of Dayton, Tennessee, to defend high school teacher John Scopes, who had been arrested for teaching the scientific theory of evolution to his students. In doing so Scopes had violated a recently enacted Tennessee law intended to uphold the traditional, Bible-based belief that God had created each species separately. Assisting the prosecution was William Jennings Bryan (1860–1925), a noted conservative politician and activist (see William Jennings Bryan's Undelivered Closing Statement from the Scopes Trial Primary Sources entry). During the trial, Darrow called Bryan to the stand to defend his literal interpretation of the Bible. Although Scopes was convicted, Darrow was credited with an intellectual victory. The next year, he successfully defended Henry Sweet, an African American charged with murder. The killing had occurred when Henry and his brother Ossian, who had moved into a white neighborhood, tried to defend Ossian's home against a hostile mob.

Darrow died in 1938. Meanwhile, Loeb was killed in a prison fight in 1936, while Leopold was paroled in 1958 and lived until 1971.

Defense attorney Clarence Darrow (center) sits with his clients Nathan Leopold (right) and Richard Loeb (left) after they are found guilty of the kidnapping and murder of Bobby Franks. *(© Bettmann/Corbis. Reproduced by permission.)*

Did you know . . .

- When questioned about why they had committed the murder, Leopold and Loeb mentioned their interest in the ideas of German philosopher Friedrich Nietzsche (1844–1900). The young men claimed to see themselves as examples of Nietzsche's "superman," who is driven by a strong will to exert power over others and who is immune to all moral and social rules.

- During their years in prison, Leopold and Loeb remained friends and worked together to set up a school for inmates. In 1936 Loeb was killed by a prisoner who claimed that Loeb had made sexual advances toward him. Leopold was released after spending thirty-three years in prison. He went to live in

Puerto Rico, where he became an ornithologist (bird expert) and published a book on the birds of his new home. He married in 1961 and died ten years later, insisting to the end of his life that it was Loeb who was primarily responsible for the murder of Bobby Franks.

Consider the following . . .

- Clarence Darrow was strongly opposed to capital punishment, even in the case of a criminal who confessed to a horrible murder. The case of Sacco and Vanzetti was very different from that of Leopold and Loeb, but it also involved the issue of the death penalty. Compare and contrast the two cases.

- Knowing the extent of the public outrage against his clients and wishing to avoid a jury trial, Darrow chose not to enter an insanity plea. If the trial took place today, do you think he would make the same decision? How much have people's ideas about the insanity defense changed or stayed the same? Research a recent court case to help you shape your thoughts.

For More Information

Books

Driemen, John E. *Clarence Darrow*. New York: Chelsea House, 1992.

Hanson, Erica. *The 1920s*. San Diego, CA: Lucent Books, 1999.

Higdon, Hal. *Crime of the Century: The Leopold & Loeb Case*. New York: Putnam, 1975.

Larson, Edward J. *Trial and Error: The American Controversy over Creation and Evolution*. New York: Oxford University Press, 1994.

Miller, Nathan. *New World Coming: The 1920s and the Making of Modern America*. New York: Scribner, 2003.

Tierney, Kevin. *Darrow: A Biography*. New York: Thomas Y. Crowell, 1979.

Weinberg, Arthur, and Lila Weinberg. *Clarence Darrow: A Sentimental Rebel*. New York: Putnam, 1980.

Web Sites

"Famous American Trials: Illinois versus Nathan Leopold and Richard Loeb." *Famous Trials by Doug Linder*. Available online at http://www.law.umkc.edu/faculty/projects/ftrials/leoploeb/leopold.htm. Accessed on June 20, 2005.

F. Scott Fitzgerald

Excerpt from **The Great Gatsby**
Published in 1925

Although F. Scott Fitzgerald (1896–1940) is now considered one of the most important figures in twentieth-century American literature, he was not highly regarded at the time of his death in 1940. He did enjoy a brief period of fame and success during the 1920s, when he used vivid language and imagery to bring the Jazz Age (a term that he himself coined) to life in his popular stories and novels.

Fitzgerald was born to fairly well-off parents in St. Paul, Minnesota. He showed an early interest in writing and drama and pursued both at Princeton University, which he attended for two years. He never graduated, leaving in 1917 to join the army. Fitzgerald served for fifteen months but, to his disappointment, was never sent overseas to fight in World War I (1914–18). While stationed at an army camp near Montgomery, Alabama, he met and fell in love with Zelda Sayre, the wealthy daughter of an Alabama Supreme Court judge.

Returning to St. Paul, Fitzgerald continued work on an autobiographical novel he had begun during his army days. Eventually titled *This Side of Paradise,* the manuscript was

"As the moon rose higher the inessential houses began to melt away until gradually I became aware of the old island here that flowered once for Dutch sailors' eyes fresh, green breast of the new world"

A scene from the 1949 film version of *The Great Gatsby.* *(© Bettmann/Corbis. Reproduced by permission.)*

accepted by Scribner's and published in 1920. Fitzgerald received rave reviews for his portrayal of Amory Blaine, who was seen as representative of postwar youth. The newly successful Fitzgerald soon married Zelda and began a life of travel and adventure with her. Over the next two years, he produced several volumes of short stories and a second novel, *The Beautiful and the Damned.*

The excerpt featured here is drawn from *The Great Gatsby,* the novel considered Fitzgerald's masterpiece. Published in 1925, it features the skillful use of a first-person narrator, young Nick Carroway. Like his creator, Nick is a native of the midwestern United States and an army veteran who now lives and works on the East Coast. The novel takes place on Long Island (located close to New York City) in the summer of 1922. Nick has rented a home on West Egg, a section of the island that is across a bay from East Egg, where the area's most established, wealthy residents live. Nick's unhappily married cousin Daisy Buchanan lives there with her husband, Tom, and their daughter. Next to Nick's modest rented cottage is a huge, extravagantly decorated home owned by Jay Gatsby, who is rumored to have grown rich through the buying and selling of illegal liquor.

Nick soon learns that Gatsby and Daisy had a brief romance several years before while Gatsby was a young soldier with little money. After Gatsby went overseas to fight in World War I, Daisy married Tom Buchanan, a member of her own social class. Gatsby still loves Daisy and involves Nick in his quest to win her back. In a tragic series of events, the characters attend a drunken party in New York, during which they quarrel and then begin the drive back to Long Island. On the way, Gatsby's car hits and kills Myrtle Wilson, Tom's mistress. Although it is assumed that Gatsby was in the driver's seat, Daisy was actually driving; nevertheless, Gatsby intends to take the blame for the accident. Meanwhile, Tom has allowed Myrtle's grief-crazed husband to believe that Gatsby is responsible. Wilson kills Gatsby and then himself. Nick arranges Gatsby's funeral, but only two other people show up: Gatsby's deluded father and one of the many guests from Gatsby's lavish summer parties. In the end, the disillusioned Nick decides to return to the Midwest.

One of the novel's dominant themes involves the decay of traditional American values in a suddenly prosperous society. Fitzgerald draws a contrast between the immorality and shallowness of the East and the innocence and virtue of the West, highlighting the persistence of illusions and dreams in the face of sordid reality.

Things to remember while reading this excerpt from *The Great Gatsby* . . .

In creating this richly detailed portrait of life among wealthy New Yorkers, Fitzgerald called upon his own experiences in that environment. Certainly he had attended many lavish Long Island parties like those Gatsby hosts, and the colorful variety of characters in the novel, from flappers to gangsters to intellectuals, no doubt reflects the spectrum of his own acquaintances.

While writing *The Great Gatsby,* **F. Scott Fitzgerald drew upon many of his own experiences as a wealthy New Yorker during the 1920s.** *(© Minnesota Historical Society/Corbis. Reproduced by permission.)*

The effects of Prohibition on U.S. society are strongly felt in the novel. Illegal or not, liquor flows freely at the parties attended by Nick and his friends, and drunkenness is a factor in the novel's final outcome. Furthermore, motivated by his deep desire to impress the wealthy, upper-class Daisy, Gatsby has made his fortune through the shady underworld of bootlegging (the producing, buying, and selling of banned alcoholic beverages).

The Great Gatsby is famous for its intriguing, sometimes ambiguous motifs and symbols. Examples include the use of East Egg to represent the corruption of the eastern United States and West Egg to stand for the Midwest and West, where traditional American values and virtues remain intact. The color green represents not only Gatsby's dream of winning back the idealized Daisy but also the broader American dream. The valley of ashes that lies between Long Island and New York City may symbolize both the moral decay of U.S. society and the plight of the poor people (including Myrtle and her husband) who live in it. Seen on a faded billboard above the valley of ashes, the eyes of Dr. T.J. Eckleburg may suggest the eyes of God, or they may be assigned different meanings by different individuals.

Excerpt from *The Great Gatsby*

(From Chapter III)

There was music from my neighbor's [Jay Gatsby's] house through the summer nights. In his blue gardens men and girls came and went like moths among the whisperings and the champagne and the stars. At high tide in the afternoon I watched his guests diving from the tower of his raft, or taking the sun on the hot sand of his beach while his two motor-boats slit the waters of the Sound, drawing aquaplanes over cataracts of foam. On weekends his Rolls-Royce became an omnibus, bearing parties to and from the city between nine in the morning and long past midnight, while his station wagon scampered like a brisk yellow bug to meet all trains. And on Mondays eight servants, including an extra gardener, toiled all day with mops and scrubbing-brushes and hammers and garden shears, repairing the ravages of the night before.

Every Friday five crates of oranges and lemons arrived from a fruiterer in New York—every Monday these same oranges and lemons left his back door in a pyramid of pulpless halves. There was a machine in the kitchen which could extract the juice of two hundred oranges in half an hour as if a little button was pressed two hundred times by a butler's thumb.

At least once a **fortnight** a corps of caterers came down with several hundred feet of canvas and enough colored lights to make a Christmas tree of Gatsby's enormous garden. On buffet tables, garnished with glittering **hors d'oeuvre**, spiced baked hams crowded against salads of **harlequin** designs and pastry pigs and turkeys bewitched to a dark gold. In the main hall a bar with a real brass rail was set up, and stocked with gins and liquors and with **cordials** so long forgotten that most of his female guests were too young to know one from another.

Fortnight: Two weeks.

Hors d'oeuvre: Foods served as appetizers.

Harlequin: In varied colors.

Cordial: A kind of liquor.

By seven o'clock the orchestra has arrived, no thin five piece affair, but a whole pitful of oboes and trombones and saxophones and viols and cornets and piccolos, and low and high drums. The last swimmers have come in from the beach now and are dressing upstairs; the cars from New York are parked five deep in the drive, and already the halls and **salons** and **verandas** are gaudy with primary colors, and hair shorn in strange new ways, and **shawls beyond the dreams of Castile**. The bar is in full swing, and floating rounds of cocktails permeate the garden, outside until the air is alive with chatter and laughter, and casual **innuendo** and introductions forgotten on the spot, and enthusiastic meetings between women who never knew each other's names.

The lights grow brighter as the earth lurches away from the sun, and now the orchestra is playing yellow cocktail music, and the opera of voices pitches a key higher. Laughter is easier minute by minute, spilled with **prodigality**, tipped out at a cheerful word. The groups change more swiftly, swell with new arrivals, dissolve and form in the same breath; already there are wanderers, confident girls who weave here and there among the stouter and more stable, become for a sharp, joyous moment the center of a group, and then, excited with triumph, glide on through the sea-change of faces and voices and color under the constantly changing light.

Suddenly one of these gypsies, in trembling opal, seizes a cocktail out of the air, dumps it down for courage and, moving her hands like Frisco, dances out alone on the canvas platform. A momentary hush; the orchestra leader varies his rhythm obligingly for her, and there is a burst of chatter as the **erroneous** news goes around that she is **Gilda Gray's understudy from the Follies**. The party has begun.

(From Chapter IX)

Most of the big shore places were closed now and there were hardly any lights except the shadowy, moving glow of a ferryboat across the **Sound**. And as the moon rose higher the inessential houses began to melt away until gradually I became aware of the old island here that flowered once for Dutch sailors' eyes fresh—green breast of the new world. Its vanished trees, the trees that had made way for Gatsby's house, had once pandered in whispers to the last and greatest of all human dreams; for a transitory enchanted moment man must have held his breath in the presence of this continent, compelled into an **aesthetic** contemplation he neither understood nor desired, face to face for the last time in history with something **commensurate** to his capacity for wonder.

Salons: An elegant drawing room.

Verandas: Long open roofed poarches.

Shawls beyond the dreams of Castile: Colorful shawls were characteristic of the traditional clothing of Spain; Fitzgerald suggests that these were even more impressive.

Innuendo: Hint.

Prodigality: Wasteful extravagance.

Erroneous: Incorrect.

Gilda Gray's understudy from the Follies: A reference to a dancer in the *Ziegfeld's Follies* musical variety shows that were popular with New York audiences.

Sound: A long passage of water often connecting two larger bodies of water.

Aesthetic: Concerned with beauty.

Commensurate: Equal.

William Faulkner: Chronicling Southern Society

Like F. Scott Fitzgerald, William Faulkner was a major twentieth-century novelist who captured the essence of a particular place and time. In Faulkner's case, the place was the southern United States, and the time was the first several decades of the twentieth century. Praised for his modernist style and the psychological depth he brought to his characters, Faulkner wrote several of his best known novels during the 1920s.

Born in 1897 in New Albany, Mississippi, Faulkner grew up in the nearby town of Oxford. He was educated sporadically after the fifth grade and never graduated from high school, but he loved to read and write.

Faulkner served briefly in the military during World War I before being discharged after being injured in an airplane crash. After spending a year as a student at the University of Mississippi in 1919, Faulkner traveled to New York City. He soon returned to Mississippi, but left again to travel in Europe. He returned to the United States in 1926.

The same year he returned from Europe, Faulkner's first novel, *Soldier's Pay*, was published, with another following in 1927. It was not until his third novel, however, that Faulkner's writing started to gain attention. *Sartoris* (1927) is the first of a series of novels Faulkner set in fictional Yoknapatawpha County, Mississippi. It centers on an alienated veteran named Bayard Sartoris, who sinks into drinking and self-destructive behavior after returning from war.

Sartoris introduces several families that are featured in many of Faulkner's novels and short stories. These include the Sartoris and Compson clans, who represent the faded southern aristocracy, and the Snopes family, who embody the South's new merchant class.

The Sound and the Fury (1929) is considered to be Faulkner's masterpiece. Focused on the tragic history of the dysfunctional Compsons, the novel is written in four parts in an untraditional, stream-of-consciousness style. Each section records the events of one day (three of them in 1928 and one in 1910) from the perspective of four different characters. The book is considered difficult to follow, but this has not affected critical praise for the book. *The Sound and the Fury* relays with loss, despair, and cruelty the Compsons' experience as their family fortunes and relationships fall apart.

Faulkner's other acclaimed novels of this period include *As I Lay Dying* (1930), *Sanctuary* (1931) and *Light in August* (1932). Most critics find Faulkner's later works inferior to those he wrote in the late 1920s and early 1930s. *Pylon* (1935) failed to earn critical praise, while the complex *Absalom, Absalom!* (1936), received mixed reviews. In addition to his many novels, Faulkner's short stories are very well regarded, and some, such as "The Bear" and "A Rose for Emily" appear often in anthologies.

Faulkner received the Nobel Prize for Literature in 1949. He lived quietly in Oxford until his death in 1962.

And as I sat there, brooding on the old, unknown world, I thought of Gatsby's wonder when he first picked out the green light at the end of Daisy's dock. He had come a long way to this blue lawn, and his dream must have seemed so close that he could hardly fail to grasp it. He did not know that it was already behind him, somewhere back in that vast obscurity beyond the city, where the dark fields of the republic rolled on under the night.

*Gatsby believed in the green light, the **orgiastic** future that year by year recedes before us. It eluded us then, but that's no matter—tomorrow we will run faster, stretch out our arms farther And one fine morning—*

So we beat on, boats against the current, borne back ceaselessly into the past.

What happened next . . .

After completing *The Great Gatsby,* Fitzgerald started writing his fourth novel. The work went slowly, due not only to the many changes the author made but also to his alcoholism, his mounting debts, and Zelda's mental illness (which, beginning in 1930, frequently required her to be hospitalized). A short story collection that appeared in 1927, *All the Sad Young Men,* contains some of his best writing. Fitzgerald worked briefly as a screenwriter in Hollywood before producing another novel, *Tender Is the Night* (1934). Although many of his friends admired the novel, which once again centers on the spiritual emptiness of rich young Americans, few reviewers and readers seemed to like it. By this time the Great Depression had begun, and it may be that audiences had little patience for the problems of the wealthy.

Throughout the 1930s, Fitzgerald lived in Maryland and North Carolina, publishing little while his debts continued to increase. In 1937 he again went to Hollywood to work as a screenwriter, employed first by the Metro-Goldwyn-Mayer film company and later becoming a freelancer. Fitzgerald worked on fourteen films, including the hugely popular *Gone with the Wind* (1939), but was credited on only one of them. His experiences in Hollywood provided material for his final novel,

Orgiastic: Unrestrained, free, limitless.

The Last Tycoon, a portrait of the filmmaking industry that he never finished. Fitzgerald died of a sudden heart attack in December 1940, at the age of forty-four. His work was mostly overlooked until the 1950s and 1960s, when his literary reputation began to improve. Fitzgerald is now regarded as a major twentieth-century author.

Did you know . . .

- Despite very positive critical reviews, *The Great Gatsby* was not popular with a broad audience at its first appearance. Only twenty-four thousand copies were printed, and the book was not reprinted during Fitzgerald's lifetime. The novel's unlikable characters and dark themes as well as its sophisticated style may have turned away many readers.

- Fitzgerald and his beautiful wife, Zelda, epitomized the glamorous, carefree life of the wealthy elite during the Roaring Twenties. In fact, Zelda is thought to have been the model for Daisy Buchanan. Like Gatsby, Fitzgerald had once been a young soldier in love with an upper-class, seemingly unattainable girl. A parallel with the Fitzgeralds' real life may also be found in *Tender Is the Night,* which chronicles a young couple's struggles with the wife's mental illness.

- Fitzgerald's friends included some of the best-known literary figures of the period. He championed the early work of innovative writer Ernest Hemingway (1899–1961), who greatly admired Fitzgerald but eventually spoke disapprovingly of him for not trying hard enough to produce his best writing. In the 1950s another close friend, critic Edmund Wilson (1895–1972), helped to restore respect for Fitzgerald's achievements.

Consider the following . . .

- How does this passage reflect the changes that were so much a part of life in the 1920s? In framing your answer, you might want to think about advances in transportation and technology, Prohibition, the emphasis on prosperity and material success, and women's roles.

- How do characters like Nick Carroway, Jay Gatsby, Daisy Buchanon, and Myrtle Wilson embody different aspects of life in the Twenties? Think about how they fit into both the specific social world around them and the wider U.S. society. Compare and contrast the characters, or do an in-depth study of one.

For More Information

Books

Bruccoli, Matthew, ed. *F. Scott Fitzgerald in His Own Times: A Miscellany.* Kent, OH: Kent State University Press, 1971.

Lehan, Richard. *The Great Gatsby: The Limits of Wonder.* Boston: Twayne, 1990.

Medlow, James R. *Invented Lives: F. Scott Fitzgerald and Zelda Fitzgerald.* New York: Houghton Mifflin, 1984.

Web Sites

The F. Scott Fitzgerald Society. Available online at http://www.fitzgerald society.org/. Accessed on June 20, 2005.

William Jennings Bryan

Undelivered Closing Statement from the Scopes Trial
Published in 1925

T he 1920s was a period of great change in the United
States, and the changes made some people uncomfortable. The clash between traditional values, especially religious
fundamentalism (a strict form of Christianity based on the
belief that the events in the Bible are true, rather than stories
told to illustrate moral lessons), and modern trends was perhaps never more apparent than during the Scopes trial. This
widely publicized, much discussed courtroom drama took
place in the summer of 1925. It featured two figures already
famous in public life: Chicago defense attorney Clarence
Darrow (1857–1938) and longtime political leader William
Jennings Bryan (1860–1925). In fact, the man who gave his
name to the trial, defendant John Scopes, seemed to play only
a minor role.

The Scopes trial began with the passage of Tennessee's
Butler Act in January 1925. People who disapproved of the
theory of evolution passed the law. This idea was closely associated with the work of naturalist Charles Darwin (1809–1882),
who outlined the progressive development of human beings
and other species over millions of years. The Butler Act made it

"The case has assumed
the proportions of a
battle-royal between
unbelief that attempts to
speak through so-called
science and the defenders
of the Christian faith,
speaking through the
legislators of Tennessee."

William Jennings Bryan delivering a speech during the Scopes trial.

(© Bettmann/Corbis. Reproduced by permission.)

illegal to teach in public schools any theory that contradicted the story of divine creation found in the Bible. This is the theory of human origin upheld by creationists (people who believe that all living things were created by God and not through evolution). Between 1921 and 1929, thirty-seven bills similar to the Butler Act were introduced in twenty states.

Soon after the passage of the Butler Act, the American Civil Liberties Union (ACLU) offered to assist any Tennessee teacher willing to go to court to test the constitutionality of the act (that is, whether it would be found acceptable under the rules set down in the U.S. Constitution). Urged on by several friends, who disapproved of the law and wanted to bring some attention to their small town, high school science teacher John Scopes accepted the ACLU's offer. Scopes was not even his high school's regular biology teacher; in the spring of 1925, he was substituting for another teacher. In any case, using the same textbook that had been used by the school district before the passage of the new law, Scopes gave his students a lesson on Darwin's theory of evolution. Two weeks later he was arrested and charged with violating the Butler Act.

The case almost immediately attracted nationwide attention, as many people realized its social and legal importance. The prosecutors accepted an offer of assistance from William Jennings Bryan, a former Nebraska congressman, secretary of state, three-time unsuccessful presidential candidate, and devoted fundamentalist (a person who believes the Bible is a complete and accurate historical record). Hearing that Bryan would be involved, the well-known attorney Clarence Darrow volunteered his own services to the defense team. Along with a host of reporters from newspapers around the country, the key players gathered in Dayton during a week of sweltering July heat.

The courtroom proceeding that would come to be known as the "Monkey Trial" (in reference to Darwin's theory about the common ancestors of primates and humans) opened on July 12. Rather than defending Scopes, who openly admitted to violating the law, Darrow planned to prove that the Butler Act was unconstitutional. He never got a chance, failing in his attempt to bring in scientists as expert witnesses to show that there need be no contradiction between religious faith and belief in scientific truths. On July 17 the judge ruled that the expert opinions were not relevant to the question at hand, whether Scopes had broken the law, and were thus inadmissible.

Disappointed and desperate, Darrow decided to put Bryan himself on the witness stand as an expert on the Bible. Despite the objections of the other prosecutors, Bryan readily agreed. Darrow then spent an hour and a half grilling Bryan about his religious beliefs. The exchange made Bryan look foolish, confused, and intellectually shallow.

The following excerpt is from a closing statement that Bryan hoped to make. He was denied the opportunity because Darrow's team chose not to make a closing statement. In the end, in fact, the defense asked the jury to find Scopes guilty so that they could appeal the case to a higher court. The jury obliged, taking only nine minutes to reach a guilty verdict. Scopes was fined one hundred dollars.

Things to remember while reading this excerpt from Bryan's closing statement . . .

The Scopes trial highlighted the 1920s conflict between old and new, between traditional beliefs and values and the modern world, where science seemed to be more influential than religion. Ironically, the man who represented the fundamentalist viewpoint had spent his whole career as a champion of progressivism (the belief that society can and should be changed for the better). William Jennings Bryan had long fought for such liberal reforms as outlawing child labor, regulating businesses, and giving women the right to vote.

According to historian Lynn Dumenil in *The Modern Temper: American Culture and Society in the 1920s,* the Scopes trial was significant because, "despite the image of the roaring twenties and the media hype surrounding the trial, it suggests that religion was a deeply contested issue that mattered to millions of Americans."

The struggle between creationism and evolution continues to this day. In recent decades, defenders of the biblical approach to humanity's origins have argued that creationism should be given equal status with evolutionary theory in the

Charles Darwin's Controversial Theory of Evolution

The conflict between traditional and modern beliefs about the origin of the human species may have come to a head in the Scopes trial, but it began long before the Roaring Twenties. An influential nineteenth-century book by a British scientist provided the original spark for the controversy.

Born in 1809, Charles Darwin studied medicine as a young man but had a passion for collecting plant, animal, and geological specimens, or samples. Offered a position as a biologist on a surveying mission aboard the British navy ship HMS *Beagle,* Darwin spent the years 1831 to 1836 traveling South America and the islands of the South Pacific. His job was to take samples and study new plants, animals, and geological formations that the mission came across. The materials he collected provided him with the foundation for his life's work.

In 1858 Darwin published a paper and, the next year, a bestselling book titled *On the Origin of the Species by Means of Natural Selection.* In it Darwin detailed his theory that different animals could have descended, or evolved, from common ancestors. He proposed that changes in species took place over millions of years and were the result of what Darwin called "natural selection," also known as survival of the fittest. For example, a chameleon has the ability to change its skin coloring to blend into its environment, making it less visible to predators. Darwin believed that survival traits like these developed gradually and were passed on to succeeding generations.

In a later work, *The Descent of Man, and the Selection in Relation to Sex* (1871), Darwin proposed that human beings had evolved from an animal closely related to the ancestors of such primates as the chimpanzee and the gorilla. This came to be referred to as the theory of evolution. Some people incorrectly interpreted this to mean that human beings were directly descended from monkeys or apes.

Darwin's theories generated much controversy, particularly in religious communities. Religious leaders condemned the theories as heretical. Christians believe that the stories told in the Bible, such as that of Adam and Eve being made by God as the first human beings, are true. Darwin's proposal that humans evolved over millions of years challenged many religions' faith that God created man. This belief came to be called Creationism. Religious leaders also feared that acceptance of Darwin's theories would result in people's denial of God.

Many scientists, though at first skeptical, gradually came to accept Darwin's theories. But the Scopes trial, which took place at a time when traditional values seemed in danger of extinction, demonstrated lingering resistance to the scientific explanation of evolution. The debate over evolution and Creationism continues into the twenty-first century, with some schools demanding that evolution be removed from classroom teachings or insisting that Creationism be taught alongside Darwin's theory.

classroom. Opponents assert that creationism has no place in public education because it is a religious belief, while evolution is a science.

Excerpt from undelivered closing statement from the Scopes trial

*Science is a magnificent force, but it is not a teacher of morals. It can perfect machinery, but it adds no moral restraints to protect society from the misuse of the machine. It can also build gigantic intellectual ships, but it constructs no moral **rudders** for the control of storm tossed human vessel. It not only fails to supply the spiritual element needed but some of its unproven **hypotheses** rob the ship of its compass and thus endangers its cargo. In war, science has proven itself an evil genius; it has made war more terrible than it ever was before. Man used to be content to slaughter his fellowmen on a single plane—the earth's surface. Science has taught him to go down into the water and shoot up from below and to go up into the clouds and shoot down from above, thus making the battlefield three times a bloody as it was before; but science does not teach brotherly love. Science has made war so hellish that civilization was about to commit suicide; and now we are told that newly discovered instruments of destruction will make the cruelties of the late war seem trivial in comparison with the cruelties of wars that may come in the future. If civilization is to be saved from the wreckage threatened by intelligence not consecrated by love, it must be saved by the moral code of the meek and lowly **Nazarene**. His teachings, and His teachings, alone, can solve the problems that **vex** heart and perplex the world. . . .*

*It is for the jury to determine whether this attack upon the Christian religion shall be permitted in the public schools of Tennessee by teachers employed by the state and paid out of the public treasury. This case is no longer local, the defendant ceases to play an important part. The case has assumed the proportions of a battle-royal between unbelief that attempts to speak through so-called science and the defenders of the Christian faith, speaking through the legislators of Tennessee. It is again a choice between God and **Baal**; it is also a renewal of the issue in **Pilate**'s court. . . .*

Rudders: Guides.

Hypotheses: Theories.

Consecrated: Made sacred or holy.

Nazarene: Jesus Christ.

Vex: Make worried.

Baal: False god or idol.

Pilate: The Roman official who condemned Jesus to death.

William Jennings Bryan pleads with the court during the Scopes trial to exclude expert scientific evidence from the case. (© *Bettmann/Corbis. Reproduced by permission.*)

*Again force and love meet face to face, and the question, "What shall I do with Jesus?" must be answered. A bloody, brutal doctrine—Evolution—demands, as the **rabble** did nineteen hundred years ago, that He be crucified. That cannot be the answer of this jury representing a Christian state and sworn to uphold the laws of Tennessee. Your answer will be heard throughout the world; it is eagerly awaited by a praying **multitude**. If the law is **nullified**, there will be rejoice wherever God is **repudiated**, the savior **scoffed** at and the Bible ridiculed. Every unbeliever of every kind and degree will be happy. If, on the other hand, the law is upheld and the religion of the school children protected, millions of Christians will call you blessed and, with hearts full of gratitude to God, will sing again that grand old song of triumph: "Faith of our fathers, living still, In spite of dungeon, fire and sword;*

Rabble: The mob that called for 'Jesus' death.

Multitude: Large number of people.

Nullified: Struck down.

Repudiated: Denied the truth of.

Scoffed: Made fun of.

O how our hearts beat high with joy Whene'er we hear that glorious word—Faith of our fathers—Holy faith; We will be true to thee till death!"

What happened next ...

Despite the guilty verdict, public opinion declared Darrow the trial's winner. Bryan died in his sleep only five days after the end of the trial, suggesting to many that the stress of the event and especially his ordeal on the witness stand had taken a heavy toll on his health. Darrow went on to achieve more courtroom victories before his death in 1938. Scopes left Tennessee to attend graduate school and, after becoming a geologist, never returned. In 1927 the Tennessee State Supreme Court overturned the Scopes verdict on a legal technicality (the lower court judge had not had the authority to impose a fine). The Supreme Court did not, however, find the Butler Act unconstitutional, and it remained in effect in Tennessee until 1967.

Did you know ...

- The Scopes trial was the first to be broadcast on the new medium of the radio. Print reporters also brought the U.S. public the news from Dayton. Foremost among them was H.L. Mencken (1880–1956), a Baltimore, Maryland, journalist known for his biting social commentary. He took a strong interest in the trial and its outcome—his newspaper paid both Scopes's bail and the fine he eventually received—and he is credited with coining the term "Monkey Trial."

- The small town of Dayton, Tennessee, was turned into a carnival during the trial, complete with street-corner preachers and prophets, hot dog and soft drink vendors, gospel singers, and monkeys both real and stuffed. One souvenir seller offered buttons that read, "Your Old Man's a Monkey."

Clarence Darrow (left) and William Jennings Bryan (right) during a break in the Scopes trial. Despite the guilty verdict, public opinion declared Darrow the trial's winner. *(© Bettmann/Corbis. Reproduced by permission.)*

- Despite his reputation as a great orator, Bryan's simple religious faith proved no match for Darrow's relentless questioning. At the end of their exchange, Bryan asked the judge to censure, or reprimand, Darrow for his slurs against the Bible. Darrow responded, "I object to your statement. I am examining you on your fool ideas that no intelligent Christian on earth believes."

Consider the following ...
- How does the Scopes trial contradict the image of the Roaring Twenties as a sunny, fun-filled period in U.S. history?

- Journalist H.L. Mencken was on hand for most of the trial and wrote a series of articles describing it. Read these articles and give your impression of Mencken's views of the event.

- Do you think that creationism should be taught in the public schools along with the theory of evolution? Write an editorial defending your views.

For More Information

Books

Anderson, David D. *William Jennings Bryan*. Boston: Twayne, 1981.

De Camp, L. Sprague. *The Great Monkey Trial*. Garden City, NY: Doubleday, 1968.

Dumenil, Lynn. *The Modern Temper: American Culture and Society in the 1920s*. New York: Hill and Wang, 1995.

Ginger, Ray. *Six Days or Forever: Tennessee Versus John Thomas Scopes*. Chicago, IL: Quadrangle Books, 1969.

Hanson, Erica. *The 1920s*. San Diego, CA: Lucent Books, 1999.

Larson, Edward J. *Trial and Error: The American Controversy over Creation and Evolution*. New York: Oxford University Press, 1994.

Miller, Nathan. *New World Coming: The 1920s and the Making of Modern America*. New York: Scribner, 2003.

Perret, Geoffrey. *America in the Twenties*. New York: Touchstone, 1982.

Scopes, John Thomas, and James Pressley. *Center of the Storm: Memoirs of John T. Scopes*. New York: Holt, Rinehart & Winston, Inc., 1967.

Tompkins, Jerry R., ed. *D-Days at Dayton: Reflections on the Scopes Trial*. Baton Rouge: Louisiana State University Press, 1965.

Web Sites

"Famous Trials in American History: Tennessee versus John Scopes, the Monkey Trial." *Famous Trials by Doug Linder*. Available online at http://www.law.umkc.edu/faculty/projects/ftrials/scopes/scopes.htm. Accessed on June 20, 2005.

8

Calvin Coolidge

"The Press under a Free Government"
Published in 1925

One of the ideas most often associated with the 1920s is that "the business of America is business." These words, spoken by President Calvin Coolidge (1872–1933; served 1923–29) in a speech to newspaper editors, did indeed capture the pro-business spirit of this economically well-to-do decade. A closer look at this speech, however, reveals a more complex picture of Coolidge's ideas about his nation.

Coolidge climbed the political ladder slowly and steadily, reaching the presidency unexpectedly when President Warren G. Harding (1865–1923; served 1921–23) died in office before the end of his first term. Born in 1872 in Plymouth Notch, Vermont, Coolidge attended Amherst College and later established a law practice in Northampton, Massachusetts. He served as a city councilman and state legislator and eventually as governor of Massachusetts. In that position Coolidge gained national recognition and praise from the Republican Party for his firm handling of a police strike in Boston. That led to his nomination as Harding's vice presidential running mate in the 1920 election. As vice president, Coolidge was a quiet presence. Thrust into the office of

"After all, the chief business of the American people is business. . . . We make no concealment of the fact that we want wealth, but there are many other things that we want very much more. . . ."

241

U.S. President Calvin Coolidge delivering his "The Press Under a Free Government" speech. *(© Underwood & Underwood/Corbis. Reproduced by permission.)*

the presidency, he vowed to carry on the policies begun by Harding.

Soon after Coolidge took office, the corruption that had riddled Harding's administration started to become public knowledge. Coolidge managed to distance himself from the scandals, partly by supporting the prosecution of the culprits and partly by his reputation for honesty and integrity. In 1924 Coolidge was re-elected on his own merits, running under the slogan "Keep Cool with Coolidge" and winning an impressive 54 percent of the popular vote.

Coolidge's laissez-faire approach (a policy of noninterference) was clearly in line with the times and with the beliefs of most U.S. citizens, as was the pro-business stance evident in this excerpt. But the speech is more than just pro-business. Coolidge highlights the importance of a free press in a democracy and, responding to fears that newspapers run by large, powerful corporations would not present the news in a fair, balanced manner, asserts that the business and editorial departments of newspapers can and should be kept separate. Coolidge is remembered for the famous line that "the business of America is business." Yet what followed was the claim that money is not everything, and that idealism is the most important characteristic of the American people.

Things to remember while reading this excerpt from "The Press under a Free Government" . . .

Even though this speech contains one of Coolidge's often-quoted phrases, it is not usually noted that he goes on to qualify the idea of business as the chief concern of the United States. He suggests, in fact, that values like peace, honor, charity, and idealism are more important than wealth.

According to New York governor and Democratic presidential candidate Alfred E. Smith (1873–1944), as quoted on the White House Web site, Coolidge was "distinguished for character more than for heroic achievement. His great task was to restore the Presidency when it had reached the lowest ebb in our history."

Although Coolidge generally opposed government intervention in business affairs, some important laws were passed during his administration that imposed restrictions on two major new industries. The Air Commerce Act put aviation under the Commerce Department's control. The Radio Commission was set up as a federal agency to regulate use of the airwaves by radio stations.

Excerpt from "The Press under a Free Government"

*The relationship between governments and the press has always been recognized as a matter of large importance. Wherever **despotism** abounds, the sources of public information are the first to be brought under its control. Where ever the cause of liberty is making its way, one of its highest accomplishments is the guarantee of the freedom of the press. It has always been realized, sometimes instinctively, oftentimes expressly, that truth and freedom are inseparable. An **absolutism** could never rest upon any thing save a perverted and distorted view of human relationships and upon false standards set up and maintained by force. It has always found it necessary to attempt to dominate the entire field of education and instruction. It has thrived on ignorance. While it has sought to train the minds of a few, it has been largely with the purpose of attempting to give them a superior facility for misleading the many. Men have been educated under absolutism, not that they might bear witness to the truth, but that they might be the more **ingenious** advocates and defenders of false standards and hollow pretenses. This has always been the method of privilege, the method of class and caste, the method of master and slave.*

*When a community has sufficiently advanced so that its government begins to take on that of the nature of a **republic**, the processes of education become even more important, but the method is necessarily reversed. It ils all the more necessary under a system of free government that the people should be enlightened, that they should be correctly informed, than it is under an absolute government that they should be ignorant. Under a republic the institutions of learning, while bound by the constitution and laws, are in no way **subservient** to the government. The*

Despotism: Rule by absolute power.

Absolutism: The idea that government should have complete, absolute authority.

Ingenious: Original, inventive.

Republic: State in which power is held by the people and their elected representatives and in which leaders are elected by the people.

Subservient: Ready to obey others unquestioningly.

principles which they **enunciate** do not depend for their authority upon whether they square with the wish of the ruling dynasty, but whether they square with the everlasting truth. Under these conditions the press, which had before been made an instrument for concealing or perverting the facts, must be made an instrument for their true representation and their sound and logical interpretation. From the position of a mere organ, constantly bound to servitude, public prints rise to a dignity, not only of independence, but of a great educational and enlightening factor. They attain new powers, which it is almost impossible to measure, and become charged with **commensurate** responsibilities. . . .

Our American newspapers serve a double purpose. They bring knowledge and information to their readers, and at the same time they play a most important part in connection with the business interests of the community, both through their news and advertising departments. Probably there is no rule of your profession to which you gentlemen are more devoted than that which prescribes that the editorial and the business policies of the paper are to be conducted by strictly separate departments. Editorial policy and news policy must not be influenced by business consideration; business policies must not be affected by editorial programs. Such a **dictum** strikes the outsider as involving a good deal of difficulty in the practical adjustments of every day management. Yet, in fact, I doubt if those adjustments are any more difficult than have to be made in every other department of human effort. Life is a long succession of compromises and adjustments, and it may be doubted whether the press is compelled to make them more frequently than others do.

When I have contemplated these adjustments of business and editorial policy, it has always seemed to me that American newspapers are peculiarly representative of the practical **idealism** of our country. Quite recently the construction of a **revenue statute** resulted in giving publicity to some highly interesting facts about incomes. It must have been observed that nearly all the newspapers published these interesting facts in their news columns, while very many of them protested in their editorial columns that such publicity was a bad policy. Yet this was not inconsistent. I am referring to the incident by way of illustrating what I just said about the newspapers representing the practical idealism of America. As practical newsmen they printed the facts. As editorial idealists they protested that there ought to be no such facts available.

Some people feel concerned about the **commercialism** of the press. They note that great newspapers are great business enterprises earning

Enunciate: Express.

Commensurate: Equal to.

Dictum: A statement expressing a principle.

Idealism: The practice of forming and trying to live up to high ideals.

Revenue statute: A law regarding a state's income.

Commercialism: Putting the strongest emphasis on earning profits.

large profits and controlled by men of wealth. So they fear that in such control the press may tend to support the private interests of those who own the papers, rather than the general interest of the whole people. It seems to me, however, that the real test is not whether the newspapers are controlled by men of wealth, but whether they are sincerely trying to serve the public interests. There will be little occasion for worry about who owns a newspaper, so long as its attitudes on public questions are such as to promote the general welfare. A press which is actuated by the purpose of genuine usefulness to the public interest can never be too strong financially, so long as its strength is used for the support of popular government.

There does not seem to be cause for alarm in the dual relationship of the press to the public, whereby it is on one side a **purveyor** of information and opinion and on the other side a purely business enterprise. Rather, it is probable that a press which maintains an intimate touch with the business currents of the nation, is likely to be more reliable than it would be if it were a stranger to these influences. After all, the chief business of the American people is business. They are profoundly concerned with producing, buying, selling, investing and prospering in the world. I am strongly of opinion that the great majority of people will always find these are moving impulses of our life. . . .

Wealth is the product of industry, ambition, character and untiring effort. In all experience, the accumulation of wealth means the multiplication of schools, the increase of knowledge, the **dissemination** of intelligence, the encouragement of science, the broadening of outlook, the expansion of liberties, the widening of culture. Of course, the accumulation of wealth can not be justified as the chief end of existence. But we are compelled to recognize it as a means to **well nigh** every desirable achievement. So long as wealth is made the means and not the end, we need not greatly fear it. And there never was a time when wealth was so generally regarded as a means, or so little regarded as an end, as today. Just a little time ago we read in your newspapers that two leaders of American business, whose efforts at accumulation had been most astonishingly successful, had given fifty or sixty million dollars as **endowments** to educational works. That was real news. It was characteristic of our American experience with men of large resources. They use their power to serve, not themselves and their own families, but the public. I feel

Purveyor: Provider or supplier.

Dissemination: Spreading out widely.

Well nigh: Almost.

Endowments: Gifts, usually of large amounts of money.

sure that the coming generations, which will benefit by those endowments, will not be easily convinced that they have suffered greatly because of these particular accumulations of wealth....

American newspapers have seemed to me to be particularly representative of this practical idealism of our people. Therefore, I feel secure in saying that they are the best newspapers in the world. I believe that they print more real news and more reliable and characteristic news than any other newspaper. I believe their editorial opinions are less colored in influence by mere **partisanship** *or selfish interest, than are those of any other country. Moreover, I believe that our American press is more independent, more reliable and less partisan today than at any other time in its history. I believe this of our press, precisely as I believe it of those who manage our public affairs. Both are cleaner, finer, less influenced by improper considerations, than ever before. Whoever disagrees with this judgment must take the chance of marking himself as ignorant of conditions which notoriously affected our public life, thoughts and methods, even within the memory of many men who are still among us.*

It can safely be assumed that self interest will always place sufficient emphasis on the business side of newspapers, so that they do not need any outside encouragement for that part of their activities. Important, however, as this factor is, it is not the main element which appeals to the American people. It is only those who do not understand our people, who believe that our national life is entirely absorbed by material motives. We make no concealment of the fact that we want wealth, but there are many other things that we want very much more. We want peace and honor, and that charity which is so strong an element of all civilization. The chief ideal of the American people is idealism. I cannot repeat too often that America is a nation of idealists. That is the only motive to which they ever give any strong and lasting reaction. No newspaper can be a success which fails to appeal to that element of our national life. It is in this direction that the public press can lend its strongest support to our Government. I could not truly criticize the vast importance of the **counting room**, *but my ultimate faith I would place in the high idealism of the editorial room of the American newspaper.*

Partisanship: Strongly supporting one side of an issue, person, or cause over another.

Counting room: The business department.

Calvin Coolidge signing the tax bill in 1926. He supported tax cuts for the rich believing that more money would be poured into investment and eventually benefit all of the nation's citizens. *(Courtesy of The Library of Congress.)*

What happened next . . .

Coolidge's administration was marked by conservatism. He supported tax cuts for the rich (believing that more money would thus be poured into investments, which would eventually benefit all of the nation's citizens), isolationism (keeping out of other countries' affairs), and restrictions on immigration. He believed that the government should not interfere in business and private affairs. Coolidge opposed efforts to provide the struggling farmers of the rural United States with more government support, which some historians feel helped to bring about the economic collapse known as the Great Depression (1929–41). Republican Party leaders were surprised when Coolidge announced that he would not run for reelection in 1929. He died in 1933.

Trickle-Down Economics

President Calvin Coolidge exercised a policy of what many refer to as "trickle-down economics," or supply-side economics. The policy is based on the theory that the pace of economic growth depends on the willingness of producers to create goods and services.

Those who follow this economic theory support government noninterference in the economy, lower income taxes, and tax incentives for businesses and the wealthy. They believe that these measures encourage producers to invest more in their industries and encourage laborers to work more. Laborers who work more will have more money to spend on products, feeding into the economic growth cycle. This is the "trickle-down" effect, where the benefits received at the top spread into and eventually benefit the overall economy. In theory, such incentives result in the generation of more jobs and the higher production of goods and services.

President Ronald Reagan, a great admirer of Coolidge, followed this economic theory throughout his two terms in office during the 1980s. Reagan's economic policies were dubbed "Reaganomics." He followed the supply-side model of tax cuts and benefits for businesses and the wealthy, and the economy experienced significant growth during his administration. Critics, however, connect the massive federal deficits incurred during this same period, from under $1 trillion before Reagan took office to $2.6 trillion at the end of his presidency, as a direct result of Reagan's economic policies.

The Keynesian theory, named after British economist John Maynard Keynes (1884–1946), proposes that consumer demand, not production, is the driving force of the economy. When demand for products falters, the economy can experience slow or negative growth. Consumers may buy fewer products for a variety of reasons, such as a loss of wages due to unemployment or an increase in the price of goods. According to the Keynesian theory, government involvement in the economy is welcome when the economy experiences difficulties.

Did you know . . .

- It was Vice President Coolidge's own father, a notary public (a person authorized to perform certain legal formalities), who gave him the oath of office (the official, verbal promise a president makes to fulfill the duties of his office). Coolidge was vacationing at his family home in Vermont when, at 2:30 AM on August 3, 1923, he received word that President Harding had died. Coolidge took the oath of office again in Washington, D.C., two weeks later.

- Despite his nickname of "Silent Cal," Coolidge was an active president who gave many press conferences and radio broadcasts and who was even willing to pose for silly photographs, dressed in cowboy or farmer costumes.

- Coolidge's reputation suffered somewhat in the years following his administration, but he was greatly admired by the nation's fortieth president, Ronald Reagan (1911–2004; served 1981–89). In fact, Reagan took down a portrait of President Harry Truman that hung in the White House and replaced it with one of Coolidge. Like Coolidge, Reagan believed in what has been called "trickle-down economics": the idea that relieving the tax burden on the wealthy frees them to put more money into investments, with benefits eventually "trickling down" to the rest of the population.

Consider the following . . .

- In another speech, Coolidge suggested that business was a temple at which U.S. citizens worshipped. Do you think that Coolidge believed that business was the best thing about the United States? Find evidence in the excerpt to support your answer.

- First, find a place in this speech where Coolidge addresses the issue of corruption. Then think about why Coolidge was reelected in 1928.

For More Information

Books

Abels, Jules. *In the Time of Silent Cal.* New York: Putnam, 1989.

Ferrell, Robert H. *The Presidency of Calvin Coolidge.* Lawrence: University Press of Kansas, 1998.

Haynes, John Earl. *Calvin Coolidge and the Coolidge Era: Essays on the History of the 1920s.* Washington, DC: Library of Congress, 1998.

McCoy, Donald R. *Calvin Coolidge: The Quiet President.* Lawrence: University Press of Kansas, 1988.

Sobel, Robert. *Coolidge: An American Enigma.* Washington, DC: Regnery, 1998.

Web Sites

"Calvin Coolidge: 30th President of the United States." *The Calvin Coolidge Memorial Foundation.* Available online at http://www.calvin-coolidge.org/index.html. Accessed on June 20, 2005.

"Calvin Coolidge." *The White House.* Available online at http://www.whitehouse.gov/history/presidents/cc30.html. Accessed on June 20, 2005.

9

Ernest Hemingway

Excerpt from The Sun Also Rises
Published in 1926

"I thought of her walking up the street and stepping into the car, as I had last seen her, and of course in a little while I felt like hell again. It is awfully easy to be hard-boiled about everything in the daytime, but at night it is another thing."

One of the most influential authors of the twentieth century, Hemingway was a leading figure among the famous U.S. expatriates (people who live outside of their home countries) who lived in Paris during the Roaring Twenties. As a young man who had participated and been wounded in World War I (1914–1918; the United States entered the conflict in 1917), Hemingway both embodied and voiced the viewpoint of the disillusioned postwar generation. His work is characterized by a spare, succinct writing style with a distinctively modern feel that, especially in the 1920s, presented a strong contrast to the ornate prose of the nineteenth century.

Born in Oak Park, Illinois, Hemingway was influenced by both his physician father, who introduced him to the joys of the outdoors, and his music-loving, rather domineering mother. Each year the family vacationed on a lake in northern Michigan, which would provide a wealth of material for Hemingway's fiction. In high school, he wrote articles for his school newspaper and also took part in athletics. After graduation, he tried to volunteer for military service in World War I, but was rejected due to poor vision. Instead of attending college, as his parents wished, he got a job as a reporter for the Kansas City *Star* newspaper. There Hemingway began to develop the clipped, concise writing style that would characterize his later work.

Unable to stay away from the war, Hemingway enlisted in the medical service of the Red Cross and was sent to Italy to serve as an ambulance driver. In that role he experienced the devastation and brutality of war first-hand. After being wounded in the knee, he managed to carry another man to safety; later, doctors removed two hundred pieces of shrapnel (jagged pieces of metal from an exploded bomb) from his legs and body. Hemingway subsequently enlisted in the Italian army and spent some more time fighting before returning to the United States. He lived for almost a year with his parents in Oak Park, writing and speaking in public about his war experiences.

Finally Hemingway was hired as a foreign correspondent by the Toronto *Star* newspaper. With his new wife, Hadley Richardson, he moved to Paris and soon became part of a group of U.S. writers who were living there, including poet Ezra Pound (1885–1972) and novelists Gertrude Stein (1872–1946) and F. Scott Fitzgerald (1896–1940). Hemingway's first book, *Three Stories and Ten Poems,* was published in 1923, followed by a collection of short stories titled *In Our Time* (1925). The second book features one of Hemingway's best known characters, Nick Adams.

The Sun Also Rises was published in May 1926, after Hemingway had returned to the United States. It opens with a quote from Gertrude Stein: "You are all a lost generation." Although Hemingway later said that he had not intended to define anyone, both the quote and the novel were interpreted as expressing the plight of those who had come of age just before, during, or after World War I. Several of the novel's characters are, like Hemingway, disillusioned veterans of the fighting who sustained physical or emotional damage (or both). All of them are now living a morally bankrupt existence of joyless drinking, dancing, and shifting sexual liaisons.

The novel is narrated by Jake Barnes, whose injury in the war resulted in impotence (the inability to function sexually). He is in love with Lady Brett Ashley, a young English woman who, after losing her fiancé in the war, married another

Gertrude Stein: An Expatriate and Modernist

Unconventional and highly intellectual, Gertrude Stein was a Roaring Twenties figure known both for her experimental literary works and as a hostess and mentor to U.S. and British expatriates. Expatriates are those who live outside of their native countries, and during the 1920s many flocked to Paris, France.

Born in 1874, in Oakland, California, Stein was the youngest child of a wealthy Jewish family. She attended noted women's college Radcliffe University and then Johns Hopkins University. Stein first studied psychiatry before determining her primary interest in literature.

After traveling around Europe and Africa with her brother Leo, Stein and her brother settled in an apartment at 27 rue de Fleurus in Paris in 1903. The apartment became a gathering place, or "salon," for artists and writers. The Steins' friends and guests included such famous painters as Paul Cezanne, Henri Matisse, and Pablo Picasso, who painted a well-known portrait of Stein. Guillaume Apollinaire and Max Jacob, young writers, were also frequent visitors.

In 1909 Stein took on a companion and secretary, California native Alice B. Toklas. That same year, Stein published her first book, *Three Lives,* which contained short novels about the lives of three female characters. *Tender Buttons* (1914), a collection of prose poems written in a distinctly modern style, was Stein's next work.

During World War I, Stein and Toklas remained in war-torn Paris, and Stein volunteered as a medical supply driver. After the war, U.S. writers and artists arrived in Paris, seeking refuge from a society they considered intolerant and materialistic. Stein welcomed them into her salon, especially the novelist and short story writer Ernest Hemingway, who quoted her in his 1926 novel *The Sun Also Rises* as having said, "You are all a lost generation." Other members of Stein's circle included F. Scott Fitzgerald, Ezra Pound, and Edith Sitwell.

Stein's literary works during the 1920s included the novel, *The Making of Americans* (1925). This complex work chronicles three generations of a German-American family similar to the Steins. It reflects Stein's interest in delving beneath the surface of personality, as well as her unconventional approach to writing. Her style features long sentences made up of simple words, with no punctuation other than periods. This kind of experimentation with form and content made her writing both purely modern and inaccessible to most readers. Nevertheless, her work was much appreciated by a small, sophisticated audience.

In the 1930s Stein published books of memoirs, plays, art criticism, and literary theory. Her most famous book was the bestselling, widely acclaimed *Autobiography of Alice B. Toklas,* which actually tells the story of Stein's life. Stein and Toklas stayed in France during World War II. After Paris was liberated from Nazi (German) occupation, Stein resumed her famous salon. She died of cancer in 1946.

man purely for the wealth and aristocratic title he could provide. She is now engaged to Mike Campbell, an alcoholic with few prospects and a brutal nature. Brett returns Jake's love, but she cannot do without the sexual relations he is unable to offer. *The Sun Also Rises* chronicles the characters' interactions in both Paris and Spain, where they travel to attend the yearly running of the bulls and the bullfighting spectacular. By the end of the novel, nothing has changed.

In the first part of this excerpt, Jake and Brett ride in a taxicab to join friends at a Paris nightclub. Their strong attraction to each other is evident, but it becomes clear to the reader that their relationship is doomed by Jake's inadequacy. In the second part, Jake goes to be alone after leaving Brett with her friends. He thinks about his injury, then goes to sleep. Later Brett arrives for a visit, eventually leaving Jake alone with his sad thoughts.

Ernest Hemingway is considered by many critics to be one of the greatest writers of the twentieth century. *(AP/Wide World Photos. Reproduced by permission.)*

Things to remember while reading this excerpt from *The Sun Also Rises* . . .

The novel is laced with references to a number of dominant issues and trends of the Roaring Twenties, including the expatriate movement, Prohibition (the Constitutional ban on alcohol, which the characters can ignore since they live outside of the United States), women's changing roles, and especially the effects of World War I. The first armed conflict to include such effective weapons as machine guns, airplanes that could drop bombs, and trench warfare, this war shocked the whole world with its toll of death and destruction. Evidence of both physical and emotional damage are evident in the character of Jake Barnes, the novel's protagonist.

The early part of the novel chronicles the characters' relentless merrymaking as they drink and dance their way around Paris. It soon becomes clear, however, that they find little joy in these pursuits and that their lives are actually meaningless and bleak.

In her pursuit of pleasure, her independence, and her appearance—featuring short hair and a man's hat pulled low on her forehead—Lady Brett Ashley embodies a new kind of woman that was beginning to emerge in the Roaring Twenties. Unlike the women of earlier decades, she drinks as much as the men around her, and seeks sexual satisfaction with a variety of partners, even rejecting Jake's love because he cannot perform sexually.

Excerpt from The Sun Also Rises

From Chapter IV

The taxi went up the hill, passed the lighted square, then on into the dark, still climbing, then leveled out onto a dark street behind St. Etienne du Mont, went smoothly down the asphalt, passed the trees and the standing bus at the Place de la Contrescarpe, then turned onto the **cobbles** *of the Rue Mouffetard. There were lighted bars and late open shops on each side of the street. We were sitting apart and we jolted close together going down the old street. Brett's hat was off. Her head was back. I saw her face in the lights from the open shops, then it was dark, then I saw her face clearly as we came out on the Avenue des Gobelins. The street was torn up and men were working on the cartracks by the light of* **acetylene** *flares. Brett's face was white and the long line of her neck showed in the bright light of the flares. The street was dark again and I kissed her. Our lips were tight together and then she turned away and pressed against the corner of the seat, as far away as she could get. Her head was down.*

"Don't touch me," she said. "Please don't touch me."

"What's the matter?"

"I can't stand it."

"Oh, Brett."

Cobbles: Round stones used to cover roads.

Acetylene: A gas that burns with a bright flame.

"You mustn't. You must know. I can't stand it, that's all. Oh, darling, please understand!"

"Don't you love me?"

"Love you? I simply turn all to jelly when you touch me."

"Isn't there anything we can do about it?"

She was sitting up now. My arm was around her and she was leaning back against me, and we were quite calm. She was looking into my eyes with that way she had of looking that made you wonder whether she really saw out of her own eyes. They would look on and on after everyone else's eyes in the world would have stopped looking. She looked as though there were nothing on earth she would not look at like that, and really she was afraid of so many things.

"And there's not a . . . thing we could do," I said.

"I don't know," she said. "I don't want to go through that . . . again."

"We'd better keep away from each other."

"But, darling, I have to see you. It isn't all that you know."

"No, but it always gets to be."

"That's my fault. Don't we pay for all the things we do, though?"

She had been looking into my eyes all the time. Her eyes had different depths, sometimes they seemed perfectly flat. Now you could see all the way into them.

"When I think of the . . . I've put chaps through. I'm paying for it all now."

"Don't talk like a fool," I said. "Besides, what happened to me is supposed to be funny. I never think about it."

"Oh, no. I'll lay you don't."

"Well, let's shut up about it."

"I laughed about it too, myself, once." She wasn't looking at me. "A friend of my brother's came home that way from Mons. It seemed like . . . a joke. Chaps never know anything, do they?"

"No," I said. "Nobody ever knows anything."

I was pretty well through with the subject. At one time or another I had probably considered it from most of its various angles, including the one that certain injuries or imperfections are a subject of merriment while remaining quite serious for the person possessing them.

"It's funny," I said. "It's very funny. And it's a lot of fun, too, to be in love."

"Do you think so?" her eyes looked flat again.

"I don't mean fun that way. In a way it's an enjoyable feeling."

"No," she said. . . .

"It's good to see each other."

"No. I don't think it is."

"Don't you want to?"

"I have to."

We were sitting now like two strangers. On the right was the Parc Montsouris. The restaurant where they have the pool of live trout and where you can sit and look out over the park was closed and dark. The driver leaned his head around.

"Where do you want to go?" I asked. Brett turned her head away.

"Oh, go to the Select."

"Café Select," I told the driver. "Boulevard Montparnasse." We drove straight down, turning around the Lion de Belfort that guards the passing Montrouge trams. Brett looked straight ahead. On the Boulevard Raspail, with the lights of Montparnasse in sight, Brett said: "Would you mind very much if I asked you to do something?"

"Don't be silly."

"Kiss me just once more before we get there,"

When the taxi stopped I got out and paid. Brett came out putting on her hat. She gave me her hand as she stepped down. Her hand was shaky. "I say, do I look too much of a mess?" She pulled her man's felt hat down and started in for the bar. Inside, against the bar and at tables, were most of the crowd who had been at the dance.

"Hello, you chaps," Brett said. "I'm going to have a drink. . . ."

I lit the lamp beside the bed, turned off the gas, and opened the wide windows. The bed was far back from the windows, and I sat with the windows open and undressed by the bed. Outside a night train, running on the street-car tracks, went by carrying vegetables to the markets. They were noisy at night when you could not sleep. Undressing, I looked at myself in the mirror of the big **armoire** beside the bed. That was a typically French way to furnish a room. Practical, too, I suppose. Of all the ways to be wounded. I suppose it was funny. I put on my

Armoire: A large chest or mobile closet for storing clothing.

A scene from the film *The Sun Also Rises* based on Ernest Hemingway's novel by the same name. *(The Kobal Collection. Reproduced by permission.)*

pajamas and got into bed. I had the two bull-fight papers, and I took their wrappers off. One was orange. The other yellow. They would both have the same news, so whichever I read first would spoil the other. Le Toril was the better paper, so I started to read it. I read it all the way through, including the Petite Correspondence and the Cornigrams. I blew out the lamp. Perhaps I would be able to sleep.

*My head started to work. The old **grievance**. Well, it was a rotten way to be wounded and flying on a joke **front** like the Italian. In the Italian hospital we were going to form a society. It had a funny name in Italian. I wonder what became of the others, the Italians. That was in the **Ospedale Maggiore** in Milano, Padiglione Ponte. The next building was the Padiglione Zonda. There was a statue of Ponte, or maybe it was Zonda. That was where the liaison colonel came to visit me. That was funny. That was about the first funny thing. I was all bandaged up. But they had told him about it.*

Grievance: Complaint.

Front: The furthest position an army has reached.

Ospedale Maggiore: The Italian hospital in which Jake's injury was treated.

Then he made *that wonderful speech*: "You, a foreigner, an Englishman" (any foreigner was an Englishman) "have given more than your life." What a speech! I would like to have it illuminated to hang in the office. He never laughed. He was putting himself in my place, I guess. **"Che mala fortuna!** Che mala fortuna!"

I never used to realize it, I guess. I try and play it along and just not make trouble for people. Probably I never would have had any trouble if I hadn't run into Brett when they shipped me to England. I suppose she only wanted what she couldn't have. Well, people were that way. . . . The Catholic Church had an awfully good way of handling all that. Good advice, anyway. Not to think about it. Oh, it was swell advice. Try and take it sometime. Try and take it.

I lay awake thinking and my mind jumping around. Then I couldn't keep away from it, and I started to think about Brett and all the rest of it went away. I was thinking about Brett and my mind stopped jumping around and started to go in sort of smooth waves. Then all of a sudden I started to cry. Then after a while it was better and I lay in bed and listened to the heavy trams go by and way down the street, and then I went to sleep.

I woke up. There was a row going on outside. I listened and I thought I recognized a voice. I put on a dressing-gown and went to the door. The **concierge** was talking down-stairs. She was very angry. I heard my name and called down the stairs.

"Is that you, Monsieur Barnes?" the concierge called.

"Yes. It's me."

"There's a species of woman here who's waked the whole street up. What kind of a dirty business at this time of night! She says she must see you. I've told her you're asleep."

Then I heard Brett's voice. Half asleep I had been sure it was **Georgette**. I don't know why. She could not have known my address.

"Will you send her up, please?"

Brett came up the stairs. I saw she was quite drunk. "Silly thing to do," she said. "Make an awful row. I say, you weren't asleep, were you?"

"What did you think I was doing?"

"Don't know. What time is it?"

I looked at the clock. It was half-past four. "Had no idea what hour it was," Brett said. "I say, can a chap sit down? Don't be cross, darling. Just left **the count**. He brought me here. . . ."

"that wonderful speech": The officer is expressing gratitude for Jake's sacrifice, especially considering that he is not even Italian.

"Che mala fortuna!": Italian for "What bad luck!"

Concierge: Resident caretaker of an apartment building.

Georgette: A women whom Jake had met earlier in the evening.

The Count: Count Mippipopolous, a wealthy Greek aristocrat.

"Where did you go with him?"

"Oh, everywhere. He just brought me here now. Offered me ten thousand dollars to go to **Biarritz** with him. How much is that in pounds?"

"Around two thousand."

"Lot of money. I told him I couldn't do it. He was awfully nice about it. Told him I knew too many people in Biarritz."

Brett laughed.

"I say, you are slow on the up-take," she said. I had only sipped my brandy and soda. I took a long drink.

"That's better. Very funny," Brett said. "Then he wanted me to go to **Cannes** with him. Told him I knew too many people in Cannes. **Monte Carlo**. Told him I knew too many people in Monte Carlo. Told him I knew too many people everywhere. Quite true, too. So I asked him to bring me here."

She looked at me, her hand on the table, her glass raised. "Don't look like that," she said. "Told him was in love with you. True, too. Don't look like that. He was . . . nice about it. Wants to drive us out to dinner to-morrow night. Like to go?"

"Why not?"

"I'd better go now."

"Why?"

"Just wanted to see you. Silly idea. Want to get dressed and come down? He's got the car just up the street."

"The count?"

"Himself. And a chauffeur in **livery**. Going to drive me around and have breakfast in the Bois. **Hampers**. Got it all at Zelli's. Dozen bottles of **Mumms**. Tempt you?"

"I have to work in the morning," I said. "I'm too far behind you now to catch up and be any fun. . . ."

"Right. Send him a tender message?"

"Anything. Absolutely."

"Good night, darling."

"Don't be sentimental."

"You make me ill."

We kissed good night and Brett shivered. "I'd better go," she said. "Good night, darling."

Biarritz: Resort area in France.

Cannes: Resort area in France.

Monte Carlo: Resort area in France.

Livery: Special uniform.

Hampers: Picnic baskets.

Mumms: A brand of champagne.

"You don't have to go."

"Yes."

We kissed again on the stairs and as I called for the cordon the concierge muttered something behind her door. I went back upstairs and from the open window watched Brett walking up the street to the big limousine drawn up to the curb under the arclight. She got in and it started off. I turned around. On the table was an empty glass and a glass half-full of brandy and soda. I took them both out to the kitchen and poured the half-full glass down the sink. I turned off the gas in the dining-room, kicked off my slippers sitting on the bed, and got into bed. This was Brett, that I had felt like crying about. Then I thought of her walking up the street and stepping into the car, as I had last seen her, . . . It is awfully easy to be hard-boiled about everything in the daytime, but at night it is another thing.

What happened next . . .

Following the success of *The Sun Also Rises*, Hemingway went on to write another acclaimed novel, *A Farewell to Arms* (1929). This book tells the story of an American ambulance driver wounded in Italy during World War I, whose idyllic love affair with an English nurse ends with her death. During the 1930s, Hemingway published two nonfiction works, *Death in the Afternoon* (1932), about bullfighting, and *The Green Hills of Africa* (1935), about his travels on that continent. Later novels include *To Have and Have Not* (1937), which centers on characters affected by the Great Depression (the period of economic downturn and widespread hardship that lasted from late 1929 until the early 1940s). *For Whom the Bell Tolls* (1940) was inspired by Hemingway's experiences as a correspondent for *Collier's* magazine during the Spanish Civil War. During World War II (1941–45), Hemingway served as both a reporter and a military volunteer.

Having divorced his first wife in 1927, Hemingway soon married Pauline Pfeiffer. While living in Key West, Florida, during the 1930s, Hemingway met Martha Gelhorn, with whom he carried on a secret affair for four years before divorcing Pfeiffer and marrying her. He and his new wife moved to Havana, Cuba, where Hemingway spent much of his time fishing. This setting and occupation provided material for one of his best novels, *The Old Man and the Sea*. This story of a Cuban fisherman's heroic struggle with a shark earned Hemingway the Pulitzer Prize in 1953. The next year, he won the Nobel Prize for Literature.

Hemingway's final years were marred by physical illness and injury as well as emotional strain. After divorcing Gelhorn, Hemingway had married Mary Welsh and moved with her to Ketchum, Idaho. About a year after treatment for depression and other ailments proved ineffective, Hemingway killed himself with a shotgun in July 1961. Since his death, Hemingway's work has been faulted by some as shallow, excessively violent, and demeaning to women. Most commentators, however, acknowledge Hemingway's influence on the writers of the later twentieth century, many of whom have imitated his spare narrative style.

Did You Know . . .

- Hemingway was passionately interested in the sport of bullfighting, which plays a prominent role in *The Sun Also Rises*. One of the few admirable characters in *The Sun Also Rises* is the young bullfighter Pedro Romero, whose skill, bravery, and good looks attract Lady Brett Ashley. Hemingway's knowledge of bullfighting rituals and figures is evident not only in this novel but in his nonfiction work, *Death in the Afternoon* (1932).

- The novel's narrator, Jake Barnes, resembles his creator in other ways. Like Hemingway in the early 1920s, Jake is a veteran wounded in World War I and an expatriate journalist living in Paris. He also shares the author's appreciation for drinking, bullfighting, and fishing, and he speaks in the same unadorned style in which Hemingway writes.

Consider this . . .

- On their way to watch the bullfights in Pamplona, Spain, Jake and his friend Bill Gorton spend some time fishing in that country's Basque region. How does this section present a different view of relationships than the other parts of the book?

- To learn more about Hemingway's life in Paris in the 1920s, read his posthumously (after death) published memoir *A Moveable Feast* (1964). Share what you've learned through a book report or other project.

For More Information

Books

Baker, Carlos. *Ernest Hemingway: A Life Story*. Philadelphia: Scribner, 1969.

Baker, Carlos, ed. *Ernest Hemingway: Critiques of Four Major Novels*. Philadelphia: Scribner, 1962.

Bloom, Harold, ed. *Ernest Hemingway's The Sun Also Rises*. New York: Chelsea House, 1995.

Hunter-Gillespie, Connie. *Ernest Hemingway's The Sun Also Rises*. Piscatway, NJ: Research and Education Association, 1996.

Lynn, Kenneth Schuyler. *Hemingway*. Cambridge: Harvard University Press, 1995.

McDaniel, Melissa. *Ernest Hemingway*. New York: Chelsea House, 1996.

Nagel, Jems, ed. *Critical Essays on Ernest Hemingway's The Sun Also Rises*. New York: G. K. Hall, 1995.

Rovit, Earl R. *Ernest Hemingway*. Boston: Twayne, 1963.

Tessitore, John. *The Hunt and the Feast: A Life of Ernest Hemingway*. New York: Franklin Watts, 1996.

Wylder, Delbert. *Hemingway's Heroes*. Albuquerque: University of New Mexico Press, 1969.

Yannuzzi, Della A. *Ernest Hemingway: Writer and Adventurer*. Berkeley Heights, NJ: Enslow Publishers, 1998.

Web Sites

Ernest Hemingway. Available online at http://www.ernest.hemingway.com/. Accessed on June 20, 2005.

"Ernest Hemingway—Biography." *Nobelprize.org*. Available online at http://nobelprize.org/literature/laureates/1954/hemingway-bio.html. Accessed on June 20, 2005.

10

Frank Kellogg and Aristide Briand

Excerpt from the Kellogg-Briand Pact
Published on August 27, 1928

World War I (1914–18) involved thirty-two countries around the globe in a conflict that took more than 15,000,000 lives. Although casualties suffered by the United States were comparatively small—130,000 were killed, and 190,000 wounded—the country joined the rest of the world in shock at the bloodshed and destruction of this war. A mood of isolationism (keeping apart) dominated the United States as people expressed their strong desire to stay well away from other nations' troubles. Lawmakers and leaders reflected this mood. In 1929, for example, the U.S. Senate voted not to join the League of Nations, the international organization originally conceived by President Woodrow Wilson (1856–1924; served 1913–21) as a way to prevent war through global cooperation. The next year, the size of the U.S. armed services was reduced from a wartime high of 4,355,000 to 250,000.

Clearly, U.S. citizens were ready for peace. One indication was a contest sponsored by the former editor of *Ladies Home Journal* magazine, Edward W. Bok. He offered

"Hopeful that . . . all the other nations of the world will join in this humane endeavor . . . thus uniting the civilized nations of the world in a common renunciation of war as an instrument of their national policy. . . ."

The signing of the Kellogg-Briand Pact. *(© Hulton-Deutsch Collection/Corbis. Reproduced by permission.)*

a $100,000 prize for the best plan to preserve international peace. Thousands responded. But it was not just isolationists who supported the idea of finding a way to end war. Others actually wanted the United States to take a more active role in an international effort to achieve that goal.

One such person was James T. Shotwell, a professor at New York City's Columbia University, who met with French foreign minister Aristide Briand (1862–1932) in Paris to discuss the possibility of a bilateral treaty (one involving two parties) that would outlaw war between the United States and France. Briand was very interested in the proposal, mostly due to his nation's fear that Germany (the main aggressor in World War I) would gain strength again and attack France. Getting the United States to agree to side with France if such an event occurred would make the French feel much safer. Instead of approaching the United States in the usual manner, through the State Department (the branch of the U.S. government that is responsible for relations with other countries), Briand sent an open letter about his proposal to the people of the United States. It was published on April 6, 1927.

Secretary of State Frank Kellogg (1856–1937) was annoyed that Briand had not gone through the usual diplomatic channels. In addition, he did not want the United States to be obligated to defend France. But it was too late. Several prominent leaders as well as many U.S. citizens liked the idea of a treaty to end war. Facing pressure from the public, Kellogg came up with another proposal. This one was to be signed not just by the United States and France but by many nations (making it multilateral), and it would allow each one to defend its own territory if necessary. In effect, this agreement meant very little, because the nations would all be allowed to decide when to defend themselves. It also provided no way to enforce the agreement or punish any nation that violated it.

Nevertheless, in August 1928, fifteen nations signed the Kellogg-Briand Pact, which stated that countries could not "resort to war" as a way to resolve conflicts. A total of sixty-two countries ultimately signed the treaty.

Treaty Namesake Frank B. Kellogg

Though the Kellogg-Briand Pact failed to achieve its aim of international peace, the efforts of the U.S. diplomat who negotiated it were recognized when he received the Nobel Peace Prize in 1929.

Born in Potsdam, New York, in 1856, Frank B. Kellogg grew up in Minnesota. He became a successful lawyer in St. Paul, Minnesota, during which period he became friends with Theodore Roosevelt, who would serve as U.S. president from 1901 to 1909. This relationship led to Kellogg's role as the federal government's prosecuting attorney in a case against the Standard Oil Company in 1911. Kellogg successfully showed that the company had violated the Sherman Anti-Trust Act, a law designed to prevent large corporations from gaining too much power.

Elected to the U.S. Senate in 1916, Kellogg was defeated in a 1922 reelection bid. He served as ambassador to Great Britain from 1923 to 1925. President Calvin Coolidge appointed Kellogg secretary of state in 1925. One of the first challenges he faced in this position was the tense relationship between the United States and Mexico because of Mexican laws that negatively affected U.S. oil companies. Kellogg's appointment of skilled diplomat Dwight Morrow as ambassador to Mexico led to a resolution.

Similarly, Kellogg's choice of Henry Stimson, who would succeed him as secretary of state, as ambassador to Nicaragua helped to smooth relations in the wake of a civil war in that Central American nation. Kellogg also helped to arrange loans to assist Germany's recovery from its economically devastating loss in World War I.

Kellogg considered his negotiation of the Kellogg-Briand Pact his crowning achievement as secretary of state. The original proposal had been for an agreement between only France and the United States, but Kellogg expanded its scope. It was eventually signed by sixty-two countries, which agreed to seek peaceful means to resolve conflicts and to consider war only as a last resort. Though the agreement later failed to prevent war, the Nobel Prize committee showed its approval of Kellogg's efforts by awarding the him the 1929 Nobel Peace Prize.

The following year, Kellogg was appointed to the Permanent Council of the Court of International Justice at The Hague, Netherlands. He held that post until 1935, and died in 1937.

Things to remember while reading this excerpt from the Kellogg-Briand Pact . . .

Supporters of the agreement included those who saw value in international cooperation, such as Columbia University president Nicholas Murray Butler (1862–1947), who wrote a pro-treaty editorial published in the *New York*

Aristide Briand (right), French Foreign Minister Myron T. Herrick (center), and Frank Kellogg (left) meeting in Paris, France, before signing the Kellogg-Briand Pact. *(© Bettmann/Corbis. Reproduced by permission.)*

Times. But isolationists also agreed with the idea of outlawing war. One of these was Senator William T. Borah (1865–1940) of Idaho, a pacifist, who spearheaded a petition drive that collected two million signatures of people in favor of the pact.

Even at the time of the signing of the Kellogg-Briand Pact, it does not seem to have been taken very seriously, at least by the government officials involved. For example, immediately after ratifying (officially approving) the treaty, the U.S. Senate passed a bill designating $247 million to be used to build warships.

Although the Kellogg-Briand Pact is considered a failure in its stated aim of preventing war, it did have some positive effects. It has served as one of the legal bases for the international rule that using military force presumptively (taking action without a just cause) is illegal. It also helped establish the idea of a crime against peace. This concept provided the basis for the Nuremburg Tribunal, at which several people were tried and sentenced for starting World War II (1939–45).

Excerpt from the Kellogg-Briand Pact

*Treaty between the United States and other Powers providing for the **renunciation** of war as an **instrument** of national policy. Signed at Paris, August 27, 1928; ratification advised by the Senate, January 16, 1929; ratified by the President, January 17, 1929; instruments of ratification deposited at Washington by the United States of America, Australia, Dominion of Canada, Czechoslovakia, Germany, Great Britain, India, Irish Free State, Italy, New Zealand, and Union of South Africa, March 2, 1929: By Poland, March 26, 1929; by Belgium, March 27, 1929; by France, April 22, 1929; by Japan, July 24, 1929; proclaimed, July 24, 1929.*

BY THE PRESIDENT OF THE UNITED STATES OF AMERICA

A PROCLAMATION

*WHEREAS a Treaty between the President of the United States Of America, the President of the German Reich, His Majesty the King of the Belgians, the President of the French Republic, His Majesty the King of Great Britain, Ireland and the British Dominions beyond the Seas, Emperor of India, His Majesty the King of Italy, His Majesty the Emperor of Japan, the President of the Republic of Poland, and the President of the Czechoslovak Republic, providing for the renunciation of war as an instrument of national policy, was concluded and signed by their respective **Plenipotentiaries** at Paris on the twenty-seventh day of August, one thousand nine hundred and twenty-eight, the original of which Treaty, being in the English and the French languages, is word for word as follows:*

THE PRESIDENT OF THE GERMAN REICH, THE PRESIDENT OF THE UNITED STATES OF AMERICA, HIS MAJESTY THE KING OF THE BELGIANS, THE PRESIDENT OF THE FRENCH REPUBLIC, HIS MAJESTY THE KING OF GREAT BRITAIN IRELAND AND THE BRITISH DOMINIONS BEYOND THE

Renunciation: Abandonment.

Instrument: Official document.

Plenipotentiaries: Official representatives.

SEAS, EMPEROR OF INDIA, HIS MAJESTY THE KING OF ITALY, HIS MAJESTY THE EMPEROR OF JAPAN, THE PRESIDENT OF THE REPUBLIC OF POLAND THE PRESIDENT OF THE CZECHOSLOVAK REPUBLIC,

Deeply sensible of their solemn duty to promote the welfare of mankind;

Persuaded that the time has, come when a frank renunciation of war as an instrument of national policy should be made to the end that the peaceful and friendly relations now existing between their peoples may be **perpetuated**;

Convinced that all changes in their relations with one another should be sought only by **pacific** means and be the result of a peaceful and orderly process, and that any **signatory power** which shall hereafter seek to promote its national interests by resort to war a should be denied the benefits furnished by this Treaty;

Hopeful that, encouraged by their example, all the other nations of the world will join in this humane **endeavor** and by **adhering** to the present Treaty as soon as it comes into force bring their peoples within the scope of its **beneficent provisions**, thus uniting the civilized nations of the world in a common renunciation of war as an instrument of their national policy;

Have decided to conclude a Treaty and for that purpose have appointed as their respective

Plenipotentiaries:

THE PRESIDENT OF THE GERMAN REICH:

Dr Gustav STRESEMANN, Minister of Foreign Affairs;

THE PRESIDENT OF THE UNITED STATES OF AMERICA:

The Honorable Frank B. KELLOGG, Secretary of State;

HIS MAJESTY THE KING OF THE BELGIANS:

Mr Paul HYMANS, Minister for Foreign Affairs, Minister of State;

THE PRESIDENT OF THE FRENCH REPUBLIC:

Mr. Aristide BRIAND Minister for Foreign Affairs;

HIS MAJESTY THE KING OF GREAT BRITAIN, IRELAND AND THE BRITISH DOMINIONS BEYOND THE SEAS, EMPEROR OF INDIA

For GREAT BRITAIN and NORTHERN IRELAND and all parts of the British Empire which are not separate Members of the League of Nations:

Perpetuated: Continued.

Pacific: Peaceful.

Signatory Power: Country that has signed the agreement.

Endeavor: Effort.

Adhering: Going along with.

Beneficent provisions: Rules that will benefit the nations that sign.

The Right Honourable Lord CUSHENDUN, Chancellor of the Duchy of Lancaster, Acting-Secretary of State for Foreign Affairs;

For the DOMINION OF CANADA:

The Right Honourable William Lyon MACKENZIE KING, Prime Minister and Minister for External Affairs;

For the COMMONWEALTH of AUSTRALIA:

The Honourable Alexander John McLACHLAN, Member of the Executive Federal Council;

For the DOMINION OF NEW ZEALAND:

The Honourable Sir Christopher James PARR, High Commissioner for New Zealand in Great Britain;

For the UNION OF SOUTH AFRICA:

The Honourable Jacobus Stephanus SMIT, High Commissioner for the Union of South Africa in Great Britain;

For the IRISH FREE STATE:

Mr. William Thomas COSGRAVE, President of the Executive Council;

For INDIA:

The Right Honourable Lord CUSHENDUN, Chancellor of the Duchy of Lancaster, Acting Secretary of State for Foreign Affairs;

HIS MAJESTY THE KING OF ITALY:

Count Gaetano MANZONI, his Ambassador Extraordinary and Plenipotentiary at Paris.

HIS MAJESTY THE EMPEROR OF JAPAN:

Count UCHIDA, Privy Councillor;

THE PRESIDENT OF THE REPUBLIC OF POLAND:

Mr. A. ZALESKI, Minister for Foreign Affairs;

THE PRESIDENT OF THE CZECHOSLOVAK REPUBLIC:

Dr Eduard BENES, Minister for Foreign Affairs;

who, having communicated to one another their full powers found in good and due form have agreed upon the following articles:

Article I

Recourse: Source of help in a difficult situation.

*The High Contracting Parties solemnly declare in the names of their respective peoples that they condemn **recourse** to war for the solution of* international controversies, and renounce it, as an instrument of national policy in their relations with one another.

Article II

The High Contracting Parties agree that the settlement or solution of all disputes or conflicts of whatever nature or of whatever origin they may be, which may arise among them, shall never be sought except by pacific means.

Article III

The present Treaty shall be ratified by the High Contracting Parties named in the **Preamble** in accordance with their respective constitutional requirements, and shall take effect as between them as soon as all their several instruments of ratification shall have been deposited at Washington.

This Treaty shall, when it has come into effect as prescribed in the preceding paragraph, remain open as long as may be necessary for adherence by all the other Powers of the world. Every instrument evidencing the adherence of a Power shall be deposited at Washington and the Treaty shall immediately upon such deposit become effective as between the Power thus adhering and the other Powers parties hereto.

It shall be the duty of the Government of the United States to furnish each Government named in the Preamble and every Government subsequently adhering to this Treaty with a certified copy of the Treaty and of every instrument of ratification or adherence. It shall also be the duty of the Government of the United States **telegraphically** to notify such Governments immediately upon the deposit with it of each instrument of ratification or adherence.

IN FAITH WHEREOF the respective Plenipotentiaries have signed this Treaty in the French and English languages both texts having equal force, and hereunto **affix their seals**.

DONE at Paris, the twenty seventh day of August in the year one thousand nine hundred and twenty-eight.

[SEAL] GUSTAV STRESEMANN

[SEAL] FRANK B KELLOGG

[SEAL] PAUL HYMANS

[SEAL] ARI BRIAND

Preamble: First part of the treaty, which lists the signing nations.

Telegraphically: Electronically sending messages over a wire using code.

Affix their seals: Guarantee authenticity.

The signatories of the Kellogg-Briand Pact, together with representative ambassadors and ministers were entertained by the French President M. Doumergue at the Chateau of Rambouillet. *(© Underwood & Underwood/ Corbis. Reproduced by permission.)*

[SEAL] CUSHENDUN

[SEAL] W. L. MACKENZIE KING

[SEAL] A J MCLACHLAN

[SEAL] C. J. PARR

[SEAL] J S. SMIT

[SEAL] LIAM T. MACCOSGAIR

[SEAL] CUSHENDUN

[SEAL] G. MANZONI

[SEAL] UCHIDA

[SEAL] AUGUST ZALESKI

[SEAL] DR EDWARD BENES

Certified to be a true copy of the signed original deposited with the Government of the United States of America.

FRANK B. KELLOGG

Secretary of State of the United States of America

AND WHEREAS it is stipulated in the said Treaty that it shall take effect as between the High Contracting Parties as soon as all the several instruments of ratification shall have been deposited at Washington;

AND WHEREAS the said Treaty has been duly ratified on the parts of all the High Contracting Parties and their several instruments of ratification have been deposited with the Government of the United States of America, the last on July 24, 1929;

NOW THEREFORE, be it known that I, Herbert Hoover, President of the United States of America, have caused the said Treaty to be made public, to the end that the same and every article and clause thereof may be observed and fulfilled with good faith by the United States and the citizens thereof.

IN TESTIMONY WHEREOF, I have hereunto set my hand and caused the seal of the United States to be affixed.

DONE at the city of Washington this twenty-fourth day of July in the year of our Lord one thousand nine hundred and twenty-nine, and of the Independence of the United States of America the one hundred and fifty-fourth

HERBERT HOOVER By the President:

HENRY L STIMSON Secretary of State

Note by the Department of State

Adhering Countries When this Treaty became effective on July 24, 1929, the instruments of ratification of all of the signatory powers having been deposited at Washington, the following countries, having deposited instruments of **definitive** adherence, became parties to it:

Additional adhesions deposited subsequent to July 24, 1929. Persia, July 2, 1929; Greece, August 3, 1929; Honduras, August 6, 1929; Chile, August 12, 1929; Luxemburg August 14, 1929; Danzig,

Definitive: Decisive and with authority.

Besides receiving the Noble Prize, Frank Kellogg also received the Grand Cross of the Legion of Honor for his work on the Kellogg-Briand Pact.

(© Corbis. Reproduced by permission.)

September 11, 1929; Costa Rica, October 1, 1929; Venezuela, October 24, 1929.

What happened next . . .

Most historians agree that the Kellogg-Briand Pact turned out to be meaningless, mainly because it lacked any measure to force nations to abide by the agreement. It also allowed for war to defend one's own territory, and it provided neither an expiration date nor a way to make needed changes or additions. During the 1930s several nations that had signed the pact ignored its terms as they took aggressive actions to expand their boundaries. For instance Japan invaded Manchuria (a region in northern China) in 1931, Italy attacked the African nation of Ethiopia in 1935, and Germany took over Austria in 1938. Three years after that, most of the countries of the world were again involved in a global conflict.

Did you know . . .

- Only fourteen years after the Kellogg-Briand Pact supposedly outlawed war, all the nations that had signed it were involved in World War II.

- Each of the two sponsors of the Kellogg-Briand Pact was awarded the Nobel Peace Prize. Briand won his in 1926, and Kellogg received his in 1929.

Consider the following . . .

- The United Nations, formed in 1945, at the end of World War II, has been more successful than either the League of Nations or the Kellogg-Briand Pact in preventing and resolving global conflicts. Why do you think this is the case?

- Imagine that you are taking part in Edward Bok's contest to propose a plan to achieve international peace. What would you suggest?

For More Information

Books

Miller, D.H. *The Peace Pact of Paris: A Study of the Briand-Kellogg Treaty*. New York, London: G. P. Putnam's Sons, 1928.

Shotwell, James T. *War as an Instrument of National Policy and Its Renunciation in the Pact of Paris*. New York: 1974.

Web Sites

"Coolidge and Foreign Affairs: Kellogg Briand Pact, August 27, 1928." *U-S-History.com*. Available online at http://www.u-s-history.com/pages/h1485.html. Accessed on June 20, 2005.

11

Robert S. Lynd and Helen Merrell Lynd

***Excerpt from* Middletown**
Published in 1929

"Boys and girls in the three upper years of high school marked the number of times they go out on school nights and the hour they get in at night more frequently than any other sources of friction with their parents. . . ."

In January 1924 a young couple arrived in Muncie, Indiana, with a special purpose in mind. They planned to conduct a study of religious life in this small town in the middle of the United States. By the time they were finished, though, the scope of their study had expanded. What they finally produced was a richly detailed portrait of how the residents of the place they called Middletown lived. The Lynds' published study gives contemporary readers a revealing peek into the day-to-day lives of ordinary people in the 1920s.

Robert and Helen Lynd had both been born and raised in the midwestern United States, but both were living on the East Coast when they met. At the time of their 1922 marriage, Helen was a schoolteacher and Robert a graduate student in religious studies. After Robert's graduation, the couple moved to Montana to work as church missionaries (those who try to convert people to their own religious beliefs). This experience helped to shift their interest from religion toward sociology, the study of human societies. In the middle of the 1920s, the Institute of Social and Religious Research

One of *Middletown*'s authors, Robert S. Lynd. *(Leonard Mccombe/Getty Images. Reproduced by permission.)*

hired Robert to conduct a series of studies on small towns. Soon the Lynds were selected to produce a similar study of Muncie, Indiana.

The Lynds' goal was to conduct a factual, highly descriptive study of what they considered an average, typical U.S. town. They would compare conditions and beliefs in the 1920s to those of the 1890s. The Lynds spent eighteen months conducting interviews, handing out surveys, and gathering statistics. They divided their study into six parts, focused on information about how people earned their living, organized their homes, raised their children, spent their leisure time, practiced their religion, and took part in community activities. The Lynds were careful to maintain an objective, nonjudgmental stance, but their work revealed much about the townsfolk's beliefs and values. In their conclusion, the Lynds called the 1920s "probably ... one of the eras of greatest rapidity of change in the history of human institutions."

Things to remember while reading this excerpt from *Middletown* ...

During the 1920s many social scientists became intensely interested in describing and analyzing U.S. society. The Lynds used what was then a new approach to research, modeling their study after the exhaustively detailed work of anthropologists (people who study human societies, cultures, and origins).

In addition to revealing the changes in how people viewed such things as raising children and spending free time, *Middletown* highlighted the 1920s trend toward consumerism (the preoccupation of a society with acquiring goods). The Lynds credited this change both to the rise of advertising and to "installment buying [purchasing things on credit and then making regular payments, which include interest, for a set period], which turns wishes into horses overnight."

When the twentieth century began, sociology was not yet widely recognized as a legitimate academic field. Through *Middletown*, as well as his later work as a researcher and professor, Robert Lynd is credited with helping elevate the status of sociology.

Excerpt from Middletown

Chapter XI: Child Rearing

Child-rearing is traditionally conceived by Middletown chiefly in terms of making children conform to the approved ways of the group; a "good" home secures the maximum of conformity; a "bad" home fails to achieve it. But today the swiftly moving environment and multiplied occasions for contacts outside the home are making it more difficult to secure **adherence** *to established group* **sanctions***, and Middletown parents are* **wont to** *speak of their "problems" as new to this generation, situations for which the* **formulae** *of their parents are inadequate. Even from the earliest years of the child's life the former dominance of*

A researcher collecting data. Due to work by people such as Robert Lynd, sociology emerged as a legitimate field during the 1920s. *(© Bettmann/Corbis. Reproduced by permission.)*

the home is challenged; the small child spends less time in the home than in the ample days of the nineties. Shrinkage in the size of the yard affords less play space. "Mother, where can I play?" wailed a small boy of six, as he was protestingly hauled into a tiny front yard from the enchanting sport of throwing ice at passing autos.... The community has recently begun to institute public playgrounds, thereby hastening the passing of the time when a mother could "keep an eye on" the children in the home yard. The taking over of the kindergarten by the public schools in 1924 offers to children of four and five an alternative to the home. "Why, even my youngster in kindergarten is telling us where to get off," exclaimed one bewildered father. "He won't eat white bread because he says they tell him at kindergarten that brown is more healthful!"...

Adherence: Remaining faithful.

Sanctions: Rules of behavior.

Wont to: What is usually done.

Formulae: Methods.

[With] entry into high school, the agencies drawing the child away from home multiply. Athletics, dramatics, committee meetings after school hours demand his support; Y.M.C.A., Y.W.C.A., Boy Scouts, Girl Reserves, the movies, auto-riding—all extra-neighborhood concerns unknown to his parents in their youth—are centers of interest; club meetings, parties, or dances, often held in public buildings, compete for his every evening. A "date" at home is "slow" compared with motoring, a new film, or a dance in a near-by town. It is not surprising that both boys and girls in the three upper years of high school marked the number of times they go out on school nights and the hour they get in at night more frequently than any other sources of friction with their parents, and that approximately half of the boys and girls answering the question say that they are at home less than four evenings out of the week. "I've never been criticized by my children until these last couple of years since they have been in high school," said one business class mother, "but now both my daughter and older son keep saying, 'But Mother, you're so old-fashioned.'" "My daughter of fourteen thinks I am 'cruel' if I don't let her stay at a dance until after eleven," said another mother. "I tell her that when I was her age I had to be in at nine, and she says, 'Yes, Mother, but that was fifty years ago.'"

With the diminishing place of the home in the life of the child comes the problem of "early sophistication," as business class parents put it, or "children of twelve or fourteen nowadays act just like grown-ups," in the words of workers' wives. A few of the wealthier parents have reluctantly sent their children away to school, largely in order that they may avoid the sophisticated, early-maturing social life which appears to be almost inescapable. As one listens to the **perplexity** of mothers today, the announcement in the local press in 1900 that "beginning March first, curfew bell will be rung at 9 p.m. instead of 8 p.m." seems very remote.

"What can we do," protested one mother, "when even church societies keep such late hours? My boy of fifteen is always supposed to be home at eleven, but a short time ago the Young People's Society of the church gave a dance, and dancing was from nine to twelve! And so few mothers will do anything about it. My son was eleven when he went to his first dance and we told him to be home by ten thirty. I knew the mother of the girl he was taking and called her up to tell her my directions. 'Indeed, I am not telling my daughter anything of the kind,' she said; 'I don't want to interfere with her good time!'"....

Perplexity: Confusion.

In *Middletown* the public was made aware for the first time of the increased social activities, such as dances, in which teenagers were participating. *(Hulton Archive/Getty Images. Reproduced by permission.)*

Almost every mother tells of compromise somewhere. "I never would have believed I would have let my daughter join so many clubs," said one thoughtful mother of a high school girl. "I have always criticized people who did it. But when it comes right down to it, I want to minimize the boy interest, and filling her life full of other things seems to be the only way to do that. She belongs to three high school clubs besides the Matinee Musicale and a Y.W.C.A. club."

Another woman, criticized by her neighbors for letting her children "run wild," insists that the only difference between her and other mothers is that she knows where her children are and the other mothers don't: "I wish you could know the number of girls who come

Dorothy Dix: Advice for Ordinary People

Between 1896 and 1951, advice columnist Dorothy Dix's words of wisdom were read by as many as sixty million people a day in newspapers across the nation. In *Middletown,* the Lynds quote Dix on such topics as marriage, child-rearing, divorce, and housework.

Born Elizabeth Meriweather in 1870, Dix grew up in a once-wealthy Tennessee family. She married at twenty-one, but her husband was mentally unstable and unable to provide for his family. Dix began to work as a freelance writer when her neighbor, Elizabeth Nicholson, publisher of the New Orleans *Picayune* newspaper, recognized the talent evident in some short pieces Dix had written. She was hired as an assistant to Nathaniel Burbank, the newspaper's editor.

Before long, Dix moved from writing death notices and other short articles to writing an advice column, called the "Sunday Salad." Since respectable women of the day did not want their names published in newspapers, she wrote under an invented name: Dorothy, a favorite name, and Dix, the name of a slave her family had owned before the Civil War. Written in an easy-going, down-to-earth style and focused on issues of concern to women—such as problems with parents, spouses, and children as well as religion, etiquette, and recipes—the column became very popular. Readers appreciated Dix's sincerity, her unsophisticated manner, and the mature approach she took to problems.

In 1901 Dix began to write for the *New York Journal.* Her new column was called "Dorothy Dix Talks." At the same time she also wrote articles on a number of sensational murder trials. Dix's ability to get victims, criminals, and family members to share details made her ideal for this work. By 1917, however, Dix decided to focus exclusively on her column. She made an exception in 1926, when she covered the Halls-Mill murder trial, a sensational case involving a minister's wife accused of killing her husband and his lover, a married member of the church choir. It is thought that Dix's sympathy for the accused influenced public opinion; the woman was ultimately found innocent.

In her column, Dix projected an outlook both traditional and modern. She believed that women should stay home with their young children if possible, and that children should obey their parents. On the other hand, she firmly supported the Nineteenth Amendment, which gave women the right to vote, and she knew from personal experience that women's employment outside the home was often a matter of survival for their families.

Dix continued to produce her column until the time of her death in 1951, when she was eighty-one years old.

over here and then go to _____ (a much-criticized public dance resort fifteen miles away). They say, 'Well, it's perfectly all right if you keep with your own crowd, but I can't explain it to mother, so I just don't tell her.'"

One working mother said that she no longer lets her children go to church on Sunday evening "because that's just an excuse to get out-of-doors and away from home."

What happened next . . .

Even though their town had not been referred to by its real name, residents of Muncie recognized themselves in the study. Some of them expressed anger, claiming that the Lynds' work was slanted and unflattering to its subjects. The book was popular with readers, though, and was reprinted six times in 1929. It also inspired other researchers to conduct sociological surveys on life in the United States. The Lynds produced a follow-up to *Middletown* in 1937, when *Middletown in Transition* was published. This study focused less on detailed description and more on the changes caused by industrialization, class differences, and the effects of the Great Depression (1929–41; the period of economic downtown and hardship that followed the prosperous 1920s). Several other studies of Muncie have since been conducted, and a six-part documentary series titled *Middletown* was filmed in the early 1980s.

Did you know . . .

- Teenagers in the 1920s looked and behaved very differently than their parents (who had grown up at the end of the nineteenth century) had as young people. Adults found it nearly impossible to understand their children. "For those with adolescent sons and daughters it was," notes historian Nathan Miller in his book *New World Coming: The 1920s and the Making of Modern America*, "by all accounts a trying time."

- Later critics noted that the Lynds' study had involved only Middletown's white residents. In *The Other Side of Middletown* (2004), a group of researchers sought to provide a more balanced view by chronicling Muncie's African American community.

Consider the following . . .

- The parents of teenagers in the 1920s were often shocked and confused by their children's behavior. In what ways do they remind you of today's parents? How do you think the adults of the 1920s would react to today's teenagers?

- Some of the practices people take for granted today, such as owning a car or going to the movies, were brand new in the 1920s. Look through *Middletown* to find examples of what people thought of these new, exciting trends.

For More Information

Books

Caplow, Theodore, et al. *Middletown Families: Fifty Years of Change and Continuity*. Minneapolis: University of Minnesota Press, 1982.

Geelhoed, E. Bruce. *Muncie: The Middletown of America*. Chicago, IL: Arcadia Publishing, 2000.

Hoover, Dwight W. *Middletown: The Making of a Documentary Film Series*. Philadelphia, PA: Harwood Academic Publishers, 1992.

Lassiter, Luke Eric, et al. *The Other Side of Middletown: Exploring Muncie's African American Community*. Walnut Creek, CA: Altamira Press, 2004.

Web Sites

"Middletown Studies Collection and Digital Archives." *Archives and Special Collections Research Center*. Available online at http://www.bsu.edu/library/article/0,,29036--,00.html. Accessed on June 20, 2005.

Where to Learn More

The following list focuses on works written for readers of middle school or high school age. Books aimed at adult readers have been included when they are especially important in providing information or analysis that would otherwise be unavailable.

Books

Abels, Jules. *In the Time of Silent Cal*. New York: Putnam, 1989.

Allen, Frederick Lewis. *Only Yesterday: An Informal History of the 1920s*. New York: Perennial, 1964.

Allsop, Kenneth. *The Bootleggers: The Story of Chicago's Prohibition Era*. New Rochelle, NY: Arlington House, 1968.

Altman, Linda Jacobs. *The Decade That Roared: America During Prohibition*. New York: Twenty-First Century Books, 1997.

Andryszewski, Tricia. *Immigration: Newcomers and Their Impact on the United States*. Brookfield, CT: Millbrook Press, 1995.

Applebaum, Stanley, ed. *The New York Stage: Famous Productions in Photographs*. New York: Dover Publications, 1976.

Bacho, Peter. *Boxing in Black and White*. New York: Henry Holt, 1999.

Bachrach, Deborah. *The Importance of Margaret Sanger.* San Diego, CA: Lucent Books, 1993.

Bains, Rae. *Babe Ruth.* Mahwah, NJ: Troll Associates, 1985.

Barry, James P. *The Noble Experiment: 1919–33.* New York: Franklin Watts, 1972.

Barry, John M. *Rising Tide: The Great Mississippi Flood of 1927.* New York: Simon & Schuster, 1997.

Bateson, Mary Catherine. *With a Daughter's Eye: A Memoir of Margaret Mead and Gregory Bateson.* New York: William Morrow, 1984.

Bergreen, Laurence. *Capone: The Man and the Era.* New York: Simon & Schuster, 1992.

Bergreen, Laurence. *Louis Armstrong: An Extravagant Life.* New York: Broadway Books, 1997.

Berg, Scott. *Lindbergh.* New York: Putnam, 1998.

Berke, Art. *Babe Ruth.* New York: Franklin Watts, 1988.

Bernstein, Irving. *The Lean Years: A History of the American Worker, 1920–1933.* Boston: Houghton Mifflin, 1960.

Berry, Michael. *Georgia O'Keeffe.* New York: Chelsea House, 1988.

Bloom, Harold, ed. *Zora Neale Hurston.* Broomall, PA: Chelsea House, 1986.

Blumhofer, Edith. *Aimee Semple McPherson: Everybody's Sister.* Grand Rapids, MI: Erdmans, 1993.

Bode, Carl. *Mencken.* Carbondale: Southern Illinois University Press, 1969.

Boer, Lawrence, and John D. Walther, eds. *Dancing Fools and Weary Blues: The Great Escape of the Twenties.* Bowling Green, OH: Bowling Green University Press, 1990.

Brittin, Norman A. *Edna St. Vincent Millay.* Boston: Twayne, 1967. Rev. ed. 1982.

Burby, Lisa. N. *Margaret Mead.* New York: Rosen, 1996.

Burlingame, Roger. *Henry Ford: A Great Life in Brief.* New York: Knopf, 1969.

Brown, Sanford. *Louis Armstrong.* New York: Franklin Watts, 1993.

Burner, David. *Herbert Hoover: A Public Life.* New York: Knopf, 1978.

Cairns, Huntington. *H.L. Mencken: The American Scene.* New York: Vintage Books, 1982.

Calhoun, Randall. *Dorothy Parker: A Bio-Bibliography.* Westport, CT: Greenwood Press, 1992.

Candael, Kerry. *Bound for Glory 1910–1930: From the Great Migration to the Harlem Renaissance.* New York: Chelsea House, 1996.

Cashman, Sean Dennis. *America in the Twenties and Thirties.* New York: New York University Press, 1989.

Chalmers, David. *Hooded Americanism: The History of the Ku Klux Klan.* Durham: Duke University Press, 1987.

Cheney, Robert W. *A Righteous Cause: The Life of William Jennings Bryan.* Boston: Little, Brown, 1985.

Chesler, Ellen. *Woman of Valor: Margaret Sanger and the Birth Control Movement.* New York: Simon & Schuster, 1992.

Cigney, Virginia. *Margaret Sanger: Rebel with a Cause.* Garden City, NY: Doubleday, 1969.

Clark, Norman H. *Deliver Us from Evil: An Interpretation of American Prohibition.* New York: W.W. Norton, 1976.

Clinton, Susan. *Herbert Hoover: Thirty-First President of the United States.* Chicago: Children's Press, 1988.

Coletta, Paolo E.. *William Jennings Bryan—Political Evangelist, 1860–1908.* Lincoln: University of Nebraska Press, 1964.

Collier, Peter, and David Horowitz. *The Fords: An American Epic.* New York: Simon & Schuster, 1987.

Cowley, Malcolm, ed. *The Stories of F. Scott Fitzgerald.* New York: Charles Scribner's Sons, 1952.

Creamer, Robert. *Home Run: The Story of Babe Ruth.* New York: Simon & Schuster, 1974.

Crouch, Tom D., ed. *Charles A. Lindbergh: An American Life.* Washington, DC: Smithsonian, 1977.

Dardis, Thomas. *Keaton: The Man Who Wouldn't Lie Down.* Minneapolis: University of Minnesota Press, 2002.

D'Augustino, Annette M. *Harold Lloyd.* Westport, CT: Greenwood Press, 1994.

De Camp, L. Sprague. *The Great Monkey Trial.* Garden City, NY: Doubleday, 1968.

Dempsey, Jack, with Barbara Piatelli Dempsey. *Dempsey.* New York: Harper & Row, 1977.

Deutsch, Sarah Jane. *From Ballots to Breadlines: American Women 1920–1940.* Oxford: Oxford University Press, 1994.

Donenberg, Barry. *An American Hero: The True Story of Charles A. Lindbergh.* New York: Putnam, 1998.

Dooley, D.J. *The Art of Sinclair Lewis.* Lincoln: The University of Nebraska Press, 1967.

Douglas, Emily Taft. *Margaret Sanger: Pioneer of the Future.* New York: Holt, Rinehart and Winston, 1970.

Downes, Randolph C. *The Rise of Warren Gamaliel Harding: 1865–1920*. Columbus: Ohio State University Press, 1970.

Dray, Philip. *At the Hands of Persons Unknown: The Lynching of Black America*. New York: Random House, 2002.

Driemen, John E. *Clarence Darrow*. New York: Chelsea House, 1992.

Dumenil, Lyn. *The Modern Temper: American Culture and Society in the 1920s*. New York: Hill and Wang, 1995.

Epstein, Daniel M. *Sister Aimee: The Life of Aimee Semple McPherson*. New York: Harcourt, 1993.

Epstein, Daniel. *What Lips My Lips Have Kissed: The Loves and Love Poems of Edna St. Vincent Millay*. New York: Holt, 2001.

Evensen, Robert J. *When Dempsey Fought Tunney: Heroes, Hokum, and Storytelling in the Jazz Age*. Knoxville: University of Tennessee Press, 1996.

Fausold, Martin. *The Presidency of Herbert C. Hoover*. Lawrence: University Press of Kansas, 1985.

Ferrell, Robert H. *The Presidency of Calvin Coolidge*. Lawrence: University Press of Kansas, 1998.

Feuerlicht, Roberta Strauss. *America's Reign of Terror: World War I, the Red Scare, and the Palmer Raids*. New York: Random House, 1971.

Finkelstein, Norman H. *Sounds of the Air: The Golden Age of Radio*. New York: Charles Scribner's, 1993.

Fisher, Jim. *The Lindbergh Case*. New Brunswick, NJ: Rutgers University Press, 1994.

Flink, Steven. *The Greatest Tennis Matches of the Twentieth Century*. Danbury, CT: Rutledge Books, 1999.

Freedman, Diane P. *Millay at 100: A Critical Reappraisal*. Carbondale: Southern Illinois University, 1995.

Freedman, Russell. *Martha Graham: A Dancer's Life*. New York: Clarion, 1998.

Fremon, David K. *The Great Depression in American History*. Springfield, NJ: Enslow Publishers, Inc., 1996.

Frewin, Leslie. *The Late Mrs. Dorothy Parker*. New York: Macmillan, 1986.

Gerstle, Gary. *Crucible: Race and Nation in the Twentieth Century*. Princeton: Princeton University Press, 2001.

Gherman, Beverly. *Georgia O'Keeffe*. New York: Atheneum, 1986.

Gilbert, Thomas. *The Soaring Twenties: Babe Ruth and the Home Run Decade*. New York: Franklin Watts, 1996.

Glabb, Charles N., in John Braemen, Robert H. Bremner, and David Body, eds. *Change and Continuity in Twentieth Century America: The 1920s.* Columbus: Ohio University Press, 1968.

Goldberg, David J. *Discontented America: The United States in the 1920s.* Baltimore: Johns Hopkins Press, 1997.

Goldston, Robert. *The Great Depression: The United States in the Thirties.* Greenwich, CT: Fawcett, 1968.

Gould, Jean. *The Poet and Her Book: The Life of Edna St. Vincent Millay.* New York: Dodd, Mead, 1969.

Gurko, Miriam. *Restless Spirit: The Life of Edna St. Vincent Millay.* New York: Thomas Y. Crowell, 1962.

Hardy, P. Steven, and Sheila Jackson Hardy. *Extraordinary People of the Harlem Renaissance.* New York: Children's Press, 2000.

Hanson, Erica. *The 1920s.* San Diego, CA: Lucent Books, 1999.

Haynes, John Earl. *Calvin Coolidge and the Coolidge Era: Essays on the History of the 1920s.* Washington, DC: Library of Congress, 1998.

Heckscher, August. *Woodrow Wilson: A Biography.* New York: Scribner, 1991.

Hemenway, Robert. *Zora Neale Hurston: A Literary Biography.* Chicago: University of Illinois Press, 1977.

Herald, Jacqueline. *Fashions of a Decade: 1920s.* New York: Facts on File, 1991.

Higdon, Hal. *Crime of the Century: The Leopold & Loeb Case.* New York: Putnam, 1975.

Higham, John. *Strangers in the Land: Patterns of American Nativism.* New York: Atheneum, 1965.

Hoffman, Frederick J. *The 1920s: American Writing in the Postwar Decade.* New York: Free Press, 1965.

Hoff-Wilson, Joan. *American Business and Foreign Policy, 1920–1933.* Boston: Beacon, 1973.

Hoff-Wilson, Joan. *Herbert Hoover: A Public Life.* Boston: Beacon, 1984.

Hoff-Wilson, Joan. *Herbert Hoover, Forgotten Progressive.* Boston: Little, Brown, 1975.

Holway, John B. *Josh and Satch: The Life and Times of Josh Gibson and Satchel Paige.* Westport, CT: Meckler, 1991.

Howard, Jane. *Margaret Mead: A Life.* New York: Simon & Schuster, 1984.

Howard, Lillie P. *Zora Neale Hurston.* Boston: Twayne, 1980.

Hutchisson, James M. *The Rise of Sinclair Lewis, 1920–1930.* University Park: Pennsylvania State University Press, 1996.

Jacques, Geoffrey. *Free Within Ourselves: The Harlem Renaissance.* New York: Franklin Watts, 1996.

Jablonsky, Edward, and Lawrence D. Stewart. *The Gershwin Years.* Doubleday and Co., 1973.

Jones, Max and John Chilton. *Louis: The Louis Armstrong Story.* Boston: Little, Brown, 1971.

Kahn, Roger. *A Flame of Pure Fire: Jack Dempsey and the Roaring 20s.* New York: Harcourt Brace, 1999.

Katz, Ephraim. *The Film Encyclopedia,* 4th ed. New York: HarperResource, 2001.

Katz, William Loren. *The New Freedom to the New Deal 19131939.* Austin, TX: Raintree Steck-Vaughn, 1993.

Kavanaugh, Jack. *Shoeless Joe Jackson.* New York: Chelsea House, 1995.

Kennedy, David M. *Birth Control in American: The Career of Margaret Sanger.* New Haven: Yale University Press, 1970.

Kerr, Walter. *The Silent Clowns.* New York: Knopf, 1975.

Kent, Zachary. *Charles Lindbergh and the Spirit of St. Louis in American History.* Berkeley Heights, NJ: Enslow Publishers, Inc., 2001.

Kimball, Robert, and Alfred Simon. *The Gershwins.* New York: Atheneum Publishers, 1972.

Kinney, Arthur. *Dorothy Parker.* Boston: Twayne, 1978.

Klein, Maury. *Rainbow's End: The Crash of 1929.* New York: Oxford University Press, 2001.

Klingman, William K. *1919: The Year Our World Began.* New York: Harper & Row, 1989.

Kobler, John. *Capone: The Life and World of Al Capone.* New York: Putnam, 1971.

LaBlanc, Michael L. *Hotdogs, Heroes & Hooligans: The Story of Baseball's Major League Teams.* Detroit: Visible Ink Press, 1994.

Lacy, Robert. *Ford: The Men and the Machine.* Boston, MA: Little, Brown, 1986.

Larson, Edward J. *Trial and Error: The American Controversy Over Creation and Evolution.* New York: Oxford University Press, 1994.

Lears, Jackson. *Fables of Abundance: A Cultural History of Advertising in America.* New York: HarperCollins, 1994.

Leavell, J. Perry, Jr. *Woodrow Wilson*. New Haven, CT: Chelsea House, 1987.

Leinwald, Gerald. *1927: High Tide of the 1920s*. New York: Four Walls Eight Windows, 2001.

Levin, Phyllis Lee. *Edith and Woodrow: The Wilson White House*. New York: Scribner, 2001.

Levine, Lawrence W. *Defender of the Faith*. Cambridge, MA: Harvard University Press, 1965.

Lichtman, Allan J. *Prejudice and the Old Politics: The Presidential Election of 1928*. Chapel Hill: University of North Carolina Press, 1979.

Lisle, Laurie. *Portrait of an Artist: A Biography of Georgia O'Keeffe*. Seaview Books, 1980.

Lucas, Eileen. *The Eighteenth and Twenty-First Amendments: Alcohol-Prohibition and Repeal*. Springfield, NJ: Enslow Publishers, 2000.

Ludel, Jacqueline. *Margaret Mead*. New York: Franklin Watts, 1983.

Lynd, Robert S., and Helen M. Lynd. *Middletown*. New York: Harcourt, Brace, 1929.

Lynn, Kenneth C. *Charlie Chaplin and His Times*. New York: Simon & Schuster, 1997.

Lyons, Mary E. *Sorrow's Kitchen: The Life and Folklore of Zora Neale Hurston*. New York: Scribner Book Company, 1990.

MacCann, Richard Dyer. *The Silent Comedians.*. Metuchen, NJ: Scarecrow Press, 1993.

Macht, Norman. *Babe Ruth*. New York: Chelsea House, 1991.

Manchester, William. *Disturber of the Peace: The Life of H.L. Mencken*. New York: Harper, 1951.

Marable, Manning. *W.E.B. Du Bois: Black Radical Democrat*. Boston: Twayne, 1986.

Marsden, George. *Fundamentalism and American Culture: The Shaping of Twentieth Century Evangelism, 1870–1925*. New York: Oxford University, 1980.

McCaffrey, Donald W. *Four Great Comedians: Chaplin, Lloyd, Keaton, and Langdon*. New York: A.S. Barnes, 1968.

McCoy, Donald R. *Calvin Coolidge: The Quiet President*. Lawrence: University Press of Kansas, 1988.

McCutcheon, Marc. *Everyday Life from Prohibition Through World War II*. Cincinnati: Writer's Digest Books, 1995.

McKissack, Patricia and Frederick McKissack Jr. *Black Diamond: The Story of the Negro Baseball Leagues*. New York: Scholastic Trade, 1994.

McPherson, Edward. *Buster Keaton: Tempest in a Flat Hat.* New York: Newmarket Press, 2005.

Meade, Marion. *Dorothy Parker: What Fresh Hell Is This?* New York: Penguin, 1989.

Meltzer, Milton. *Langston Hughes.* Brookfield, CT: Millbrook Press, 1997.

Milford, Nancy. *Savage Beauty: The Life of Edna St. Vincent Millay.* New York: Random House, 2001.

Miller, Nathan. *New World Coming: The 1920s and the Making of Modern America.* New York: Scribner, 2003.

Milton, Joyce. *Loss of Eden: A Biography of Charles and Anne Morrow Lindbergh.* New York: HarperCollins, 1993.

Moore, Edward A. *A Catholic Runs for President: The Campaign of 1928.* New York: Ronald Press, 1956.

Moore, Gloria. *Margaret Sanger and the Birth Control Movement: A Bibliography, 1911–1984.* Metuchen, NJ: Scarecrow Press, 1986.

Mowry, George E., ed. *The Twenties: Fords, Flappers, and Fanatics.* Gloucester, MA: Peter Smith/Prentice Hall, 1963.

Nash, George H. *The Life of Herbert Hoover, Vol. I.* New York: Norton, 1983.

Ness, Eliot. *The Untouchables.* New York: Messner, 1957; 1987 reprint.

Nevins, Allan, and F.E. Hill. *Ford: The Times, the Man, the Company.* New York: Scribner, 1954.

Nierman, Judith. *Edna St. Vincent Millay: A Reference Guide.* Boston: G.K. Hall, 1977.

Noggle, Burl. *Into the Twenties: The United States from Armistice to Normalcy.* Urbana: University of Illinois, 1974.

Noggle, Burl. *Teapot Dome: Oil and Politics in the 1920s.* New York: Greenwood Press, 1980.

Nye, Frank T., Jr. *Door of Opportunity: The Life and Legacy of Herbert Hoover.* West Branch, IA: The Herbert Hoover Presidential Library Association, 1988.

Ogren, Kathy J. *The Jazz Revolution: Twenties America and the Meaning of Jazz.* New York: Oxford University Press, 1989.

O'Keeffe, Georgia. *Georgia O'Keeffe.* New York: Viking Press, 1976.

Orgill, Roxanne. *If I Only Had a Horn: Young Louis Armstrong.* Boston: Houghton Mifflin, 1997.

Orgill, Roxanne. *Shout, Sister, Shout! Ten Girl Singers Who Shaped a Century.* New York: Margaret McElderry, 2001.

Paige, Leroy "Satchel" and David Lipman. *Maybe I'll Pitch Forever.* Garden City, NY: Doubleday, 1962.

Parker, Dorothy. *Enough Rope.* New York: Boni & Liveright, 1928.

Parrish, Michael E. *Anxious Decades: America in Prosperity and Depression.* New York: Norton, 1992.

Pegram, Thomas. *Battling Demon Rum: The Struggle for a Dry America, 1800–1933.* Chicago, IL: Ivan R. Dee, 1998.

Perret, Geoffrey. *America in the Twenties.* New York: Touchstone, 1982.

Polikoff, Barbara G. *Herbert C. Hoover: 31st President of the United States.* Ada, OK: Garrett Educational Corporation, 1990.

Randolph, Blythe. *Charles Lindbergh.* New York: Franklin Watts, 1990.

Reef, Catherine. *George Gershwin: American Composer.* Greensboro, NC: Morgan Reynolds, 2000.

Ribowsky, Mark. *Don't Look Back: Satchel Paige in the Shadows of Baseball.* New York: Simon & Schuster, 1994.

Roberts, Randy. *Jack Dempsey: The Manassa Mauler.* Baton Rouge: Louisiana State University Press, 1979.

Robinson, David. *Chaplin: His Life and Art.* New York: McGraw-Hill, 1985.

Russo, Guy. *The Outfit: The Role of Chicago's Underworld in the Shaping of Modern America.* New York: Bloomsbury, 2001.

Ruth, George Herman. *The Babe Ruth Story as Told to Bob Considine.* New York: E.P. Dutton, 1948.

Sanger, Margaret. *An Autobiography.* New York: W.W. Norton & Company, 1938.

Schlesinger, Arthur M., Jr. *The Crisis of the Old Order, 1919–1933.* Boston: Houghton Mifflin, 1957.

Schoenberg, Robert. *Mr. Capone: The Real—and Complete—Story of Al Capone.* New York: Morrow, 1992.

Schorer, Mark. *Sinclair Lewis: An American Life.* New York: McGraw-Hill, 1961.

Schroeder, Alan. *Charlie Chaplin: The Beauty of Silence.* New York: Franklin Watts, 1997.

Schwartz, Charles. *Gershwin: His Life and Music.* Indianapolis: Bobbs-Merrill Co., 1973.

Seymour, Harold. *Baseball: The Golden Age.* New York: Oxford University Press, 1971.

Sharman, Margaret. *1920s.* New York: Raintree Steck-Vaughn Publishers, 1992.

Shirley, David. *Satchel Paige.* New York: Chelsea House, 1993.

Sinclair, Andrew. *Prohibition: The Era of Excess*. New York: Harper Colophon, 1964.

Slayton, Robert A. *Empire Statesman: The Rise and Redemption of Al Smith*. New York: Free Press, 2001.

Smith, Robert. *Pioneers of Baseball*. Boston: Little, Brown, 1978.

Smith, Toby. *Kid Blackie: Jack Dempsey's Colorado Days*. Ouray, CO: Wayfinder Press, 1987.

Sobel, Robert. *Coolidge: An American Enigma*. Washington, DC: Regnery, 1998.

Sobel, Robert. *The Great Bull Market: Wall Street in the 1920s*. New York: Norton, 1968.

Stenerson, Douglas C. *H.L. Mencken: Iconoclast from Baltimore*. Chicago: University of Chicago Press, 1971.

Stevenson, Elizabeth. *Babbitts and Bohemians: The American 1920s*. New York: Macmillan, 1967.

Stieglitz, Alfred. *Georgia O'Keeffe: A Portrait*. New York: Metropolitan Museum of Art, 1978.

Teachout, Terry. *A Life of H.L. Mencken*. New York: HarperCollins, 2002.

Thomas, Lately. *Storming Heaven: The Lives and Turmoils of Minnie Kennedy and Aimee Semple McPherson*. New York: Ballantine Books, 1973.

Tierney, Kevin. *Darrow: A Biography*. New York: Thomas Y. Crowell, 1979.

Tessitore, John. *F. Scott Fitzgerald: The American Dreamer*. New York: Franklin Watts, 2001.

Trani, Eugene P., and David L. Wilson. *The Presidency of Warren G. Harding*. Lawrence: Regents Press of Kansas, 1977.

Turnbull, Andrew. *Scott Fitzgerald*. New York: Scribner, 1962.

Wagenheim, Karl. *Babe Ruth: His Life and Legend*. Chicago, Olmstead Press, 2001.

Ward, Geoffrey, and Ken Burns. *Jazz: A History of America's Music*. New York: Knopf, 2000.

Weinberg, Arthur, and Lila Weinberg. *Clarence Darrow: A Sentimental Rebel*. New York: Putnam, 1980.

Weiner, M.R., and John Starr. *Teapot Dome*. New York: Norton, 1965.

Whittingham, Richard. *Rites of Autumn: The Story of College Football*. New York: Free Press, 2001.

Woog, Adam. *Louis Armstrong*. San Diego, CA: Lucent Books, 1995.

Wukovitz, John F. *The 1920s*. San Diego, CA: Greenhaven Press, 2000.

Yanuzzi, Della A. *Ernest Hemingway: Writer and Adventurer*. Springfield, NJ: Enslow Publishers, 1998.

Yanuzzi, Della A. *Zora Neale Hurston: Southern Story Teller*. Springfield, NJ: Enslow Publishers, 1996.

Yapp, Nick, ed. *The 1920s*. New York: Konemann, 1998.

Ziesk, Edna. *Margaret Mead*. New York: Chelsea House, 1990.

Web Sites

America from the Great Depression to World War II: Photos from the FSA-OWI, 1935–1945. Library of Congress. Available online at http://memory.loc.gov/ammem/fsowhome.html. Accessed on August 4, 2005.

American Cultural History, Decade 1920-1929. Kingwood College Library. Available online at http://kclibrary.nhmccd.edu/decade20.html. Accessed on August 4, 2005.

Best of History Websites. Available online at http://www.besthistorysites.net/USHistory_Roaring20s.shtml. Accessed on August 4, 2005.

Clash of Cultures in the 1910s and 1920s. Available online at http://history.osu.edu/Projects/Clash/default.htm. Accessed on August 4, 2005.

Christy's Fashion Pages: Flapper Fashion. Available online at http://www.rambova.com/fashion/fash4.html. Accessed on August 4, 2005.

Harlem: Mecca of the New Negro. Available online at http://etext.lib.virginia.edu/harlem/. Accessed on August 4, 2005.

Interpreting Primary Sources. Digital History. Available online at http://www.digitalhistory.uh.edu/historyonline/us16.cfm. Accessed on August 4, 2005.

Jazz Age Culture. Available online at http://faculty.pittstate.edu/knichols/jazzage.html. Accessed on August 4, 2005.

The Jazz Age: Flapper Culture & Style. Available online at http://www.geocities.com/flapper_culture/. Accessed on August 4, 2005.

Linder, Douglas. "Tennessee vs. John Scopes, The Monkey Trial, 1925." *Famous Trials in American History*. Available online at http://www.law.umkc.edu/faculty/projects/ftrials/scopes/scopes.htm. Accessed on August 4, 2005.

New Deal Network. Available online at http://newdeal.feri.org/. Accessed on August 4, 2005.

The 1920s Experience. Available online at http://www.angelfire.com/co/pscst/index.html. Accessed on August 4, 2005.

"Prosperity and Thrift: The Coolidge Era and the Consumer Economy." *Library of Congress*. Available online at http://lcweb2.loc.gov/ammem/coolhtml/coolhome.html. Accessed on August 4, 2005.

Index

Holmes, Oliver Wendell 13
Home to Harlem (McKay) 129
Hoover, Herbert
  accomplishments of 34
  biographical information and
    working experience of 32–33
  business and government
    philosophy of 39–40, 162
  on causes of Great Depression
    165
  farming sector and 54
  Great Depression and 35, 166
  leadership style of 34
  optimism of 160
  as Secretary of Commerce 23
  Stock market crash and 164
Hoover, J. Edgar 103
Hopper, Edward 134
Hot Chocolates (Broadway show)
  131
How to Write Short Stories (Lardner)
  124
Hubble, Edwin 69
Huck, Winnifred Mason 78, 79
  (ill.)
Hughes, Charles Evans 26
Hughes, Langston 129, 169,
  204–11, 210 (ill.)
Humor 124–25
Hurston, Zora Neale 130
Hygiene 58

I

Idols. *See* Celebrities
"I'll Say She Is" (musical comedy)
  147
Immigration
  anti-immigration laws 107
  changes in 24–25
  discrimination and 96
  impact upon society 77
  legislation related to 26
  new patterns and sources of 41
  overview of 6
  restrictions put on 24–25
  tensions created by changes in
    41
Indoor plumbing 58, 71–72
Industrialization. *See also* Big
  business; Laissez-faire
  philosophy of economics;
  Urbanization

assembly line production and
  46–47
labor unions and 51–53
management principle changes
  and 45–46
overviews of 5–6, 41
scientific management
  principles and 45–46
technology and 140–41
Influenza ("flu") epidemic 14–15,
  14 (ill.)
In Old Arizona (movie) 68
In Our Time (Hemingway) 253
Installment plan 47–48
Institute of Social and Religious
  Research 278, 280
Insulin 71
Investment 34–35
Isolationism 1, 267, 269; *see also*
  World War I
*Is Sex Necessary? Or, Why You Feel
  the Way You Do* (Thurber and
  White) 125

J

Jackson, Joe ("Shoeless") 149
Japan 36
Jazz 5, 130–33, 206 (ill.)
Jazz Age 119, 130, 169
Jazz Singer, The (movie) 68, 146–47
Jim Crow laws 108–09, 148
Johnson, William Julius ("Judy")
  152
Jolson, Al 68, 140, 146, 147
Jones, Bobby 140, 154–55, 155 (ill.)
Joyce, James 122
Jung, Karl 122, 215
"Justice Denied in Massachusetts"
  (Millay) 123
J. Walter Thompson (advertising
  agency) 50

K

Kaufman, George S. 126
Keaton, Buster 144
Kellogg-Briand Pact 31–32,
  265–77, 266 (ill.), 274 (ill.)
Kellogg, Frank B. 32, 266 (ill.),
  267–77, 269 (ill.), 276 (ill.)
Kelly, Alvin ("Shipwreck") 145

Shebas 85
Sheiks 85
Sheik, The (movie) 144
Sheppard-Towner Act 70–71
Sherman Antitrust Act of 1980 43
Shotwell, James T. 32, 267
Showboat (Broadway musical) 147
Shuffle Along (Broadway play) 127
Sikorsky, Igor 63–64
Simmons, William J. 109, 111
Sinclair, Harry F. 28, 28 (ill.)
"Sixth Avenue Elevated at Third
    Street" (painting by Sloan) 134
Skyscrapers 135
Slang 189
Slipher, Vesto M. 69
Sloan, Alfred P. 47, 61, 160
Sloan, John 134
Smart Set, The (magazine) 193
Smith, Al 102, 104
Smith, Alfred E. 33, 243
Smith, Bessie 133, 133 (ill.)
Snyder, Ruth 114
Social changes 75–91; *see also*
    Women
Socialism 6, 20
Social science. *See* Sociology
Sociology 278–86, 281 (ill.)
Soldier's Pay (Faulkner) 227
Sound and the Fury, The (Faulkner)
    227
Soup kitchens 166
Southern Renaissance 123–24
Speakeasies 2 (ill.), 101; *see also*
    Eighteenth Amendment;
    Prohibition
Spirit of St. Louis 64–65
Sports
    baseball 148–52
    boxing 152–53
    celebrities 140
    college football 153–54
    golf 151 (ill.), 154–55
    Jim Crow laws and 148
    overview of 147–49
    stars 140
    swimming 155–56
    tennis 155
Stage 126–27; *see also* Broadway
    musical comedies
Stanton Elizabeth Cady 8
Stein Gertrude 121, 253, 254
Stieglitz, Alfred 134
Stock market 34–35, 49, 160–61

Stock market crash 158–64, 159
    (ill.), 161–62, 163 (ill.),
    164–65, 166–70
Stream-of-consciousness 122, 123
Strikes 12, 41, 61; *See also*
    Industrialization; Labor
    unions
St. Valentines Day Massacre
    100–01
Style. *See* Fads; Fashion; Flappers
Suffragists 196
Sun Also Rises, The (Hemingway)
    121, **252–64**, 259 (ill.)
Survey Graphic (magazine) 205
Swanson, Gloria 144
Sweet, Ossian 112–13
Swimming 155–56

T

Talented Tenth 129, 206–07
Tales of the Jazz Age (Fitzgerald)
    119
"Talkies" 140; *see also* Movies
Tammany Hall 104
Taylor, Frederick 45, 59
Taylor, William Desmond 114
Teapot Dome scandal 27–28, 180
Technology 4, 71–72, 140–41
Teenagers 84–85, 283 (ill.)
Telephones 72
Television 68–69
Temperance movement 7, 97–99
Tennis 155
Theater 126–27; *see also* Broadway
    musical comedies
Their Eyes were Watching God
    (Hurston) 130
This Is Confusion (Fauset) 130
This Side of Paradise (Fitzgerald)
    119, 125, 221, 223
Thomas, Norman 20
Three Stories and Ten Poems
    (Hemingway) 253
Thurber, James 125
Thurman, Wallace 129
Tilden, Bill 140, 155
Time (magazine) 4, 50
Tin Lizzie. *See* Model T Ford
Toll of the Sea, The (movie) 68
Toomer, Jean 129
Transportation 42, 47, 62
Treaty of Versailles 19, 21